Four Generations of Norteños

CCIS Anthologies, 5

CENTER FOR COMPARATIVE IMMIGRATION STUDIES, UCSD

FOUR GENERATIONS OF NORTEÑOS

NEW RESEARCH FROM THE CRADLE OF MEXICAN MIGRATION

edited by

Wayne A. Cornelius

David S. Fitzgerald

Scott Borger

LA JOLLA, CALIFORNIA

CENTER FOR COMPARATIVE IMMIGRATION STUDIES, UCSD

Printed in the United States of America

Cover design by Debra B. Topping.

ISBN–13: 978-0-9800560-0-6 (paper)
ISBN–13: 978-0-9800560-1-3 (cloth)

Library of Congress Cataloging-in-Publication Data

Four generations of norteños : new research from the cradle of Mexican migration / edited by Wayne A. Cornelius, David S. Fitzgerald, Scott C. Borger.
    p. cm. -- (CCIS anthologies ; 5)
  Includes bibliographical references.
  ISBN 978-0-9800560-0-6 (pbk.) -- ISBN 978-0-9800560-1-3 (cloth cover)
  1. Mexicans--United States--Case studies. 2. Alien labor, Mexican--United States--Case studies. 3. Mexicans--Employment--United States--Case studies. 4. Mexico--Emigration and immigration--Case studies. 5. United States--Emigration and immigration--Case studies. 6. Mexico--Relations--United States--Case studies. 7. United States--Relations--Mexico--Case studies. 8. Tlacuitapa (Mexico)--Emigration and immigration. I. Cornelius, Wayne A., 1945- II. Fitzgerald, David, 1972- III. Borger, Scott C. (Scott Charles), 1976- IV. University of California, San Diego. Center for Comparative Immigration Studies. V. Title. VI. Series.

E184.M5F694 2008
305.800972--dc22

2007050007

CONTENTS

The highlands of Jalisco are the historical cradle of Mexican migration to the United States. Four generations have made their way north from small towns like Tlacuitapa, a two-hour drive northeast of the state capital of Guadalajara. Since the 1970s, researchers from the United States and Mexico have studied patterns of migration from Tlacuitapa to gain an intimate understanding of who migrates and why, as well as the effects of migration on its people who stay home and those who migrate to the United States. Five different studies of migrants and potential migrants in the town have been conducted, in 1975–76, 1987–88, 1995, 2005, and 2007.[1] The survey and ethnographic data reported in this volume come from field research conducted in 2007 by the Mexican Migration Field Research and Training Program (MMFRP), based in the Center for Comparative Immigration Studies at the University of California, San Diego.

The extensive body of research conducted in Tlacuitapa over more than three decades has established an excellent baseline for understanding contemporary migration patterns. The town's evolution as a migrant-sending community and its changing engagement with U.S. immigration law and policy can be seen clearly in the field research data, from the heavy participation of Tlacuitapeños in the Bracero Program, through which most of the town's present-day transborder migratory networks were established, to their continued migration—as *indocumentados*—after that program ended in 1964, to the wave of legalizations in the late 1980s made possible by the U.S. Immigration Reform and Control Act (IRCA) of 1986, and to the current era of tougher border enforcement, in which Tlacuitapeños risk their lives and pay thousands of dollars to *coyotes* (people-smugglers) to assist them through the obstacle course that has been created on the border since 1994.

The present study reveals with particular intensity several broader patterns in Mexican migration to the United States and why current U.S.

---

1. This research is reported in Cornelius 1976, 1989, 1991, 1992, 1998; Cornelius and Salehyan 2007; and Cornelius and Lewis 2007.

policy is ill equipped to meet these challenges. Chapter 1 explains who decides to migrate and how the usual intention to return home quickly generally stretches into indefinite settlement in the United States. Nearly 60 percent of Tlacuitapeños are now settled in the United States.

Chapters 2 and 3 help explain the tendency toward increased settlement by asking whether U.S. border enforcement policy is working. Close to 40 percent of the migrants in our sample were apprehended at the border in their most recent journey to the United States, but nearly 100 percent eventually entered the United States on that trip. Migrants whom we interviewed were far more concerned about the physical dangers of crossing remote wilderness areas and the presence of border bandits preying on migrants than they were about apprehension by the Border Patrol, new fencing, or the deployment of National Guard troops. The percentage of unauthorized migrants using professional people-smugglers and the fees charged by coyotes have been increasing in tandem with the number of Border Patrol agents trying to stop them. Chapter 3 draws on a unique set of extensive interviews with coyotes and migrants to explain how the coyote business works, the fee structure for different kinds of clients and services, and why the post-1993 U.S. border buildup has been a bonanza for smugglers.[2] In short, these findings show that rather than deterring unauthorized migration, current U.S. policy is bottling up unauthorized migrants in the United States. Once they have made the expensive and dangerous crossing, migrants are less likely to return to Mexico than in years past.

Why do potential migrants from Tlacuitapa not simply get in line and migrate legally? Chapter 4 explains the process through which some can migrate legally but also why most do not, at least initially. For those without immediate family members in the United States or advanced degrees, legal channels are not a realistic option. Many townspeople react to a mismatch between U.S. demand for low-skilled labor and an immigration policy that all but shuts out low-skilled laborers by migrating without papers. The inflow of remittances that migrants send home has not been a prescription for self-sustaining economic development as an alternative

---

2. In 1976, we found that 41 percent of undocumented Tlacuitapeños had used a coyote on their most recent trip to the United States. In our 2007 survey we found that 100 percent of clandestine border crossings made by interviewees since 2003 had been coyote-assisted.

to emigration, as chapter 5 shows, but remittances have improved the lot of most Tlacuitapeños who remain in the town and they have created a social safety net. The town today is visibly more prosperous than the place we began studying in 1975, with virtually none of the low-end poverty that could be observed then.

Chapters 6 and 7 take an innovative approach toward understanding the cultural shifts caused by migration. How do migrants differ from those who stay behind? We explain how migrants increasingly shift their primary political interests toward the United States over time and come to identify with the broader Latino/Latin American community. Levels of religiosity decline moderately. In the household sphere, we find strong reasons to be skeptical of claims that migration to the United States leads to increased egalitarianism in marriages. While there is a widespread belief that migrant men are less "macho" than nonmigrants, migrant men are actually more likely than nonmigrants to report patriarchal attitudes in our anonymous survey. The authors explain this paradox by suggesting that migrant men strategically present themselves publicly as more willing to accept female equality when returning to the community to search for what they really want—a suitably "traditional" woman to take back to the United States.

Finally, chapter 8 examines the "Latino health paradox," which holds that Latino immigrants are healthier on average than would be expected given their overall socioeconomic profile. In our study of both migrant and nonmigrant Tlacuitapeños, we found that migrants report better health than nonmigrants, and the principal reason for this is migrant selectivity: healthier members of the community decide to migrate in the first place.

METHODS

The Mexican Migration Field Research and Training Program seeks to document and explain changes in migration and settlement behavior by restudying, in great depth, the same set of three migrant-sending communities in rural Mexico and their U.S. satellite communities, at two- or three-year intervals. The fieldwork is conducted each year by a binational research team consisting of between thirty-two and thirty-four U.S. and Mexican interviewers, all native-level Spanish speakers, who are trained by the MMFRP to conduct survey research, ethnographic observation, and unstructured interviewing. The substantive foci vary from year to year, but one constant is the impact of changes in U.S. immigration law and policy on migration, return migration, and U.S. settlement behavior. Since 2005 the MMFRP has been documenting the effectiveness and unintended consequences of the U.S. border enforcement strategy. These data sets, gathered from the people whose behavior has been targeted by the U.S. strategy, constitute the most direct and up-to-date evidence of whether it is actually keeping undocumented migrants out of the United States. The MMFRP's research sites were selected purposively to enable us to test our research hypotheses in diverse socioeconomic and cultural contexts. The migrant-sending communities included in the program differ markedly in terms of levels of economic development (they are classified by Mexico's National Population Council as high, medium, and low-marginality *municipios*), ethnic composition (one is *mestizo*; two are indigenous–Maya and Mixteco), and density of U.S. migration experience (ranging from 37 to 70 percent of residents having migrated internationally). All are small towns, ranging in size from 1,264 to 2,812 inhabitants in 2005.

The universe for standardized survey interviews is every adult aged 15 to 65 residing in the migrant-sending community. Since the entire adult population is interviewed in each field study, there is no sampling and therefore no sampling error. We make no claim that the resulting samples are statistically representative of larger universes of Mexican migrants and potential migrants. However, the research sites selected for the MMFRP are broadly representative of high-emigration communities in west-central and southern Mexico, as documented in dozens of survey and ethnographic studies conducted in such communities since 1975 (see, for example, Cohen 2004; Durand and Massey 2004).

The total number of standardized survey interviews conducted by the MMFRP with migrants and potential migrants in the four studies conducted to date is 3,008, which includes 603 interviews in Jalisco and Zacatecas (2005), 724 in Yucatán (2006), 860 in Jalisco (2007), and 821 in Oaxaca (2007–08). Where migrants were absent throughout our fieldwork period, we asked their closest family member for contact information to enable us to communicate with the migrant in his/her U.S. receiving city.

A snowball sample of U.S.-based migrants from each sending community was interviewed in the two months immediately following our interviews with Mexico-based respondents. In the sending communities, information was gathered from neighbors on the former occupants of all uninhabited houses encountered in the town, to document cases of whole-family migration to the United States and enable us to include these families in our U.S.-based snowball samples.

The people of Tlacuitapa, on both sides of the border, have generously cooperated in this ongoing research for the last two generations of their hometown's migration history. We thank them for sharing their compelling stories. We are also indebted to the Ford Foundation, the Tinker Foundation, the Foundation on Population, Migration, and Environment, and Eleanor Roosevelt College and the Senior Vice Chancellor for Academic Affairs at the University of California, San Diego, for their financial support of the MMFRP.

Wayne A. Cornelius

David Fitzgerald

Scott Borger

La Jolla, California

January 2009

References

Cohen, Jeffrey H. 2004. *The Culture of Migration in Southern Mexico.* Austin, TX: University of Texas Press.

Cornelius, Wayne A. 1976. "Outmigration from Rural Mexican Communities." In *The Dynamics of Migration: International Migration.* Washington, DC: Smithsonian Institution, Interdisciplinary Communications Program, Occasional Monograph Series No. 5, Vol. 2: 1–40.

———. 1989. "Impacts of the 1986 U.S. Immigration Law on Emigration from Rural Mexican Sending Communities," *Population and Development Review* 15, no. 4 (December): 689–705.

———. 1991. "Labor Migration to the United States: Development Outcomes and Alternatives in Mexican Sending Communities." In *Regional and Sectoral Development in Mexico as Alternatives to Migration,* ed. Sergio Díaz-Briquets and Sidney Weintraub. Boulder, CO: Westview Press.

————. 1992. "From Sojourners to Settlers: The Changing Profile of Mexican Migrants to the United States." In *U.S.-Mexico Relations: Labor Market Interdependence*, ed. Jorge A. Bustamante, Clark W. Reynolds, and Raúl Hinojosa Ojeda. Stanford, CA: Stanford University Press.

————. 1998. "Ejido Reform: Stimulus or Alternative to Migration?" In *The Transformation of Rural Mexico: Reforming the Ejido Sector*, ed. Wayne A. Cornelius and David Myhre. La Jolla, CA: Center for U.S.-Mexican Studies, University of California, San Diego.

Cornelius, Wayne A., and Jessa M. Lewis, eds. 2007. *Impacts of Border Enforcement on Mexican Migration: The View from Sending Communities*. La Jolla, CA: Center for Comparative Immigration Studies, University of California, San Diego.

Cornelius, Wayne A., and Idean Salehyan. 2007. "Does Border Enforcement Deter Unauthorized Immigration? The Case of Mexican Migration to the United States of America," *Regulation & Governance* 1, no. 2: 139–53.

Durand, Jorge, and Douglas S. Massey, eds. 2004. *Crossing the Border: Research from the Mexican Migration Project*. New York: Russell Sage Foundation.

Pablo Amézquita, webmaster of the town's Web site, www.tlacuitapa.com, who lives in Los Angeles and returns to Tlacuitapa for Christmas vacations.

1   The Dynamics of Migration: Who Migrates? Who Stays? Who Settles Abroad?

Justin Jarvis, Anita Ponce, Soledad Rodríguez, and Laura Cajigal García

This chapter seeks to explain why the people of Tlacuitapa decide to migrate to, and often settle in, the United States. Our analysis focuses on the interplay between the macro- (state), meso- (community), and micro-level (individual) forces that influence an individual who, as a rational actor, makes a cost-benefit choice in the decision to migrate. We argue that an individual's migration decision is made in response to the confluence of forces coming from these three levels (see figure 1.1).

Figure 1.1 The Migration Decision Process

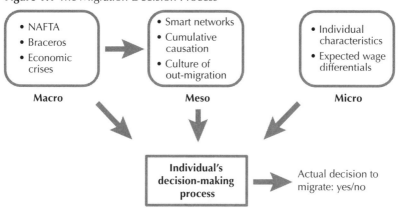

We establish the influence of macro-level factors through historical accounts of the initiation of state-directed migration from the region as well as academic research indicating the effects of national-level market-oriented policies. These initiatives have had deep impacts on individual

communities, especially those in the heart of Mexico's traditional migrant-sending region. Consequently, these macro-level factors have embedded migration in the communities and spurred the creation of the meso-level factors, which by definition influence everyone in the community and are unique to the given community (Faist 2000, 33).

Our analysis of the meso-level factors that influence the migration decision in communities with extensive migration histories reveals Tlacuitapa as a unique environment, with relatively detailed and accurate information about the migration experience and with extensive social networks. Tlacuitapa also exemplifies cumulative causation and demonstrates a culture of out-migration, all of which, as meso-level factors, promote and reinforce the decision to migrate.

Finally, we describe the micro-level factors that are unique to the individual and are instrumental in influencing the decision to migrate. By definition, individual factors vary from person to person, whereas macro-level factors change based upon one's country and meso-level factors differ according to one's community. Through multivariate regression analysis we identify the micro-level variables that make individual Tlacuitapeños more likely to migrate.

Because men and women calculate the migration decision differently, we deviate from the traditional approach by separating our regressions by sex. The basic model for the migration decision explains a migrant's initial decision to migrate to the United States. A second model predicts the odds of a migrant being in the United States in any given year based on the influence of different variables. Our ultimate aim is to explain both return migration and settlement in the United States.

THE PENDULUM MODEL: A VISUAL REPRESENTATION OF THE DECISION TO MIGRATE

Only by exploring the macro-, meso-, and micro-level forces at work in Tlacuitapa—the "unusual circumstances . . . that make migration appear to be a good and reasonable investment of time and resources"—can we offer a complete account of why individuals decide to migrate (Massey et al. 1998, 10). We hold that Tlacuitapeños' preferred and natural choice is to remain at home. The calculus only shifts in favor of migration because of "unusual circumstances." As long as these circumstances persist, so will migration. A migrant makes an individual decision to "stay migrated" based upon inputs received from the macro, meso, and micro arenas. If a migrant chooses to remain migrated for a sufficiently long period, the migrant effectively becomes settled in the host country.

For ease of conceptualization, we visualize Mexican migration as a pendulum, with its point of equilibrium representing the geographic location of Mexico. Absent any disturbing force, our pendulum will remain in position A (see figure 1.2). An outside force can move the pendulum to position B or C, but when that force is removed the pendulum returns to equilibrium at point A. The same is true of a potential migrant. Absent a disturbing force, a potential migrant will not migrate but will prefer to remain in the place to which he or she is socially and culturally bound. Highly revealing of this feeling of rootedness in Mexico is our finding that 78 percent of Tlacuitapeño migrants stated a preference for retiring in Mexico rather than the United States.

Figure 1.2 Pendulum Theory of Migration

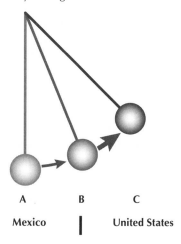

A	B	C
Mexico	|	United States

However, micro-, meso-, and macro-level factors can push the pendulum away from its point of equilibrium. A potential migrant who is at point B in figure 1.2 is seriously considering crossing the border, and a migrant at point C has already crossed. In this chapter we discuss the push factors that move a potential migrant away from his or her home, the "unusual circumstances" that drive a decision to migrate. Over time, these original "push" factors may be replaced by new societal forces that act on the migrant while in the United States and may lead to the migrant's decision to settle in the host country.

Representing migration in this way provides simple yet powerful answers to two key questions: How do we explain return migration? And why doesn't everyone in Mexico come to the United States? It is difficult to answer the first question if we view migration as a mountain, as it is often conceptualized. A great deal of effort is required to cross the mountain and reach the other side (the United States), but an equal effort is required to crest the mountain in the opposite direction and return to Mexico. Under the pendulum model, the return involves only a relaxation or weakening of the push factors that initially caused an individual to migrate. Regarding the second question, because a potential migrant's natural preference is to remain in Mexico, only forces acting on the individual can compel the decision to migrate. For some individuals, the factors do not push with sufficient force to disrupt equilibrium.

MACRO-LEVEL ANALYSIS

The macro-level factors that spurred Mexicans' first migration include the Bracero Program, a series of economic crises in Mexico in the 1970s and 1980s, and the implementation of the North American Free Trade Agreement (NAFTA) in 1994. The Bracero Program, a contract labor program that operated from 1942 to 1964, gave millions of Mexicans an opportunity to migrate to the United States for the first time. In the 1970s and 1980s, Mexico's recurrent economic crises and currency devaluations (1976, 1981–82, 1994–95), coupled with the dismantling of the government's system of subsidies to small-scale producers and consumers and other neoliberal economic policies, made Mexico's rural dwellers prime candidates for migration to the United States. Figure 1.3 illustrates the possible impact of the peso devaluations on out-migration from Tlacuitapa. Given that this community established extensive social networks in the United States during the 1970s and 1980s, the significance of above-trend growth in the number of trips suggests that macroeconomic factors might have been influencing migration.

Figure 1.3 Undocumented Migration from Tlacuitapa, 1960–2005

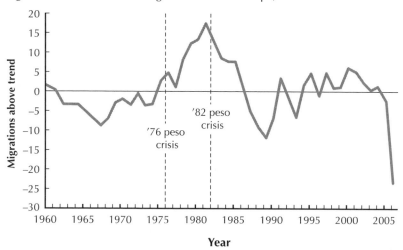

NAFTA, another important macro-level factor, was originally presented as a way to reduce Mexican migration to the United States—in the short run by stimulating job creation in Mexico's export sector, and in the long run by equalizing wage differentials between the two countries (Cornelius 2002, 287). However, the outcome has been the opposite. Job creation in Mexico's export sector has been more than offset by the number of sectors that are languishing (Dussel Peters 2000). Even where exports have risen, as in Jalisco, which saw a 500 percent increase, out-migration rates have not been affected. Contrary to the predictions of NAFTA's proponents, areas like Jalisco have experienced high export growth *and* high emigration to the United States simultaneously (Alba and Dussel Peters 2001). Nor has NAFTA diminished wage differentials between Mexico and the United States, which are in fact increasing. NAFTA may have actually encouraged out-migration by increasing the disposable income of potential migrant families, enabling members to make the trip north (Weintraub 1990, 270; Portes and Bach 1985, 387). Overall, NAFTA has not eased the economic pressure to migrate and seems to have inadvertently increased the flow of migrants it was supposed to stop.

MESO-LEVEL ANALYSIS

Using "community" as a level of analysis allows us to consider character-istics specific to places like Tlacuitapa that have extensive migratory ex-perience. These characteristics include social networks, cumulative cau-sation, and a culture of out-migration, all of which facilitate and promote individual Tlacuitapeños' decisions to migrate.

Social Networks

According to Bourdieu and Wacquant (1992, 332), social capital is "the sum of the resources, actual or virtual, that accrue to an individual or a group by virtue of possessing a durable network of more or less institu-tionalized relationships of mutual acquaintance and recognition." For our purposes, this social capital takes the form of friends and relatives who have already migrated.

Massey, Goldring, and Durand (1994, 1492) classified friends and rela-tives in the United States, or "social networks," as a form of social capital. These networks transmit information back to their hometowns through returning migrants, information that is received by potential migrants and incorporated into their individual decisions to migrate.

Migrants' networks reduce the risks a potential migrant runs. That is, worries about finding a job and housing in the United States, paying for the trip, and adjusting to a foreign language and culture may be so great that a potential migrant decides not to migrate. But social networks can give the potential migrant accurate information about job availability, wages, border enforcement, and other crucial details that can tip the deci-sion in favor of migration. Furthermore, a social network in the United States can help the migrant fund the trip, find a job, and obtain housing. Because such assistance reduces the financial and psychological costs of migration, we would expect migrants to have larger transborder social networks than those who have not migrated.

An analysis of the transborder social networks of migrants and peo-ple who have never migrated shows that migrants do indeed have much larger networks. Our interviewees with U.S. migration experience have an average of nineteen people from their extended family and about five from their nuclear family living in the United States. Nonmigrants aver-age only eleven extended family members and about two nuclear family members in the United States. A regression analysis discussed later in this chapter reveals that an increase in the size of one's social network corresponds to an increase in the likelihood of migration, especially among women. But did the sum of U.S.-based family members induce a decision to migrate, or did the migrant, after migrating, encourage many more of his relatives to come? To answer this question, we need to specify the number of family members living in the United States *before a person migrates for the first time* in order to control for any possible simultaneous causality bias that could arise when reporting relatives. By determining the number of relatives living in the United States before one's first migration, we can capture the effects of the social network free of bias. Our findings indicate that a large social network facilitates migration, not the other way around.

Cumulative Causation

The high density of Tlacuitapa's social networks produces another important phenomenon at the meso level that contributes to the decision to migrate. In communities with a deep migratory tradition, we often find "cumulative causation," with migration becoming a cause in itself, a giant snowballing social convention that in time outstrips the economic motivations that initiated it (Massey, Goldring, and Durand 1994). Every migrant who crosses the border becomes an asset to friends and family and can be tapped for advice, money, job referrals, and any other resource that could lower the costs of migration. Thus, as more migrants cross, the costs to other potential migrants decrease and, as a result, more would-be migrants head north. Massey and his colleagues caution that this system of cumulative causation cannot increase ad infinitum; a saturation point is reached when each additional migrant's marginal reduction in the cost for others to migrate equals or approaches zero. At this point, we would expect to see a leveling off in the number of new migrants.

An examination of the annual density of first-time migrations from Tlacuitapa to the United States reveals that the number of first-time male migrants increased until the 1968–1975 period (see figure 1.4), after which it seems to have reached a saturation point. That is, by this period roughly all potential first-time migrants for whom the benefits outweigh the costs have already taken their first trip to the United States.

Figure 1.4 Annual Migration Density of First-Time Crossers

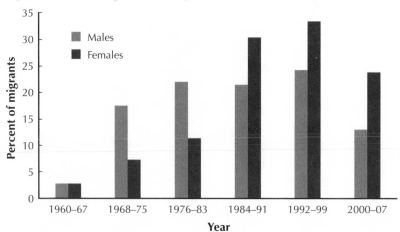

Note: The decline in 2000–2007 reflects the fact that many first-time migrants who migrated during these years had not yet returned to Tlacuitapa at the time of our study and hence were not interviewed.

Although the number of male migrants (who constitute the majority of migrants interviewed) seems to have stabilized, women migrants may not yet have reached their saturation point. This suggests that women require a much higher density in their social networks; these networks continue lowering women's costs of migration long after men have reached saturation.

The Culture of Out-Migration

Cornelius notes that "in communities with a multigenerational history of migration to the United States, new and repeat migration is also impelled by a very pronounced culture of out-migration." This culture of out-migration involves "a set of interrelated perceptions, attitudinal orientations, socialization processes and social structures, including transnational social networks, growing out of the international migratory experience, which constantly encourage, validate and facilitate participation in this movement" (1990, 24). For example, many young males may make their first trip to the United States, not because of purely economic and familial considerations, but in response to peer pressure or even as a rite of passage—considerations that are not explicitly recognized but which are embedded in the community.

Because of Tlacuitapa's intense migratory history, we would expect that the culture of out-migration continuously validates Tlacuitapeños who make the decision to migrate by perpetuating a view of migration as a natural and preferred choice, especially for first-time migrants. Unfortunately, because this hypothetical effect is "difficult to quantify and objectively assess" (Massey et al. 1998, 105), we examine Tlacuitapa's culture of out-migration through observation and life-history interviews.

The impacts of migration are clearly evident in Tlacuitapa. Although the town lies deep in Mexico's interior, cars there have license plates from across the United States. Regional Mexican music plays alongside American hip-hop, and conversations can take place in either English or Spanish.

Historical macro-level factors such as the Bracero Program are largely responsible for embedding migration as a rational economic strategy in Tlacuitapa, creating a social space that "encourages, validates and facilitates participation" in migrating (Cornelius 1990, 24). Although individuals rarely acknowledge the role that the culture of out-migration plays in the decision to migrate, it is crucial. Even young children recognize migration as a valid, viable, and often necessary economic and social strategy, something they learn from their fathers or other relatives. We focus on the way in which community perpetuates migration by generating transnational networks and engendering an inherent understanding about the migratory experience among migrants and nonmigrants alike. We document the understanding of migration as a custom in Tlacuitapa through life histories and measures of the townspeople's unwillingness to invest in education. The high probability that Tlacuitapeños will become migrants is depicted in figure 1.5.

Guadalupe, a 57-year-old experienced migrant, described Tlacuitapa's culture of out-migration in this way: "Everyone in our little town has the custom of going over there [the United States]. And because there are no sources of work here, more and more people keep going. . . . It is an ideology the people have. My boy, who is 12 years old, is already thinking of going." Interestingly, Guadalupe observes that migration occurs not just because it is a behavioral norm but also because there are no jobs in Tlacuitapa. Although he first noted that migration was a "custom," he also characterized it as a valid strategy for economic improvement. The cumulative experience of migration in Tlacuitapa deeply affects how the town socializes its residents and unwittingly promotes migration in subsequent generations.

Figure 1.5 Share of the Population with Migration Experience

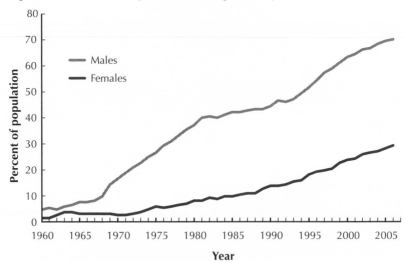

The decision to migrate is not taken immediately preceding someone's first trip as a working adult. It takes shape at a much younger age, as illustrated by two local schoolteachers, who lamented the lack of investment in education, especially for young boys: "When we arrived here, the children were only interested in going to the United States. It didn't matter whether they studied, they said, because even without an education they would earn more in the United States than we would here." School-age children view migration as a good "career alternative," one that offers earnings that surpass anything available in Tlacuitapa.

Peer pressure also encourages first-time migration decisions. Such was the case with Roberto, who finished middle school in Tlacuitapa and now works with livestock and operates agricultural machinery. Roberto's first attempt at migration, made when he was in his late twenties and newly married, did not fall neatly into an economic calculation of costs and benefits. He reported that he left Tlacuitapa to better his economic situation, but he added, "My two friends invited me. I didn't want to go, because it's hard to leave your family." Yet he undertook the trip because his friends encouraged him.

Roberto and his friends tried to cross into the United States by running through a legal port of entry, where they were detained. Once back in Tlacuitapa, they made no further attempts to migrate, an uncommon choice among would-be migrants. Because Roberto's attempted border crossing was so poorly strategized, it is clear that his migration decision was not driven by necessity, but rather by an unwillingness to refuse his friends' invitation.

MICRO-LEVEL ANALYSIS

Our micro-level analysis includes the individual-level factors that contribute to a decision to migrate, including age, marital status, education, legal status, birth order, and number of children. These are the factors that most precisely answer the question of "who migrates."

Harris and Todaro (1970) pioneered the model of the individual as a rational actor who decides to migrate. They argue that the primary motivator for an individual to migrate is the wage differential. If the discounted present value of the benefit to movement (in the form of a higher income stream) is higher than the costs incurred, then the individual will move. In the case of Tlacuitapa, we collected data on expected wage differentials and on the amounts paid to people-smugglers (see chapter 3 in this volume) in an attempt to quantify the explicit costs of movement. We are unable to quantify the psychological costs incurred when leaving one's hometown and resettling elsewhere. However, following Harris and Todaro's logic, we can assume these costs to be less than the difference between the expected benefit and the explicit costs. If the situation were otherwise, the individual would not move.

The wage differential between Tlacuitapa and the United States accounts for much of the economic rationale underlying the decision to migrate. Among respondents who reported a wage in both Tlacuitapa and the United States, the average wage gain for migrants working in the

United States was US$6.45 per hour, with a standard deviation of $4.17. Migrants from Tlacuitapa generally work in agriculture at home, but in the United States they are employed predominantly in nonprofessional services, so the wage differential is between different economic sectors.

Consistent with Harris and Todaro's framework, comparing the average wage differential with the cost of migrating reveals whether migration is a reasonable choice. On their most recent clandestine crossings, Tlacuitapeños paid people-smugglers an average fee of about $2,100, an amount that would require between eight and nine 40-hour weeks of work to repay.

The relatively short duration of the payback period returns us to a question asked earlier: Why doesn't everyone in Mexico come to the United States? The immeasurable implicit costs of migration are quite large when compared to the explicit costs of migration. Harris and Todaro posit that border-crossing costs determine the equilibrium wage differential between two locations. However, because migration flows from Tlacuitapa seem to have reached an equilibrium point, as discussed above, and observed wage differentials remain large, we suggest that some very high but unobservable migration-associated psychological costs are at work.

MODELING THE DECISION TO MIGRATE

In this section we identify the variables that most strongly influence an individual Tlacuitapeño's decision to migrate. We estimate two multivariate models, one for first-time migrants and one for the odds of a person being in the United States in a given year. For the first model we examine the historical incidence of migration for every migrant in our sample, using a panel data set created from detailed migration histories taken in our survey of Tlacuitapeños. From this information, we can extrapolate the state of all independent variables at the time of a person's first migration. We regress these variables on the probability of being a migrant to the United States for the first time.

Using the same data set, we look at the state of the variables for every person from the ages of 15 to 65 for every year. This forms the basis for our second regression, giving the probability of a person being in the United States in any given year. These multivariate regressions test demographic variables in addition to social networks, position in the family, and number of relatives currently in the United States for the probability of being in the United States in a given year. Therefore, through these regressions we can identify those demographic variables that raise or lower the likelihood that a given person will migrate.

First-Time Migration

For the men of Tlacuitapa, the average age at first migration is quite constant at about 20 years, with a slight downward trend over time (see figure 1.6). For women, average age at first migration fluctuates, but it appears to follow an upward trend in recent years. These fluctuations may indicate that women are more sensitive to variations in macro-level policies; however, because of the smaller sample size for women, their averages are more susceptible to variation.

Figure 1.6 Average Age at First Migration

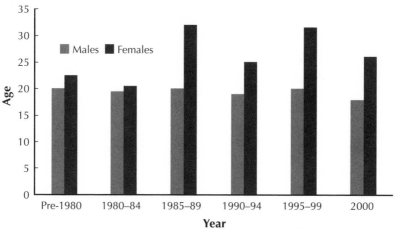

Figure 1.7 shows the documentation status of our interviewees at the time of first migration and the time of the interview. Men are much less likely to cross legally on their first trip, but they had a significantly higher rate of legal status at the time of our interviews. Women's first migration also tends to be undocumented, although not at the rate we found among male migrants.

Figure 1.7 Documentation Status of Migrants, by Sex,
at First Migration and Time of Interview

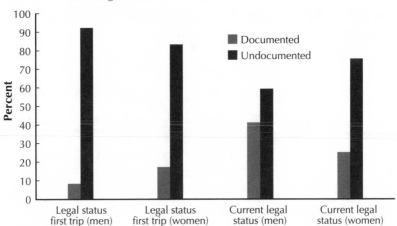

Another characteristic that varies significantly between men and women migrating for the first time is marital status. Only 16 percent of first-time male migrants to the United States were married, versus 56 percent of the women, which suggests that women migrate primarily in response to a spouse's prior migration.

The results of our regression analysis of first-time migration are reported in table 1.1. As demographic and control variables, we use age, years of education, number of children, marital status (a dummy variable), legal status, birth order (1 indicates youngest child), and number of family members in the United States.

We find that age, marital status, legal status, and family members in the United States are significant predictors of the decision to migrate for the first time among both men and women. Age has a negative effect on the decision to migrate for the first time for both men and women. Age makes men 17 percent less likely to migrate and women 16 percent less likely to migrate for the first time. As mentioned previously, men tend to migrate for the first time at around 20 years of age, while the average age for women fluctuates (see figure 1.6). Thus men will be less likely to migrate for the first time with each successive year; the age variable also affects women but not to the same extent. Our model also allows flexibility in the impact of age on migration by including age-squared. For women in Tlacuitapa, their age at first migration could be conceptualized as an inverted U, with women taking their first trip at a much older age to reunite their family on the other side of the border.

Table 1.1 Characteristics of First-Time Migrants (maximum-likelihood logistic estimation)

	Model 1 β Males	Model 2 β Females	Model 1 Odds-Ratio Males	Model 2 Odds-Ratio Females
Age	−0.148*** (.059)	−0.157*** (.061)	0.862*** (.050)	0.854*** (.050)
Age²	0.001 (.001)	0.002*** (.001)	1.001 (.001)	1.002*** (.001)
Education	−0.031 (.020)	−0.019 (.031)	0.969 (.019)	0.981 (.030)
Children	0.000 (.084)	−0.262*** (.095)	1.000 (.084)	0.770*** (.073)
Married	−0.633*** (.238)	0.922*** (.337)	0.531*** (.127)	2.515*** (.848)
Legal	−1.085*** (.393)	0.375 (0.397)	0.338*** (.133)	1.455 (0.577)
Birth order	0.129 (.274)	−0.035 (0.405)	1.138 (.312)	0.966 (0.391)
Family in United States	0.030* (.018)	0.103*** (0.025)	1.031* (.018)	1.108*** (0.028)
Chi-square	173.32	67.40	173.32	67.40
Pseudo-R²	.1526	.0513	.1526	.0513
N	6403	7063	6403	7063

* 90%, ** 95%, *** 99% confidence levels; robust standard errors in parentheses.

Being married is statistically significant for both male and female first-time migrants, but in opposing directions: negative for men and positive for women. A married man is only half as likely as an unmarried man to be a first-time migrant; and women are two and a half times more likely to be married when they migrate for the first time. This confirms our earlier assertion that men usually make their first migration at a young age and while still single. However, the majority of women migrate after marriage, which accords with the Mexican tradition that a woman should not leave her parents' home until she is married.

Men who migrate to the United States for the first time are very unlikely to have U.S. legal status. However, the lack of statistical significance of legal status for women indicates that although more women have legal documentation when they migrate for the first time, this is not a significant determinant in their decision.

The regression analysis also shows that having a social network in the United States makes migration more likely for both men and women. Each additional member in the social network makes men about 3 percent and women 11 percent more likely to migrate for the first time. Because social networks typically comprise multiple members, this statistic highlights the importance of social networks for women, who are much more likely to migrate in the presence of a strong social network.

Odds of Being in the United States in a Given Year

Our second multivariate regression analysis seeks to predict the odds of a Tlacuitapeño being in the United States in a given year (see table 1.2). As in the previous analysis, the demographic variables include the respondent's age, years of education, number of children, marital status, legal status, birth order, and number of family members in the United States. An additional variable is whether a female migrant gave birth to a child in a given year. The purpose of this model is to separate the decision to migrate for the first time from the decision for subsequent or repeat trips. The model uses a maximum-likelihood fixed-effects logit estimation approach, where the fixed effect estimation controls for yearly macroeconomic and policy impacts. As discussed previously, there have been surges in migration flows from Mexico associated with macro-level factors. Because our models control for these effects, they provide better estimates of the demographic and network characteristics of Tlacuitapa migrants in the United States.

We find that years of education, number of children, legal status, and number of family members in the United States are all statistically significant for men and women. Marriage is statistically significant for women only. Birth order and age-squared are significant for men only, but the effect of age-squared is so close to zero that it has no quantitatively noticeable effect.

Table 1.2 Odds of Being in the United States in a Given Year
(maximum likelihood fixed-effects logistic estimation)

	Model 1 β Males	Model 2 β Females	Model 1 Odds-Ratio Males	Model 2 Odds-Ratio Females
Age	**0.036***** **(.005)**	−0.004 (.008)	**0.964***** **(.005)**	0.996 (.007)
Education	0.008 (.010)	**0.118***** **(.016)**	1.008 (.011)	**1.125***** **(.018)**
Children	**−0.069***** **(.020)**	**−0.259***** **(.036)**	0.934*** (.019)	0.772*** (.027)
Married	−0.036 (.082)	**1.636***** **(.160)**	0.964 (.079)	**5.135***** **(.819)**
Legal	**1.463***** **(.082)**	**3.116***** **(.129)**	**4.319***** **(.082)**	**22.551***** **(2.919)**
Birth order	**−.249**** **(.115)**	0.130 (.188)	**.780**** **(.090)**	1.139 (.214)
Family in United States	**0.129***** **(.008)**	**0.184***** **(0.013)**	**1.137***** **(.009)**	**1.202***** **(0.015)**
Child born	—	0.159 (0.151)	—	1.173 (0.177)
LR Chi-square	1249	1906	1249	1906
N (person years)	6297	6826	6297	6826

* 90%, ** 95%, *** 99% confidence levels; robust standard errors in parentheses.

Unlike in the models presented in table 1.1, education has a significant positive effect in this model for both men and women. An extra year of education makes men about 3 percent and women about 11 percent more likely to be in the United States in any given year. The number of children is also statistically significant, in a negative direction, in explaining the odds of a person being in the United States in a given year. Each additional child makes men about 5 percent more likely to remain in Tlacuitapa, and women about 20 percent more likely to remain there. Having more children appears to have a greater negative effect for women, the traditional caregivers. Men have more freedom to be away from home for part of the year and to seek employment in the United States. Further, the more children a woman has in Mexico, the less likely she is to jeopardize their safety in a clandestine crossing and the more likely she will wait until the children are older or until they can enter legally in order to reunite the family across the border.

Legal status proves to be the most significant determinant, making both men and women much more likely to migrate during a given year. For women, legal status makes them twenty-two times more likely to be in the United States in a given year. Men, while less influenced by legal status, are still nearly five times more likely to be in the United States if they have documents. The powerful effect of legal status can be explained as follows: Men who have legal status may be more likely to take return trips from Mexico to the United States, continuing their migration careers and perhaps positioning themselves and their dependents for permanent settlement in the United States. For women, legal status can eliminate one of migration's greatest costs—the intrinsic dangers of clandestine entry, which for women include kidnapping and rape. Yet even though legal status makes men and women more likely to migrate during any given year, undocumented status does not significantly deter women from becoming migrants (see figure 1.7).

Having a network of family members in the United States makes a potential migrant more likely to be in the United States. For each additional person in a potential migrant's social network, women are about 20 percent more likely and men about 10 percent more likely to be in the United States.

As in our analysis of first-time migration, marriage is a significant predictor of migration in a given year, with a married woman being five times more likely to be in the United States. Although women are capable of influencing the migration decision in their household, they nevertheless migrate primarily as "tied movers" accompanying their husbands (see chapter 7, this volume). Thus marriage makes a woman much more likely to be in the United States, particularly if her husband is a migrant.

Birth order only affects males, and the effect is in a negative direction. First-born males are much more likely to be in the United States, reflecting the likelihood that the family, as a decision-making unit, allocates family members to different labor markets in an effort to increase earnings and decrease unemployment risk. This constraint is relaxed for each subsequent child, because the family is likely to already have an earlier child in the United States.

Why Separate Explanatory Models for Men and Women?

There are pronounced differences in how men and women calculate the migration decision. To date, "migration theories have not addressed the gender aspects of international migration partly because of the assumption that most migrant workers were men, and women their dependents" (Oishi 2002, 4). Traditional approaches to the decision to migrate often do not apply to women. This may be the case simply because women are still not seen as primary breadwinners, or on a more complex level it may reflect the social and cultural expectations for women in the household, labor market, and community. In any case, the independent variables' differential effects on men and women in their calculation to migrate may often go unnoticed.

The effect of marriage on first-time migration, for example, points out the utter ineffectiveness of a single model. Marriage means very different things for men and women within the culture of Tlacuitapa. For a man, marriage means responsibility as the primary breadwinner for a household; for a woman it means she may leave her parents' home and establish a new home with her husband. Although not calculated in this research, these differential effects of a single variable are also seen in macro- and meso-level factors, which can mean different things for men and women. We must acknowledge, therefore, that even though we separate men and women in our models, a full modeling of the decision to migrate should also account for how macro- and meso-level factors influence women's expectations and their subsequent decision to migrate differently than men. Nevertheless, ours is an important step in recognizing that no discussion of the decision to migrate is complete without noting how this calculation is very different for women and men.

Smith-Lovin and McPherson (1993) define gender as the product of social relationships in which men and women are embedded and note its influence in individual decisions and actions. Further, "migration decisions are made within a context of socially recognized and mutually reinforcing expectations that reflect several dimensions of gender relations between individuals, within families, and in societal institutions" (Kanaiaupuni 2000, 1312). With respect to our model, we envision gender as directly influencing how a woman will rationalize the decision to migrate based on gender-specific expectations within Mexican patriarchal society, specifically with regard to economic and familial considerations. We were able to capture the importance of gender in the decision to migrate by running separate models for men and women using the same independent variables. As expected, the coefficients on any given variable were slightly different for men and women because of social constructions of gender roles.

Among the key differences captured by our separate models for men and women was the strong impact of marriage in increasing the likelihood that a woman would migrate: 56 percent of women are married on the first trip, compared to only 16 percent of men. Another key variable in the women's decision to migrate is the presence of social networks, which makes women 11 percent more likely to take their first trip, compared to 3 percent among men. Although the percentage of women who are married on their first trip to the United States is high, at 56 percent, the remaining 44 percent of women migrants are not married on their first trip. For these cases we postulate that family members other than a husband form their social network. The role of marriage and/or social network for would-be women migrants speaks to the family considerations that dominate in the rural environment of Tlacuitapa and to the characteristics of Mexican patriarchal society (see chapter 7 in this volume).

THE SETTLEMENT PROCESS

After a migrant arrives in the United States, the push factors that drove migration are often replaced by others related to the migrant's integration in the host society. These factors "hold" the migrant in the host society, increasing the likelihood that he or she will "stay migrated" and not return to the home community. Given that the decision-making process to migrate is continuous—to be or not to be "migrated"—the implications of the decision to migrate to the United States may be felt years after the decision has been made.

Settlement as a choice reflects a migrant's intention to stay in the destination country (Piore 1979). This intention can only be formulated after a migrant has accumulated experience in the host country, and most first-time migrants—who tend to be male, young, and unmarried—in fact do not intend to settle. They must first experience the host country's labor market, something done while still migrating on a "trial basis" (Gmelch 1980, 138). After a migrant's initial trip and perhaps years of circular migration, his or her life in the United States evolves from temporary to permanent as family members—principally wives and children—join the migrant. This gradual movement toward settlement is the unintended consequence of the original decision to migrate and the societal integration process that develops through unforeseeable life events, such as obtaining stable employment, the birth of a child, the child's entry into the U.S. school system, or the purchase of a home to accommodate a growing family.

We measure settlement via respondents' answers when asked where they had spent most of the last five years. Those who had spent most of that time in the United States we designate as "settlers" or as U.S.-based. Those who had spent more time in Mexico are "non-settlers" or Mexico-based. Time spent in either location need not be consecutive, breaking from Massey's model which defines a settler as someone who has spent three consecutive years in the United States (Massey 1986, 681). Although extended residence in the United States may indicate that a migrant has chosen that country as home, indicating a certain degree of satisfaction on the migrant's part, we caution against viewing this as absolute. For example, an unauthorized migrant who has not returned to Mexico may have remained in the United States, not because he or she prefers the host country to the home country, but because strict border enforcement has raised the cost and risk of reentry after a home visit. Our research in Tlacuitapa shows that settlement as an unintended consequence is often a result of heightened border enforcement. Borrowing Riosmena's analogy (2004, 266), U.S. policies have "greased the gears of migrant settlement." Therefore, we can describe undocumented Tlacuitapeño migrants as experiencing "temporary sedentary living" because they have been prevented from maintaining circular migration and have been forced to "stay put." Another indicator of border enforcement's effects on settlement is the rising number of uninhabited houses in Tlacuitapa (see chapter 2, this volume).

Permanent settlement by Mexican migrants to the United States began rising in the 1970s and then accelerated in the 1980s (Cornelius 1992, 175; Marcelli and Cornelius 2001, 106). The family reunification provisions contained in the Immigration Reform and Control Act of 1986 (IRCA) encouraged migrants to apply for legalization and then bring their spouses and children to the United States, strengthening the incentives to remain there permanently. It has also been suggested that the more trips a migrant makes and the more experience he or she accumulates, the more likely the migrant will settle in the United States (Massey 1986, 671), attesting to the gradual movement from sojourner to settler as one integrates into the host society. A thorough understanding of how integration occurs under-pins an understanding of settlement because it highlights the importance of social networks, use of institutions, and nonseasonal employment, fac-tors that become stronger as migratory experience accumulates. High U.S. demand for year-round low-skilled labor is also contributing to rooting migrants in the United States (Cornelius 1992, 176).

Settlement often leads to retirement in the United States. Neverthe-less, when Tlacuitapeño migrants were asked where they wanted to retire, the overwhelming majority stated a desire to retire in Mexico. Of course, there is a difference between intention and outcome. Family ties and so-cial services in the United States may keep most settled migrants there after retirement. Those who follow through on their intention to retire in Tlacuitapa are responding to a mix of lifestyle preference and family networks; these conditions must be just right before migrants decide to relocate their lives post-retirement.

To describe how migrants "remain migrated" in the United States, we refer to the "settlement phase" of Massey's model (1986, 671). In this phase, migrants have been joined by wives and children, have developed widespread contacts with people and institutions in the United States, and have identified with their host community. We compare our settled and non-settled survey populations using variables that we believe influence and indicate settlement: legal status, family reunification, kinship/friend-ship networks, identification with members of the host society, English language acquisition, school enrollment of children, employment, hav-ing a bank account, property ownership, and remitting. These variables fall into the subcategories of social interaction, institutional incorporation, economic integration, and remittance behavior.

About 60 percent of migrants in our study are U.S.-based, or settled (see table 1.3). Of these, almost three-quarters are documented. Many migrants from Tlacuitapa likely received legal status through IRCA and then submitted applications for family members through its family reuni-fication provisions. Eighty-three percent of our respondents who were amnestied under IRCA are settled in the United States. Men make up 64 percent of the population of documented settled migrants and 82 per-cent of the undocumented cohort of settled migrants. The undocumented male population in the United States most likely comprises recent migrants who have had fewer opportunities for becoming legalized. Because most new migrants tend to be male, this accounts for the lower number of women among the undocumented migrants.

Table 1.3 Settlers versus Non-Settlers: Demographic, Social, and Economic Attributes

Attributes	Mexico-based (N = 168)	U.S.-based (N = 244)
% of combined population	40.8	59.2
Gender		
Male	69.9%	67.8%
Female	30.1%	32.2%
Legal Status		
Documented	28.1%	73.8%
Undocumented	71.9%	26.3%
Social Networks		
Median # relatives living in U.S. (absolute number)	15	21
Median # nuclear family members in U.S. (absolute number)	4	7
Spouse in U.S. (N = 325)	12.0%	71.6%
At least 1 child in U.S. (N = 408)	39.4%	65.0%
At least 1 U.S.-born child (N = 412))	16.1%	49.2%
Employment in U.S.		
Construction (N = 37)	13.4%	19.3%
Agriculture (N = 58)	31.5%	12.5%
Nonprofessional service (N = 36)	11.4%	21.6%
Institution Use		
Bank account (N = 164)	9.5%	64.3%
Children sent to school (N = 131)	17.4%	89.1%
Other		
Understand English well (N = 167)	17.7%	57.7%
Speak English well (N = 77)	3.6%	29.5%
Own property in U.S. (N = 135)	6.5%	53.4%
Have requested citizenship (N = 71)	6.5%	30.8%

Social Interaction

Social network theory, which explains how having contacts in the host society facilitates and encourages migration, can also explain the tendency
to settle. Increased border enforcement is prompting undocumented migrants to send for their dependents rather than run the risk of repeated
return trips, and this move toward family reunification has resulted in
longer stays. Migrants' wives and children, especially U.S.-born children,
become strong "supporters" of settling in the United States (Cornelius
1992, 176), and ties with the home country lessen. In our survey, just
under three-fourths of the U.S.-based migrants have their spouses with
them in the United States; this is true for only 12 percent of Mexico-based
migrants. Nearly half have at least one U.S.-born child, compared to only
16 percent for non-settled migrants. About two-thirds of U.S.-based migrants have at least one child who resides in the United States, versus only
40 percent for Mexico-based migrants. On average, settled migrants have
three more nuclear family members and six more relatives living in the
United States than do non-settled migrants. And documented U.S.-based
migrants have five more relatives and four more nuclear family members
in the United States on average than do undocumented settled migrants,
thanks to the former group's access to family reunification options. Approximately 60 percent of undocumented migrants based in the United
States have their spouses with them, compared to almost 80 percent for
U.S.-based migrants with legal documents.

In addition to encouraging migration in the first place, kinship and
friendship networks also help reduce the costs and risks of long-term
stays in the United States and facilitate integration by providing support
systems for dependent family members (Cornelius 1992, 176). For example, we observed how social networks link migrants to work opportunities; two-thirds of settled and about 80 percent of non-settled migrants
found their most recent U.S. employment through friends or relatives.
The numbers are almost the same when we focus on legal status: 60 percent of settled migrants with documents obtained their most recent job
through a friend or relative, and over 80 percent of undocumented settled
migrants relied on a contact. Not having papers clearly makes it more
difficult to find a job on one's own because of the risks associated with
undocumented status. Regardless of legal status, however, most migrants

rely on social networks to find work, demonstrating these networks' importance for integrating into the host society.

Another important part of social integration is contact and identification with others in the host society (Massey 1986, 673). Migrants are initially concerned primarily with maximizing their earnings, leaving little time for much else. But as migrants move away from this "ideal of economic men" and develop recreational interests, socializing becomes more important (Massey 1986, 674). Friendship networks may develop through participation in community groups such as soccer teams.

Our research team conducted interviews in Union City, California, a major receiving area for Tlacuitapeño migrants, where our researchers observed active friendship networks. Union City–based Tlacuitapeños played on a soccer team that included two Guatemalans and three native-born Americans of non-Mexican descent. The league in which the team plays, "La Liga México," also has players from Afghanistan. Danny, a 20-year-old team co-captain and player whose family is from Tlacuitapa, described the team's makeup:

> Two Guatemalans have played for us. They are close friends of people from Tlacuitapa. Like Oscar; he isn't from Tlacuitapa but we see him as one of us. They were the only non-Mexican Latinos on the team.

When asked about the relationship between the non-Tlacuitapeño team members (Guatemalan and American) and those from Tlacuitapa, Danny responded:

> We're really good friends. The only reason they are on the team is because they know lots of people from Tlacuitapa and they have a strong relationship with us. If we didn't know who they were, they wouldn't have been on our team, no matter how well they played.

The mix of Americans, Tlacuitapeños, and other Latin American migrants on the soccer team reveals the high degree of contact that Tlacuitapeños have with other members of the community. And the fact that these contacts are all based on friendship underscores the important role friendships play in community cohesion. Danny explained that he met most of the non-Tlacuitapeños in high school. Participation in soccer teams also makes it easier for Tlacuitapeños to keep in touch with friends and relatives and to introduce new arrivals to the established migrant community (Massey 1986, 675). In January 2007, the Tlacuitapa team played a team that included migrants from Oaxaca, demonstrating that the weekly games also broaden contacts with migrant groups from other regions in the home country. Danny spoke of the friendship between opposing teams: "Most of the time we make friends with other teams in the league and invite them out. For example, there is a team from San Juan de los Lagos, basically where we're from. We always kick the ball around with them and it makes for a great rivalry when we play them."

Following the games, the team gathers to eat and socialize. When asked if non-Tlacuitapeño players are involved in the postgame events, Danny remarked: "Yes; when people play in a team it gives us a sense of brotherhood."

Settled migrants tend to identify more than non-settled migrants with people outside of their ethnic group in the United States, reflecting their development of friendship ties that link them to U.S. society and culture. When we asked settled and non-settled migrants if they identified with people from Tlacuitapa, Jalisco, and Mexico, their responses were nearly identical. When the question was rephrased to include other ethnic groups, both settled and non-settled migrants indicated high levels of identification with groups linked to Latin America, though this identification was stronger among settled migrants (see figure 1.8). For example, 56 percent of settled migrants identified closely with Latin Americans, compared to 48 percent of non-settled migrants. Similarly, three-quarters of settled migrants reported a close identification with Latinos, versus 60 percent of non-settled migrants. The only two groups that ranked relatively low in terms of migrants' co-identification were North Americans and Americans. The settled migrants' stronger identification with a broader range of community members suggests that the more time a migrant has spent in the United States, the more likely he or she will develop friendship ties, which facilitate deeper integration in the host society.

Language acquisition is another indicator of settlement. More experience in the host society and more interaction with English-speaking community members lead to a higher level of English proficiency. Settled migrants self-reported much higher in terms of their ability to understand and speak English well. Nearly 60 percent of settled migrants reported that they understand English well, and almost 30 percent reported speaking English well. Among non-settled migrants, less than a fifth said they understand English well, and a mere 4 percent said they spoke English well.

Figure 1.8 Settled and Non-Settled Migrants' Identification with Other Ethnic Groups

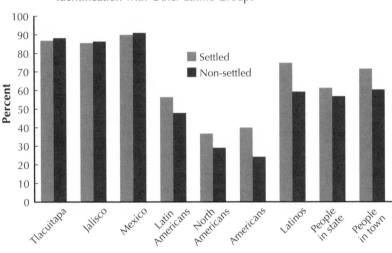

Institutional Incorporation

Enrolling one's children in U.S. schools is one of the most important forms of incorporation into U.S. society and a strong indicator of settlement. Schools connect children with U.S. culture, and they are second in importance only to the home in terms of young people's socialization. The children of migrants undergo a process of acculturation in U.S. schools that ties them to the United States and makes it difficult for them to return to and be incorporated in Mexican society. Parents also connect with other members of the community through the school system via parent-teacher interaction and parent-led groups. Most migrants want their children to have a better education and a better job than they themselves have (Chávez 1992, 182), and parents make keeping their children in U.S. schools a priority.

Nearly 90 percent of the settled Tlacuitapeño migrants we interviewed sent their children to school during their last trip to the United States (9 percent sent their children to a private school). Seventeen percent of non-settled migrants sent their children to public school (none to private school). In terms of documentation status, a higher percentage of documented settled migrants sent their children to school (91 percent) than did undocumented settled migrants (76 percent).

Economic Integration

The transition from temporary, seasonal employment to more stable year-round employment as migrants move from agricultural to nonagricultural work also contributes to long-term residence, thus increasing the opportunities for interaction with institutions in the host society (Massey 1986, 673). Settled migrants in our study are most likely to be employed in the nonprofessional service sector (22 percent), followed closely by construction (19 percent). Agriculture provides work for only about one in ten settled Tlacuitapeños. By contrast, over a third of non-settled—or "circular"—Tlacuitapeño migrants work in agriculture.

The low number of settled migrants in agriculture reflects the fact that migrants employed in nonagricultural work are less likely to return to Mexico. Of all migrants we surveyed, only 18 percent reported that they are currently employed in the agricultural sector, following a trend dating from the late 1960s, when Mexican immigrants began moving out of agriculture and into year-round employment, typically in low-skill jobs (Cornelius 1992, 177). In a 1976 study of Tlacuitapa, 55 percent of migrants had worked most recently in agriculture, but in a 1988–1989 survey only 21 percent were employed in agriculture during their most recent trip (Cornelius 1992, 180). The move from seasonal to year-round work has brought economic security and stability, creating an environment that favors settlement.

As migrants become embedded in the United States, their chances of finding better-paid work increase. The converse is true as well: getting a better-paid job leads many migrants to decide to stay. As settled migrants earn more, they need access to a banking institution in which to deposit their growing earnings; and as their work becomes more regularized, their need to make payments in a more formal manner translates into a need for a checking account. In sum, settled migrants require a more standard way to handle their earnings. Of our settled migrants, 64 percent have a U.S. bank account, versus only 10 percent of our non-settled cohort.

And as migrants remain longer in the United States, find more stable employment, earn higher wages, and use banks, property ownership becomes an option. The decision to buy property means that a migrant has resolved to remain in the United States long term, and, in complementary fashion, home mortgages and other financial obligations increase the probability of settlement because of the debt owed (Cornelius 1992, 176). Over half of our settled migrants reported owning property in the United States, compared to 7 percent of non-settled migrants. The purchase of a home symbolizes the shift from one society to the other, and it also demonstrates migrant families' desire for the comforts and conveniences that come with living in the United States. Growing families want a space of their own, protected from rent hikes and landlords' whims. The decision to buy a home can represent a gradual easing into life in the United States, building on earlier life choices such as the purposeful schooling of children in the United States.

María, a single mother and former U.S. resident who returned to Tlacuitapa five years ago to retire, underscored the importance of a home in feeling settled. When asked what it meant to be "settled" in the United States, she responded:

> For me, to be settled in the United States is to have a house, to buy a house of my own, to be settled and have a means of living over there, to have a good pension, because you need money to be there. My family is already settled. They have their houses, they have their families. If I want, I can go there and stay with my son, my daughter, my brothers. They're settled, I'm not. Since I don't have a house, I'm not settled in the United States. For me, there is no stability there. This is where I have my stability.

Remittance Behavior

During their most recent stay in the United States, some 85 percent of non-settled migrants and about 77 percent of settled migrants sent money to Tlacuitapa. The lower proportion among settled migrants accords with the fact that settled migrants, whose lives are centered in the United States, spend more of their money in the host society (Massey 1986, 677). A stronger measure is the percentage of income sent as remittances. Non-settled migrants send a third of their earnings back to Tlacuitapa, versus 16 percent among settled migrants, whose ties with the home community have weakened. Of U.S.-based migrants who sent money home, over half sent remittances to their mothers; 44 percent of Mexico-based migrants did so.

Of particular interest is the percentage of migrants who sent money to their wives. Over 40 percent of Mexico-based migrants sent money to their wives, but only 13 percent of U.S.-based migrants did so, confirming that members of the latter group were more likely to be accompanied by their wives in the United States. Indeed, of the 23 percent of U.S.-based migrants who did not send remittances to Tlacuitapa, nearly two-thirds said they had no one there to send money to. Given that most settled migrants have already been joined by their family members, sending remittances is unnecessary. Among the non-settled migrants who did not remit money, two-thirds reported they did not earn enough to send money home.

MODELING THE DECISION TO SETTLE

We used a maximum-likelihood logit estimation approach to model the decision to settle. The model in table 1.4 provides insight into the characteristics of migrants who settle in the United States. It considers only those respondents with migration experience and uses the variable that is employed throughout this section as the dependent variable: whether the interviewee indicated that he or she had spent more time over the last five years in the United States or in Mexico.

The analysis produced some interesting results. First, legal status is a highly significant predictor of settlement; those who are documented were more than three times more likely than undocumented migrants to be settled in the United States. We also found that men are more likely than women to have settled, but this is the result of a demographic imbalance, with more male migrants being in the United States at any given time.

Table 1.4 Characteristics of Migrants Who Settle in the United States

	Model 1 β	Model 1 Odds-Ratio
Male	0.965*** (.355)	2.626*** (.932)
Age	−0.044*** (.014)	0.957*** (.014)
Spouse in U.S.	1.045** (.455)	2.844** (1.294)
Education	0.031 (.059)	1.031 (.061)
Relatives in U.S.	0.011* (.006)	1.011* (.007)
U.S.-born child	0.131 (.402)	1.140 (.458)
Legal	1.185*** (.341)	3.270*** (1.115)
Agriculture	−0.819* (.437)	0.441* (.193)
Own U.S. property	1.207** (.517)	3.342** (1.730)
U.S. bank account	1.403*** (.441)	4.066*** (1.793)
Chi-square	85.81	85.81
Pseudo-R^2	.392	.392
N	340	340

* 90%, ** 95%, *** 99% confidence levels; robust standard errors in parentheses.

Second, social networks contribute positively to the likelihood that the respondent reported being settled in the United States. If the respondent reported having a spouse in the United States, he or she was almost three times more likely to state being settled. Further, there is a small but statistically significant increase in the likelihood of being settled with each additional relative the respondent currently has living in the United States.

Third, two variables decreased the likelihood of settlement: age and agricultural labor. Age had a statistically significant impact, with each additional year decreasing the likelihood of settlement by 4 percent. And, as expected, persons who reported working in the highly seasonal U.S. agricultural sector were more than twice as likely to report living primarily in Mexico.

Fourth, owning property and having a bank account in the United States were significant indicators of likelihood of settlement. Respondents who reported owning property or having a bank account were three and four times more likely, respectively, to report being settled.

Finally, the respondent's education level and whether he or she had a child born in the United States did not differ significantly between those reporting that they lived primarily in the United States and those reporting that they lived primarily in Mexico.

RETURN MIGRATION FOR RETIREMENT

Due to the transnational nature of migrants' lives, the possibility to return home is always present. However, because the conditions that initially favored U.S. settlement do not disappear at retirement, some specific considerations must come into play before a settled migrant decides to return to Tlacuitapa for retirement. Some Tlacuitapeños are making this decision even after having been settled in the United States for years, and Tlacuitapa may become a budding "retirement center for returnees" (Mines and de Janvry 1982, 453). In its favor, the cost of living in Tlacuitapa is much lower than in the United States, although services such as health care are not as developed. We have analyzed the impact of certain demographic variables and behavioral attributes on retirement preference, including whether the migrant has children in the United States, has requested U.S. citizenship, citizenship status, institution use, property ownership, and language attainment.

We asked our informants to specify their preferred location for retirement. Among non-settled migrants, 88 percent said they preferred to retire in Mexico, and 13 percent said they wished to retire in the United States. Of settled migrants, three-fourths want to retire in Mexico and one-fourth prefer the United States. Although migrants show a strong desire to return to Mexico regardless of their settlement location, the probability that settled migrants will actually return is very low due to familial ties in the United States (Chávez 1992, 176).

Even so, some of our respondents had recently returned to Tlacuitapa to retire after having lived in the United States for long periods and despite having close family members, including U.S.-born-and-raised children, remaining in the United States. Some studies have documented that "time in the U.S. is not related with intention to retire in the United States" (Aguilera 2004, 12). For example, María, who was quoted previously, went to the United States with her parents as a *mojada* at age four and grew up there, moving from state to state as her parents worked in agriculture. A trip to Tlacuitapa kindled her desire to return there one day:

> I came [to Tlacuitapa] when I was 18 years old. I graduated from high school over there and came here. This is where I met my grandparents, all of my relatives. I saw the town where they grew up and I liked it a lot. And I said, "I'm going to go back there one day." And that's what happened. Here I am.

María's case confirms that the desire to return to the homeland often begins with a vacation trip (Gmelch 1980, 139). Her example differs, however, from the general pattern by which a migrant's "center of gravity" tends to shift to the United States as their children marry and raise families there (Chávez 1992, 176). When María's children were young, she thought she would stay in the United States for the rest of her life. However, she later divorced, and she felt differently as she watched her children form families of their own: "As they began to get married and have children, I said, 'No, this is not for me.' I remembered my dream, to return. When everything's said and done, well, they have another life and I'm all alone."

Although migrants with no children in the United States were more likely to express a desire to retire in Mexico, having children residing in the United States does little to tie migrants there, at least in terms of their stated retirement preference. Indeed, three-fourths of the migrants with children currently living in the United States expressed a desire to return to Mexico, not too far below the nearly 90 percent of migrants with no children in the United States who wish to retire in Mexico. Among married migrants settled in the United States, one-fourth wish to remain, and two-thirds wish to retire in Mexico. Beatriz, a widowed, childless migrant who lived in the United States for over fifty years, expressed her desire to return to Tlacuitapa after her husband's death: "I always had that in mind. I always thought that one day I was going to come here. This is where my family is." Beatriz also mentioned that she could not survive in the United States on her Social Security pension.

The decision to seek U.S. citizenship may be seen as a decisive step toward settlement, but continuing settlement into retirement does not appear to be related to citizenship status. Over two-thirds of the interviewed migrants who have requested citizenship still state a preference for retiring in Mexico. We might better view a request for citizenship as a strategy to ease the difficulties of a migrant's transnational life. Such is the case with José Arturo, who is in his thirties, married to a U.S. citizen, and living in Oklahoma City for the past ten years. He expressed a desire to return to Tlacuitapa after retirement but also gave his reasons for wanting U.S. citizenship: "to help my parents and to get more help from the U.S. government. As a citizen, one can get more benefits."

Having actually obtained U.S. citizenship also has little impact on a migrant's retirement preference. About half of those with citizenship expressed a desire to retire in the United States, and the other half preferred Mexico. Of those who do not have citizenship, however, an overwhelming majority (about 85 percent) wish to retire in Mexico.

With regard to institution use and property ownership, migrants who have a U.S. bank account, sent their children to school during their last trip, and own property in the United States are more likely to want to retire in the United States. But more than a third of migrants who own property in the United States nevertheless want to retire in Mexico. For this group, the property owned in the United States is viewed as an asset that can be sold to support their retirement years in Tlacuitapa. Such is the case for a second María, a married mother who lived and worked with her husband for nearly twenty-five years in Las Vegas, Nevada:

> Well, with what we worked all those years, saving and saving, we were able to build this house in Tlacuitapa. We sold our house in the United States, and it was the money from

that house that we used to construct this one and to do other things to build a future here so that we would not be over there [the United States] just to be slaves to our jobs.

The ability to understand English also correlates strongly with retirement location preference. Of the migrants who self-reported understanding English well, over two-thirds want to retire in the United States, whereas two-thirds of the migrants who understand English poorly want to retire in Mexico.

According to Gmelch (1980, 139), noneconomic factors such as open space and an easy pace of life can influence the decision to return. For María and her husband, who worked in Las Vegas restaurants and hotels, the husband's health was a big factor in the decision to return to Tlacuitapa. The chemicals in the hotel carpets and the city's general pollution constituted a health hazard for him. On why they wanted to return to Tlacuitapa, María offered the following:

> To retire and to rest. You know what life is like over there—very fast. People need a bit of calm, and my husband would get very sick there. He suffers badly from asthma. He would say, "If I have to go on living like this, I won't last very much longer. I already feel really bad. Sometimes I feel like I'm dying." So his need was behind the decision to leave Las Vegas; it was just too much.

Tlacuitapa is also seen as a good final resting place. For our first María, who was raised primarily in the United States: "Hopefully it will be here that I die. I don't want to be buried. I want them to cremate me and throw my ashes to the winds here in Tlacuitapa—over there, in a high place, so that my ashes can fly."

What we have observed among retired migrants and currently settled migrants who expressed a desire to return to Tlacuitapa is that having established families in the United States does not always deter people from returning. Further, the absence of extensive nuclear families in the United States can influence migrants to return. Requesting and even obtaining U.S. citizenship does not lead migrants to prefer retirement in the United States. Nor do a U.S. bank account, children enrolled in U.S. schools, or property owned in the United States shift migrants' retirement preferences away from Tlacuitapa. Absent the factors that originally propelled them to the United States, Tlacuitapa becomes the natural place for them to be. Since retired migrants no longer need to support growing families, their desires may become the key determinants in where they retire. Language attainment, however, does influence retirement location preference in favor of the country in whose language the migrant is most proficient. Health issues and pace of life also play a role in migrants' preference for retirement in Tlacuitapa, along with a desire to rest eternally in one's native land.

CONCLUSION

This chapter presents the decision to migrate, not as a function of one predominant causal factor, but rather as the result of a diverse set of factors operating at the macro, meso, and micro levels that converge to influence an individual's migration decision. Using multivariate regressions, we were able to quantify many demographic characteristics that make a migrant more likely to migrate for the first time, to be in the United States, and to settle in the United States.

We find that settlement is best viewed as a continuation of the decision to migrate. Among the nearly 60 percent of Tlacuitapeños now settled in the United States, settlement was rarely the intent prior to migration; it was an unintended consequence of longer stays, often encouraged by increased border enforcement or year-round U.S. employment. Greater interaction with U.S. society also strengthens migrants' incentives to remain.

What are the implications for U.S. policy prescriptions? We argue that Mexican migrants prefer to stay in their place of birth, but a confluence of macro-, meso-, and micro-level factors drive the migration decision. We have shown that migration will continue as long as these push factors persist. What is needed is an immigration control policy grounded in the realities of migrant-sending communities. Investing in a physical barrier at the border will not affect these causal factors nor the emigration they cause. In order to make any noticeable impact, investments must be directed toward reducing the causal factors and giving Mexicans the opportunity to stay in Mexico, their preferred place.

References

Aguilera, Michael Bernabé. 2004. "Deciding Where to Retire: Intended Retirement Location Choices of Formerly Undocumented Mexican Migrants," *Social Science Quarterly* 85, no. 2: 340–60.

Alba, Carlos, and Enrique Dussel Peters. 2001. "Effects of Export-led Growth on the Structure of Mexican Industrial Production." In *U.S.-Mexican Economic Integration: NAFTA at the Grassroots,* ed. John Bailey. U.S.-Mexico Policy Report No. 11. Austin, TX: University of Texas at Austin.

Bourdieu, Pierre, and Loïc J. D. Wacquant. 1992. *An Invitation to Reflexive Sociology.* Chicago, IL: University of Chicago Press.

Chávez, Leo R. 1992. *Shadowed Lives: Undocumented Immigrants in American Society.* Fort Worth, TX: Harcourt, Brace, Jovanovich College Publishers.

Cornelius, Wayne A. 1990. *Labor Migration to the United States: Development Outcomes and Alternatives in Mexican Sending Communities.* La Jolla, CA: Center for U.S.-Mexican Studies, University of California, San Diego.

———. 1992. "From Sojourners to Settlers: The Changing Profile of Mexican Immigration to the United States." In *U.S.-Mexico Relations: Labor Market Interdependence,* ed. Jorge Bustamante, Clark W. Reynolds, and Raúl A. Hinojosa Ojeda. Stanford, CA: Stanford University Press.

———. 2002. "Impacts of NAFTA on Mexico-to-U.S. Migration." In *NAFTA in the New Millennium,* ed. Edward J. Chambers and Peter H. Smith. La Jolla, CA and Edmonton: Center for U.S.-Mexican Studies, University of California, San Diego, and University of Alberta Press.

Dussel Peters, Enrique. 2000. *Polarizing Mexico: The Impact of Liberalization Strategy.* Boulder, CO: Lynne Rienner Publishers.

Faist, Thomas. 2000. *The Volume and Dynamics of International Migration and Transnational Social Spaces.* New York: Oxford University Press.

Gmelch, George. 1980. "Return Migration," *Annual Review of Anthropology* 9: 135–59.

Harris, J., and M. Todaro. 1970. "Migration, Unemployment & Development: A Two-Sector Analysis," *American Economic Review* 60, no. 1: 126–42.

Kanaiaupuni, Shawn Malia. 2000. "Reframing the Migration Question: An Analysis of Men, Women, and Gender in Mexico," *Social Forces* 8, no. 4: 1311–47.

Marcelli, Enrico A., and Wayne A. Cornelius. 2001. "The Changing Profile of Mexican Migrants to the United States: New Evidence from California and Mexico," *Latin American Research Review* 36, no. 3: 105–31.

Massey, Douglas S. 1986. "The Settlement Process among Mexican Migrants to the United States," *American Sociological Review* 51, no. 5: 670–84.

Massey, Douglas, et al. 1998. *Worlds in Motion: Understanding International Migration at the End of the Millennium*. New York: Oxford University Press.

Massey, Douglas, Luin Goldring, and Jorge Durand. 1994. "Continuities in Transnational Migration: An Analysis of Nineteen Mexican Communities," *American Journal of Sociology* 99, no. 6: 1492–1533.

Mines, Richard, and Alain de Janvry. 1982. "Migration to the United States and Mexican Rural Development: A Case Study," *American Journal of Agricultural Economics* 64, no. 3: 444–54.

Oishi, Nana. 2002. "Gender and Migration: An Integrative Approach." CCIS Working Paper No. 49. La Jolla, CA: Center for Comparative Immigration Studies, University of California, San Diego. http://repositories.cdlib.org/ccis/papers/wrkg49.

Piore, Michael J. 1979. *Birds of Passage: Migrant Labor and Industrial Societies*. New York: Cambridge University Press.

Portes, Alejandro, and Robert L. Bach. 1985. *Latin Journey: Cuban and Mexican Immigrants in the United States*. Berkeley, CA: University of California Press.

Riosmena, Fernando. 2004. "Return versus Settlement among Undocumented Mexican Migrants, 1980 to 1996." In *Crossing the Border: Research from the Mexican Migration Project*, ed. Jorge Durand and Douglas S. Massey. New York: Russell Sage Foundation.

Smith-Lovin, Lynn, and J. Miller McPherson. 1993. "You Are Who You Know: A Network Approach to Gender." In *Theory on Gender/Feminism on Theory*, ed. P. England. New York: Aldine de Gruyter.

Weintraub, Sidney. 1990. *A Marriage of Convenience: Relations between Mexico and the United States*. New York: Oxford University Press.

Wall full of offerings and thank-you notes left for Padre Toribio Romo, patron saint of undocumented border crossers, at Romo's shrine near Jalostotitlán, Jalisco.

2   Is U.S. Border Enforcement Working?

JESSICA SISCO AND JONATHAN HICKEN

> *In 1999 there were ten of us crossing and the coyote lost his way. Because we had little water, people starting falling behind. I left my cousins and went ahead following another guide. Four of us and the guide made it to the river. We had left everyone behind at this point. The thirst was killing them off, four of them. We walked a maximum of sixteen hours. They were between 14 and 16 years old, although one was 25. We had food, yes, but it was water that we lacked, and the heat was so intense, around 114 degrees out there. There were originally two guides. One disappeared and we followed the other; it was with him that we finally made it.*—Javier, a 30-year-old experienced migrant.

The U.S. government has invested considerable resources in militarizing its border with Mexico since 1993. It has more than tripled the number of Border Patrol agents, and the border enforcement budget is six times what it was in 1993 (Cornelius and Salehyan 2007). During the same period, the number of unauthorized Mexican migrants living in the United States has almost tripled; as of 2005 it was estimated at 11.1 million (Passel 2007). The objective of heightened border enforcement programs—namely, to deter unauthorized immigration—has not been achieved. What, then, *are* the results of this tremendous investment in border control? Fearing apprehension by Border Patrol agents, migrants are increasingly enlisting the services of *coyotes* (people-smugglers). They, in turn, are charging more per trip because of increased migrant demand as well as the fact that they must travel increasingly isolated and dangerous routes to avoid apprehension by the Border Patrol. Once in the United States, unauthorized migrants are now staying longer, both to recoup the cost of the trip and because the routes they must follow to avoid apprehension make the crossing much more arduous.

Tlacuitapeños have a long history of sending unauthorized migrants across the border, and recent increases in border enforcement have not discouraged them from going north. As we report in this chapter, unauthorized migrants from Tlacuitapa generally continue their attempts at entry until they are successful, over 90 percent eventually do cross, and knowledge of the risk of apprehension does not affect their intent to migrate. However, heightened border enforcement has made border crossing more difficult, and migrants are consequently choosing to minimize the number of trips they make—*not* by electing not to go to the United States in the first place but by minimizing the number of *return trips* to Mexico.

This chapter builds on previous studies of undocumented migration from Mexican sending communities, particularly CCIS field research in Tlacuitapa, Jalisco, and Tunkás, Yucatán, by highlighting the intensification of several trends identified in these studies and relating them to recent developments in U.S. immigration control policy. The studies in Tlacuitapa (2005) and Tunkás (2006) found that stronger border enforcement had not significantly reduced unauthorized migration to the United States; our study yielded the same conclusion.

Nevertheless, President George W. Bush and the Border Patrol contend that their strategies have indeed been effective. The Border Patrol reported a steep decline in apprehensions of migrants along the southwest U.S. border during the second half of 2006 and continuing into 2007—a change that President Bush attributed to stronger enforcement measures. In the concluding section of this chapter we offer several alternative explanations for the decline in recorded apprehensions and demonstrate why official apprehension figures do not reflect a slowing of illegal immigration into the United States.

THE POLICY ENVIRONMENT

We begin our discussion of key policy developments with the 1980s (table 2.1), when oil prices collapsed and Mexico's inflation levels soared (Massey, Durand, and Malone 2002, 78). Coincidentally (or perhaps not), the U.S. Congress passed the Immigration Reform and Control Act (IRCA) in 1986, which made employment of an unauthorized immigrant a criminal offense punishable by fines and imprisonment for repeat offenders. IRCA also offered amnesty to certain unauthorized immigrants and provided a framework for expansion of the Border Patrol. This pattern of augmenting border enforcement resources via legislation has persisted ever since.

Table 2.1 Key Developments in U.S. Border Enforcement Policy, 1986–Present

1986	Immigration Reform and Control Act
1990	Immigration Act of 1990
1993	Operation Hold the Line; El Paso, TX
1994	Operation Gatekeeper; San Diego, CA
1995	Operation Safeguard; Nogales, AZ
1996	Operation Rio Grande; Southeast TX
2006	Secure Border Initiative Secure Fence Act Operation Jumpstart Operation Streamline

Four years after IRCA, Congress passed the Immigration Act of 1990 to correct apparent shortcomings in the former legislation, given that more, not fewer, immigrants were flowing into the United States. Under the 1990 Act, more Border Patrol agents were hired, employer sanctions were tightened, penalties were increased, and processes were streamlined (Massey, Durand, and Malone 2002, 91). The 1990 Act also established limits and requirements for legal migration, including a cap on the number admitted, a shift in preferences toward European immigrants, and more visas for highly skilled workers.

In 1993 President Bill Clinton established his standard for immigration control policies along the U.S.-Mexico border, titled "prevention through deterrence." Under Operation Hold the Line, fences were erected, high-intensity floodlights were installed, and the number of Border Patrol agents was increased in the El Paso area. A year later a similar initiative, Operation Gatekeeper, began on the San Diego–Tijuana border. In 1995 and 1996, Operation Safeguard in Nogales, Arizona, and Operation Rio Grande in southeast Texas were implemented. President Clinton then passed the 1996 Illegal Immigration Reform and Immigrant

Responsibility Act (IIRIRA), authorizing one thousand new Border Patrol agents per year through 2001. From that point forward, measures were passed every few years to increase the number of Border Patrol agents, to strengthen physical barriers, and, more recently, to introduce advanced technology along the border in hopes of deterring migrants before they attempted a crossing (Bean and Lowell 2007).

On December 6, 2005, Representative James Sensenbrenner (R) introduced H.R. 4437, or the "Border Protection, Antiterrorism, and Illegal Immigration Control Act of 2005." This bill proposed erecting up to seven hundred miles of additional fencing (physical and virtual) along the border; increasing fines across the board for violations such as entering with fraudulent documents, reentering after deportation, and employing undocumented migrants; and giving state and local authorities more immigration control powers. Another significant clause made assisting undocumented migrants in any way a felony.

Though H.R. 4437 ultimately did not become law, it did spur a number of significant intimidation-heavy border enforcement–related developments in 2006. One was the Secure Border Initiative (SBI), which called for an increase in "virtual" fencing (unmanned vehicles, watchtowers equipped with infrared cameras, GPS systems in patrol cars, and so on) and increased investment in physical barriers. The U.S. Congress and President Bush also signed the Secure Fence Act of 2006, authorizing billions of dollars for seven hundred miles of new border fencing. Also in 2006, the Bush administration launched Operation Jumpstart to deploy six thousand unarmed National Guard troops along the border to assist in seizing unauthorized crossers. Another strategic initiative, Operation Streamline, also implemented in 2006, required that all illegal entrants apprehended in the Del Rio, Texas, sector be incarcerated in temporary detention facilities for up to 180 days, the goal being to reduce repeat crossing attempts.

AN UNINTENDED CONSEQUENCE: THE DECLINE IN CIRCULAR MIGRATION

Contrary to its stated objective, and with significant implications for the stock of undocumented migrants in the United States, the buildup at the border appears to have dramatically altered the temporal patterns of *return* migration only. Tlacuitapeño migration, which formerly displayed a cyclical pattern, is now characterized by longer tenures in the United States, an unintended consequence of the border buildup.

From the start of the Bracero Program in 1942 to the 1970s, Mexican migration was largely temporary and circular. More Mexicans began to settle in the United States during the 1980s, but it was not until the 1990s that permanent settlement increased notably (Marcelli and Cornelius 2001, 114). Riosmena (2004, 265–66) argues that the upsurge in social networks composed of migrants amnestied under IRCA, along with the increased "psychic and economic" costs of border crossing resulting from increased enforcement, has decreased return migration and facilitated the growth of the stock of unauthorized Mexican migrants in the United States. Other scholars have identified additional factors as potentially responsible for the increase in undocumented Mexicans in the United States: poor economic conditions in Mexico and U.S. demand for labor (Marcelli and Cornelius 2001, 122). A study by the Public Policy Institute of California found that migrants were staying longer during the late 1990s, when tighter border enforcement was being implemented, but the authors were unable to confirm a cause-and-effect relationship (Reyes, Johnson, and Van Swearingen 2002, 36).

One key indicator of decreased circularity is the robust growth of the stock of unauthorized immigrants living in the United States. That number has increased steadily during the post-1993 period and particularly in the late 1990s, as the United States' border enforcement strategy has functioned to keep unauthorized migrants from going home (see figure 2.1).

On their most recent (or current) trip to the United States, 37 percent of the unauthorized migrants we interviewed in 2007 had stayed longer in the United States than they had expected. More than half reported that at least one of their relatives had remained in the United States due to border enforcement. Figure 2.2 shows the steady increase in duration of stay among undocumented migrants in the United States. The decline in trip duration in 1985–1989 is probably due to IRCA's impacts; migrants newly legalized under IRCA were able to come and go more easily, thus augmenting circular migration. Since then, various legislative initiatives have made return trips to Mexico less viable. Evidence of this is the increase in trip length starting in 1990 and resuming in 1994 following a slight decline. The median duration of migrants' stays has increased by 50 percent since 2000 and more than doubled since the mid-1980s.

Figure 2.1 Estimated Number of Unauthorized Immigrants in the United States, 1980–2007

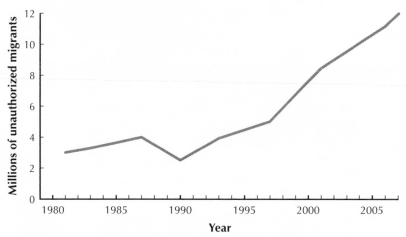

Source: Passel 2007, 3.

Figure 2.2 Duration of U.S. Trips among Unauthorized Migrants from Tlacuitapa, 1980–2003

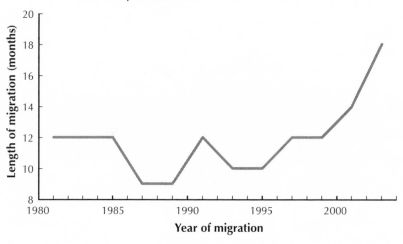

In January 2007, 81 percent of U.S.-based migrants from Tlacuitapa did not return to their hometown for the annual fiesta. Their absence was notable. We observed that social gatherings during fiesta week were poorly attended in comparison with the same events in 2005. Figure 2.3 presents the reasons our interviewees gave for failing to return to Tlacuitapa in 2007.

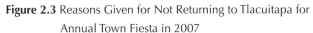

Figure 2.3 Reasons Given for Not Returning to Tlacuitapa for Annual Town Fiesta in 2007

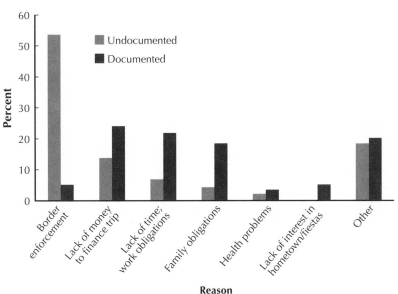

Over half of our undocumented interviewees responded that border enforcement was the primary factor for not returning to their hometown.[1] This includes not only fear of the Border Patrol and other border enforcement measures but also the unintended consequences that we discuss throughout the chapter. Documented migrants pointed relatively equally to financial constraints, work obligations, and family responsibilities as the reasons they did not return. Undocumented migrants also identified financial

---

1. Five percent of documented migrants responded that they did not return due to border enforcement, probably because some family members did not have legal status or because they were visa overstayers (documented at time of entry but undocumented at time of survey).

constraints as a significant obstacle, citing transportation costs and the ever-increasing fees charged by people-smugglers. Juan José, an experienced 42-year-old migrant who once made fifteen crossing attempts on the same trip to the border before succeeding, explained why Tlacuitapa migrants are reluctant to return home once they have made it to the United States:

> Well, I imagine it's the cost, the elevated prices that [people-smugglers] charge you to cross. They're charging $3,000 dollars. If I'm lucky enough to get there, I'll have to stay a long time to pay $3,000. No, paying $3,000 and having to support my family here in Mexico? I'm going to have to go a long time without coming back. For that reason, many people prefer not to come back to Mexico.

Indeed, coyote fees appear to be proportional to the level of border enforcement. As Border Patrol linewatch hours increased over recent decades, coyotes' fees rose in tandem (see figure 2.4). The increased fees reflect higher demand for the coyotes' services as migrants seek ways to offset the increased risk of apprehension, but also the fact that border enforcement has made border crossing more arduous and more dangerous. As Juan José noted, because the cost of a clandestine border crossing has risen, migrants must stay longer to make the trip financially worthwhile (see figure 2.5).

Figure 2.4 Border Patrol Linewatch Hours and Median Coyote Fees, Pre-1980 to 2004

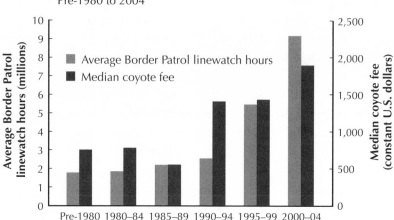

Figure 2.5 Coyote Fees and Work Hours Required to Repay Them, Pre-1980 to 2004

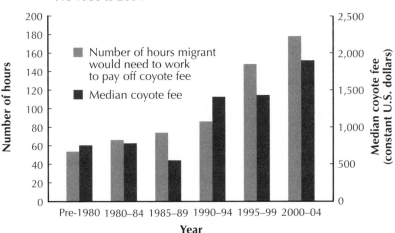

Not only are U.S. immigration policies keeping undocumented migrants in the United States, they are also promoting family reunification on the U.S. side of the border. Male heads of household, anticipating long stays in the United States, are bringing their dependents to the United States more quickly than in the past. According to Bustamante, Reynolds, and Hinojosa Ojeda (1992), "U.S.-born children and wives quickly become strong supporters of remaining permanently in the United States," thus decreasing migrants' need to return to the sending community for anything other than recreation. A key indicator of the incidence of whole-family migration from Tlacuitapa to the United States is the sharp increase in the number of uninhabited houses in the town (see figure 2.6).

As migrants come to view their stay in the United States as long term, they begin investing in the host community. More than a third of the migrants interviewed in our 2007 survey owned property in the United States. Though home ownership in the United States is mainly confined to migrants with legal status (53 percent of them reported owning property in the United States), nearly one in ten undocumented interviewees also reported owning U.S. property. By contrast, new house construction and home remodeling in Tlacuitapa have declined in recent years, according to local builders.

Figure 2.6 Number of Uninhabited Houses in Tlacuitapa, 1995–2007

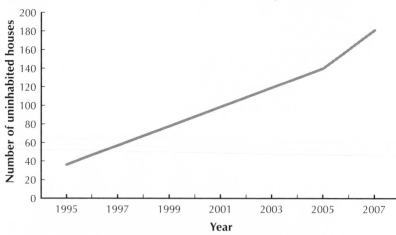

Note: No data points available between 1995 and 2005.

Total income, time in the United States, and life stage are key factors in property ownership. Because U.S. property is a huge investment, migrants must remain longer in the United States to accumulate the capital that property ownership requires. We have already seen that migrants' stays have lengthened dramatically since 2000. Additionally, migrants are increasingly bringing their entire families to settle in the United States permanently. Marriage and children correlate positively with home ownership among Mexican migrants. Whether documented or not, migrants are purchasing property and making the United States their permanent home (McConnell and Marcelli 2007, 203–205).

The resulting reduction in circular migration holds implications for the future development of migrant-sending communities like Tlacuitapa. As more migrant families settle in the United States, remittances to sending communities will decline, since fewer dependents remain in the place of origin (see chapter 4, this volume).

MIGRATION STRATEGIES

Though heightened border enforcement may not be deterring unauthorized migrants from crossing into the United States, the border buildup is affecting migrants' border-crossing strategies by, for example, increasing the need to cross with the help of a coyote. Our data show that some 93 percent of undocumented migrants from Tlacuitapa who made their last U.S. trip since 2000 used a coyote to enter the United States, compared to only 71 percent who crossed prior to 2000. Since 2003, *all* crossings that our interviewees reported were made with the assistance of a coyote (figure 2.7).[2]

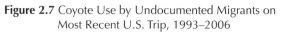

Figure 2.7 Coyote Use by Undocumented Migrants on Most Recent U.S. Trip, 1993–2006

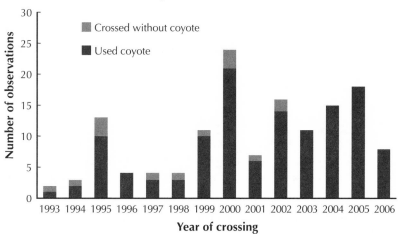

Migrants believe that using a coyote improves their chances for a successful border crossing. El Piloto, a middle-aged migrant who crossed the border clandestinely five times between 1992 and 2004, put it this way: "You could say that people-smugglers are necessary because sometimes we wouldn't make it without them. Their help is illegal, but who is going to help us if they don't?" Yet despite this sentiment, we found no significant difference in success rates between migrants who used coyotes and those who did not.

In the past, scholars and policy makers debated how immigration enforcement affected migrants' choice of border-crossing strategies, but because of their increased reliance on coyotes, today's migrants may no

2. This trend is consistent with a previous study of Tlacuitapa (Cornelius and Lewis 2007), which found that coyote use by migrants from Tlacuitapa increased to 89.8 percent in the post-1993 period.

longer be the key decision makers. While potential migrants still make the decision of whether or not to migrate, our data suggest that migrants are increasingly leaving the logistics of border crossing to the coyotes. One experienced migrant explained: "The guide is the one who calls the shots. You don't know where they'll take you. If the guide says 'that way,' then you go that way. Like chickens; we behave like chickens." Another migrant noted: "More and more coyotes are appearing around here. They come and tell you they can cross you more easily, more quickly, for a cheaper price, but, no, none of that is true. They are all liars. They'll charge what they want, and they'll take you where they want."

Thus, in assessing the impact of U.S. border enforcement policy on migration patterns, we need to understand how people-smugglers are responding to changes in policy. The remainder of this section addresses the roles of coyotes and migrants in formulating migration strategies and the ways in which these strategies are adapted to respond to changes in enforcement policy.

Over 70 percent of undocumented migrants from Tlacuitapa who crossed between 2000 and 2006 walked through the desert with a coyote (table 2.2, figure 2.8). Given that 93 percent of recent migrants crossed with coyotes, the shifts that we observe from urban to rural crossing points and the increase in the proportion of people crossing on foot are not surprising. Further, migrants who secured the services of a coyote in Mexico (in their hometown or at the border) are more likely to cross in a rural area (64.5 percent) than are migrants who retained their coyotes through contacts in the United States (68.3 percent of migrants who obtained their coyotes through U.S. contacts reported crossing in urban areas).

In an attempt to explain how the unauthorized Mexican population in the United States could have increased concurrent with an increase in the number of Border Patrol officers, Bean and Lowell (2007) posit that Mexican migrants may be turning to fake documents or visa-overstaying. While it would seem logical for migrants from Tlacuitapa to pursue means of entry other than a dangerous desert crossing, our findings reveal a decline in crossings through official ports of entry, from 36 percent prior to 2000 to 22 percent post-2000 (see table 2.3).

Table 2.2 Mode of Clandestine Entry on Most Recent U.S. Trip (percentages)

Mode of Entry	Pre-1993 (N = 70)	1993–99 (N = 37)	2000–06 (N = 88)
Walking	50.0	65.7	70.5
Hidden in vehicle	15.7	2.9	14.8
Driving own vehicle	2.9	2.9	0.0
Swimming	12.9	5.7	4.6
"Raitero" drove through port of entry	7.1	8.6	5.7
In boat or raft	4.3	8.6	2.3
By plane	1.4	2.9	0.0
Other	5.7	2.9	2.3

Figure 2.8 Undocumented Crossings in Urban versus Rural Areas

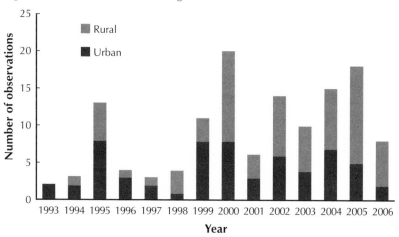

Table 2.3 Use of Official Ports of Entry by Undocumented Migrants

Use of Ports of Entry	Pre-1993	1993–99	2000–06
Crossed through official port of entry	37.1%	33.3%	21.8%
Did not cross through official port of entry	62.9%	66.7%	78.2%
N	70	39	87

Table 2.4 shows that the majority of migrants who have crossed through official ports of entry since 2000 have done so hidden in vehicles (82 percent) rather than by carrying fake, borrowed, or stolen papers, as had been the case previously.[3] Yet crossing with falsified or borrowed papers would appear to be a viable option. Pedro, an experienced migrant in his twenties, reported that a person could "borrow" papers for roughly $3,000 that would allow the border crosser to enter through a port of entry in his or her own vehicle. "It's easy to cross this way as long as you have the money," he added.

Table 2.4 Mode of Entry through Official Port of Entry (absolute frequencies)

Mode of Entry	Pre-1993	1993–99	2000–06
Hidden in vehicle	9	2	14
Bribing a U.S. official	1	2	1
Paying a coyote	0	1	0
Showing false or borrowed papers	13	6	2
N	23	11	17

If Pedro is correct, why are Tlacuitapeños still choosing to cross through the desert? Why are coyotes continuing to take people through the desert when they could charge more by selling fake papers or hiding migrants in cars and trucks? Seventeen migrants from Tlacuitapa reported paying $2,463 on average to a coyote to pass through a port of entry post-2000, roughly in line with Pedro's estimate of $3,000. Given that the average fee to cross through the desert post-2000 is $1,966, one might guess that coyotes would move into the more lucrative market. However, various other factors may affect the choice of a border-crossing strategy:

- *Coyotes can make a great deal of money by crossing migrants through the desert.* According to migrants from Tlacuitapa, coyotes can move up to one hundred people per night through the desert. At an average coyote fee of $2,000, this means that a coyote potentially can earn up to $200,000 per crossing. There is an economy of scale in crossing people through the desert; it may take considerably more effort

---

3. Prior to 2000, only 31 percent of migrants reported crossing hidden in cars, while 54 percent crossed by presenting false papers.

and investment to produce one hundred fake documents or secure passage in vehicles for one hundred migrants.

- *The legal repercussions for both coyotes and migrants are much less severe for crossing through the desert.* According to the Congressional Budget Office (2006, 14), "noncriminal, unauthorized aliens attempting entry may be offered voluntary departure in lieu of formal removal. Aliens who are allowed to depart voluntarily must admit that they were in the country illegally and agree to a witnessed departure, but they are not barred from seeking legal admission at a later time." Migrants attempting to pass through an official port of entry using false documents or falsely claiming to be U.S. citizens would not be eligible for voluntary deportation. Migrants are well aware that they can opt for "voluntary departure" if apprehended while attempting a clandestine entry through the desert. Further, whether legal penalties are actually less severe is irrelevant; if migrants *perceive* that "catch and release" in the desert presents less risk, a desert crossing becomes a more likely strategy of choice (Singer and Massey 1998; Heyman 1995).

- *Migrants may be unwilling and/or unable to pay the increased coyote fee to pass through official ports of entry.*

- *Migrants may not feel that they can "pull off" using fake papers at a legal port of entry.* When asked why more people do not use fake papers instead of walking through the desert, El Piloto responded: "You have to have the right state of mind to be able to fool the Border Patrol." Another experienced migrant explained why people from Tlacuitapa do not use fake papers: "The *migra* aren't foolish enough to say, 'ah, yes, your papers are in order, go on through.' They have everything in their computer, fingerprints, everything. So, no, I don't think people from Tlacuitapa use fake papers. And even if some do cross this way . . . they would need to know English very well. . . . Where are you going to find an illegal immigrant who knows English well? Passing with fake papers? No. It's very hard."

- *Walking across the border has been the primary means of crossing for so long that it is now viewed as a rite of passage for migrants, especially young men.*

- *Desert crossings may have a higher perceived rate of success.* We analyzed the success rate of migrants who crossed with and without coyotes in both urban and rural areas, and found no statistically significant differences between these groups, primarily because nearly all respondents succeeded, with or without coyotes and in urban or rural areas. Nevertheless, migrants may *perceive* that crossing through the desert with the help of a coyote has a higher probability of success.

Although coyotes are sticking to their traditional method of walking groups of migrants across the border, they *are* adapting to changes in border enforcement in one important respect: they are changing routes to avoid points of concentrated border enforcement. Ernesto, an experienced migrant, described why he thinks coyotes are choosing new routes and how fees are affected in turn: "Since the coyotes are also taking risks and don't want to be caught by the migra, they are retreating to the more isolated and dangerous areas, and I think that is why they charge more."

Prior to 2000, most undocumented migrants from Tlacuitapa crossed through Texas (40 percent) and California (primarily at San Diego; 36 percent) (see table 2.5). In October 1994 the Border Patrol commenced Operation Gatekeeper in the San Diego sector, which aimed to turn back unauthorized migrants through increased numbers of agents, miles of new fencing, and underground sensors to detect migrants (Nevins 2002, 4). As enforcement increased in the San Diego sector, migrants and coyotes sought new routes with greater likelihood of success. As one experienced migrant from Tlacuitapa put it, "They used to go through Tijuana, but it has become a hotspot for border vigilance. Now they're crossing through Aguaprieta, Sonora. There you'll find the most traffic."

Our data support this assertion. Most post-2000 undocumented migrants reported passing through Arizona (59 percent), with 25 percent crossing through Texas and 16 percent through California (figure 2.9). National-level data show the same shifts away from heavily enforced areas (Orrenius 2004; Trejo Peña 2006). Crossings through central Arizona (Nogales) have increased sharply in the post-1993 period of tightened border control, while crossings through San Diego (Tijuana) have declined markedly, as suggested by the numbers of "returned" migrants (figure 2.10; Trejo Peña 2006).

Table 2.5 Crossing Points by State (absolute numbers of migrant crossings among Tlacuitapeño interviewees)

Crossing Points	Pre-1993	1993–99	2000–06
ARIZONA			
Nogales/Tucson	1	1	22
Other Arizona	3	7	31
CALIFORNIA			
San Diego	28	13	9
Other California	5	4	5
TEXAS			
El Paso	7	5	14
Other Texas	26	7	8
NEW MEXICO	2	0	0
Other	2	3	1
TOTAL	74	40	90

Figure 2.9 Undocumented Migrants' Crossing Points Post-2000

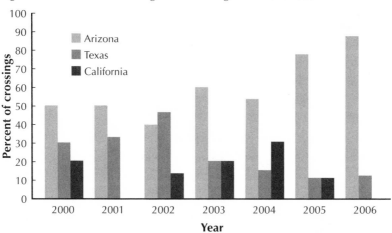

Ernesto, a Tlacuitapa migrant who has crossed the border several times, made his last trip in 2005. He reported that he would not go again because the journey through remote areas was too arduous; he preferred to be "poor and with his family." According to Ernesto, "It is easy to avoid

the Border Patrol because the places where migrants cross are dangerous and too isolated for Border Patrol, so they don't get that deep." By
contrast, Eduardo, another experienced migrant, said that necessity often trumps the risks of crossing through the desert. After witnessing the
deaths of four fellow migrants in the desert in 1999, Eduardo held out
five years before economic pressures prompted him to cross through the
desert again: "Necessity drove me to try again, and I began walking."

Figure 2.10 Percentage of Migrants Returned to Mexico, by Border-Crossing
Sector

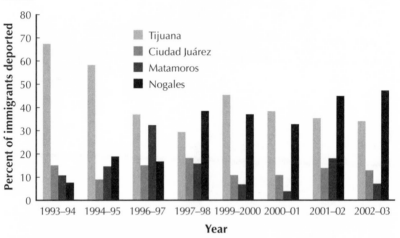

Source: Trejo Peña 2006; adapted from EMIF data.

The trends in migration strategies outlined above appear to be a direct
response to U.S. border enforcement levels and tactics. As enforcement
strategies change, coyotes respond by altering their crossing locations or
methods, the Border Patrol then responds again, and so on. Based on their
performance under heightened border enforcement since 1993, coyotes
appear willing to go to whatever lengths necessary to adapt to changes in
border control strategy and to deliver on their promises to migrants.

DOES BORDER ENFORCEMENT AFFECT MIGRATION OUTCOMES?

U.S. border enforcement post-1993 aims to deter illegal entries by increasing the probability of apprehension. Our data show that recent migrants

have a somewhat higher probability of apprehension than their predecessors (figure 2.11). Approximately 38.2 percent of recent migrants reported being apprehended at the border one or more times, whereas only 22.4 percent of migrants were apprehended multiple times prior to 2000 (see table 2.6).

Figure 2.11 Apprehensions of Undocumented Migrants, Pre-1993 to 2006

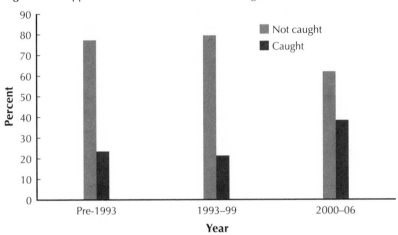

Table 2.6 Border Patrol Apprehensions of Undocumented Migrants on Most Recent U.S. Trip

Number of Apprehensions per Migrant	Pre-1993	1993–99	2000–06
0	71.8%	78.9%	61.8%
1	16.9%	13.2%	23.6%
2	5.6%	0%	7.9%
3	1.4%	5.3%	2.2%
4 or more	4.2%	2.6%	4.5%
N	71	38	89

However, higher probability of apprehension does not necessarily translate into a decreased likelihood of eventual success in crossing; only one of seventy-six respondents who attempted to cross between 1993 and 2006 reported being unable to gain entry. Our results are consistent with models that attempt to predict the crossing success of apprehended migrants. These models assume that apprehended illegal migrants will keep trying until they succeed. For example, according to Espenshade (1995, 550), "there is a convincing rationale for believing that virtually every would-be undocumented migrant who wants to enter the United States can and will—if not on the first attempt, then on a second, third, or fourth." Espenshade's "repeated trials model" assumes that all migrants are eventually able to cross because they will keep trying until they succeed. Another modeling exercise, based on Espenshade's methodology and using data from fiscal years 2005 and 2006, predicts an undocumented migrant's probability of success on the second or third try of approximately 90 percent (Chang 2007), which is roughly in line with our findings from Tlacuitapa. Thus apprehensions cannot be equated with success in keeping undocumented migrants out of the United States.

El Piloto describes a border-crossing experience in 1997 that culminated in successful entry on the fourth attempt:

> We were held for 28 hours in the detention center. Afterward they let us go right there. You sign that you accept to voluntarily return to your country. So they just leave us, being Mexicans, on the other side. If we're Latinos [from elsewhere in Latin America], they'll send us to our own countries. But we're Mexican, so they drop us off right there. So we get back to our hotel and turn right around and try again, until we reach our objective. The Border Patrol catches us over and over again, four times on the same route in the same hour. There is a guide that goes on ahead, and if he doesn't guide us well, we get caught. So we continue trying until he gets it right: we make it across. If one guide is incompetent, they replace him. . . . They punish the first guide for his failures and replace him with someone more capable. And the one who is successful, with fifty "puppets," he is awarded $5,000 per night.

In recognition of the migrants' persistence, the Border Patrol has implemented various programs aimed at reducing recidivism. During fiscal years 2004–2006, the Border Patrol implemented the Interior Repatriation Program under which the Border Patrol deported some detained migrants to cities in the interior of Mexico. In our 2007 survey, only ten respondents claimed to have been repatriated to the interior. For those who had never been subject to deep repatriation, about a third claimed it would affect their intent to migrate, though the impact may well be stronger on someone who actually experiences deep repatriation.

PERCEPTIONS OF BORDER-CROSSING OBSTACLES

It is clear that enhanced U.S. border enforcement is not reducing undocumented entries by Tlacuitapa migrants, but the building of hundreds of miles of new fencing and the deployment of thousands of National Guard troops on the border may be changing the way in which migrants *perceive* border crossing. To gauge the salience of these enforcement measures, we showed our interviewees a series of photographs, depicting, respectively, the National Guard on patrol, natural hazards, a Border Patrol vehicle, the border fence, Mexican police, minutemen/citizen vigilantes, and border bandits (see figure 2.12). We then asked them to identify the three factors that most worried them upon crossing or thinking of crossing the border.

The results demonstrate that Mother Nature—not the border fence, National Guard, or any other factor—is the principal source of worry for both experienced and potential migrants (figure 2.13). Nearly half—48 percent—were most concerned about climate extremes in the desert or mountains. Such concerns are well founded; the leading causes of death for undocumented migrants since 1995 are dehydration, heat stroke, and hypothermia. On their multi-day treks, migrants often endure life-threatening heat or cold. Since the ratcheting up of border enforcement in 1993, deaths due to environmental factors have jumped sharply (Cornelius 2001, 670). The second source of worry was Mexican bandits, at 14.9 percent. Many crossing parties are ambushed by these gangs, who beat, rob, and rape the migrants. The presence of Border Patrol agents ranked third, at 13.1 percent. Very few migrants responded that recent border enforcement strategies such as new fencing and the deployment of National Guard troops on the border were significant sources of concern; the fence was mentioned as the primary concern by only 11.2 percent of migrants, and the National Guard by a mere 5 percent.

Figure 2.12 Factors of Concern to Respondents Considering Migrating to the United States

Figure 2.13 Relative Importance of Deterrence Factors

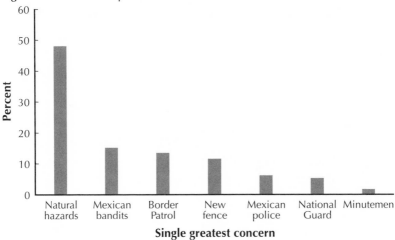

N = 221.

A weighted average of respondents' first, second, and third choices produces virtually the same order (see figure 2.14). The only significant change is that concern about the National Guard moves to fifth place but still represents only 7.5 percent of migrants' cumulative concerns.

Figure 2.14 Relative Importance of Deterrence Factors, Weighted Averages

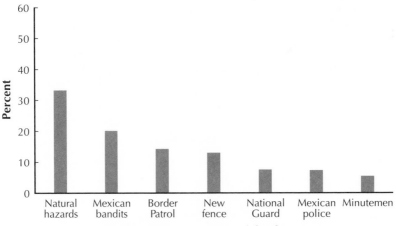

N = 221.

Our respondents' perceptions of obstacles to crossing are rooted in considerable knowledge about what is happening on the border. Migrants and nonmigrants alike are well aware of the enforcement measures the United States has implemented and the dangers associated with them. In 2007, 97 percent of our respondents believed that it was "very dangerous" to cross the border clandestinely. Forty-two-year-old Tlacuitapa migrant Juan José exhibited the detailed knowledge that he, and many others like him, possess:

> It has gotten more and more difficult to cross the border. We already know that sometimes we'll come across the National Guard, later the Border Patrol, and they're tough; they've got it really reinforced now. And now with the fence. . . . Well, that's why people don't come back to Tlacuitapa.

Despite their routine use of professional people-smugglers, unauthorized migrants still suffer significant physical hardship and expose themselves to life-threatening hazards as they attempt to cross in more isolated, rural, and dangerous areas. According to the Border Project of the California Rural Legal Assistance Foundation, there have been 4,123 migrant deaths since 1995, including 91 through the first third of 2007. In 2005, 516 migrants died crossing the border, more than in any previous year (see figure 2.15).

Between 1990 and 2005, the Pima County Medical Examiner's Office reported that 927 undocumented border crossers died in the county, making Pima the leading border county in the number of undocumented border-crosser deaths. Of the 927 deaths, 553, or nearly 60 percent, were due to exposure, up from 39.2 percent in 1990–1999 (Rubio-Goldsmith et al. 2006, 48).

As increasing numbers of women are joining the flow of undocumented border crossers, women are also dying at the border. Women accounted for 13.6 percent of border-crosser deaths in the years up to 2000 but 22.6 percent between 2000 and 2005. Further, women are almost three times more likely than men to die from exposure, holding age constant (Rubio-Goldsmith et al. 2006, 49).

Figure 2.15 Migrant Death Count

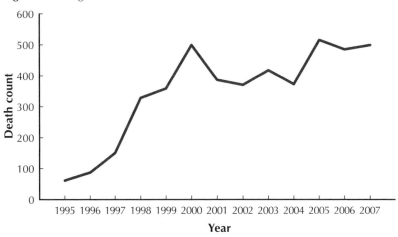

Note: Death count for 2007 is partial, from January1 to April 16.

A DEATH AT THE BORDER

Because of the remote crossing areas now preferred by undocumented migrants, there are almost certainly many more dead in the borderlands whose bodies have not yet been discovered. They are unrepresented in the official death statistics. In Tlacuitapa, 80 percent of our interviewees in 2007 knew someone who had died during the journey crossing the border. The most widely known border-crossing fatalities occurred in 1998, when a group of twelve Tlacuitapeño men headed north. Their story follows.

Javier Cárdenas, 17 years old, a gentle boy who works at the small church in Tlacuitapa asks his father for permission to migrate illegally to the United States. Pablo is in his mid-fifties, and he recalls his own testing migration experiences in the 1980s. He urges his son not to go: "Look, son, the journey is extremely dangerous. You're going to have to walk several days. I've done it before, and that's why I'm telling you." He understands that the border has become even more dangerous, but he does not forbid Javier to go.

"I didn't want to let him go; I didn't want to let him. But what can you do? I said to him, 'Listen, son. At your age, don't go! Stay put a little longer; we don't lack anything here,'" Pablo recalls with obvious emotional difficulty. However, as a strong young man with the desire to return to

Tlacuitapa financially well-prepared for marriage, Javier did not heed his father's warnings and decided to migrate. In June 1998, a group of twelve men headed for Ciudad Acuña, in the Mexican state of Coahuila. Here, like many others, they would begin their journey to *el norte*.

On the eighth day after Javier's departure, Pablo received a call from the border. A parent's nightmare: His son had been found dead; he had drowned in the Río Bravo. Pablo immediately left for the border. After identifying his son in a photograph by his tennis shoes, Pablo placed a marble cross in Ciudad Acuña's cemetery, his son's name engraved into it: Javier Cárdenas Márquez. There, alone, Pablo laid his son to rest and returned to Tlacuitapa to begin the mourning process.

Five weeks after losing his son, Pablo received a second unexpected call from the border. They informed him that they had found his son in the desert; this time they had found Javier's middle school ID card with his name and photo. Despite Pablo's confusion and his grief at losing his son for a second time, he again boarded a bus for the border.

Javier Cárdenas begins his journey to the United States in Ciudad Acuña, a border city roughly 150 miles west of San Antonio, Texas. He travels with eleven other men, most of whom are from Tlacuitapa or other nearby towns. Their guide, or coyote, is Javier's brother's father-in-law. Migrants leaving from Ciudad Acuña must drive five or six hours in a truck to a place called La Puerta del Consuelo—Consolation Gate—and then continue on foot. This fateful day, however, the truck breaks down several hours short of La Puerta. Given that the walk from La Puerta to the Río Bravo takes six hours, the group knows that they have at least doubled the length of their hike. Regardless, they turn their backs to the south and proceed onwards.

The men were no match for the heat. The El Niño phenomenon was driving temperatures in Del Rio to record highs. Even in the shade, the heat in Del Rio during the summer of 1998 sometimes reached 110 degrees. *Not expecting to have their truck break down early, the men do not have enough water for the walk. Only a few hours into the walk, one of the men, a pestilent drunk, runs out of water. He pleads with the others for water, but they refuse: "It's either him or us. Let's go!" they say. Javier can't bear to see this man die alone, no matter his moral character; he offers the man his small jug.*

At this point in his retelling of events, Pablo became visibly agitated, "It's a traitorous life," he said. *The man hastily takes several swigs of the water.*

Suddenly he raises the jug above his head and pours it over himself, wasting what little remained of Javier's water. Approximately half a mile ahead Javier takes his last breath, an undeserved return for a selfless act.

After lying in the desert for a month and a half, Javier's body was severely decayed. At the municipal morgue, his father was unable to recognize his own son. When asked how he felt when he saw Javier's body, Pablo replied: "I didn't want to see his face because I could already imagine how his body would be. A month and a half, imagine, lying on the hill, in the desert. . . . It was devastating."

Pablo had to identify his son by his ID card and his shoes. He later learned that the body of the first boy he had identified as his son was indeed wearing his son's shoes. Somewhere on their trek, Javier had given this other boy, who was from the neighboring town of San Antonio de la Garza, a pair of shoes to wear. Pablo knew, however, that Javier had two pairs of shoes with him, and the body he now witnessed wore the second pair: heavy-duty work boots. Yet, still unable to contemplate the horror of the situation, Pablo asked the mortician for more evidence. The mortician pulled out a green camouflage-style backpack, and at that moment Pablo had to accept the truth.

Out of respect for their fallen compañero, the other travelers wrap his body in plastic bags which they had brought to keep their clothing dry as they swam naked across the Río Bravo. They remove Javier's watch and wallet. Two weeks later, those who make it to the United States send Javier's belongings to his father in Tlacuitapa.

Pablo, already shaken, was not yet through his ordeal. The men who found Javier's body (and that of a third man who had died in the same trip) claimed that they were migrants who had sacrificed their own border-crossing plans in order to return with the two bodies. For this "good deed" they demanded that Pablo compensate them for the money they had paid to their coyote. Feeling that he was being taken advantage of, Pablo refused. He subsequently learned from a municipal authority that the men were not fellow migrants but were scouts from the district office whose job it was to seek out fallen migrant compatriots.

After seeing now three men fall, their dried tongues falling to the back of their equally dry throats, the rest of the group had no choice but to continue onward. Another migrant in the group, also named Javier, describes their despair: "Every hour we left another person behind. We continued with all our might, but we never knew how many of us would make it, and who wouldn't." *They make it to the river, barely alive. One man sees the water in a haze, as if it were a dream. He falls to his knees, gathers the water in his cupped hands, and brings life back into his dying body. With these same life-giving hands, he then splashes his body down, attempting to revive himself. He turns, half-conscious, only to spot another member of the group stumble toward him. Not fully cognizant, he watches the agonized boy from San Antonio de la Garza tumble into the unforgiving river and disappear: four of twelve innocent migrants dead. Two of the four will be forgotten, not counted in the official death count of the year 1998: 329.*

Pablo called another son, who lived in Oklahoma City, to come with his truck to Ciudad Acuña. They were going to carry the two bodies, Javier's and the other man's, back to their hometown. Pablo and his son, with the two bodies in boxes, began the fifteen-hour drive to Tlacuitapa. Not far out of Ciudad Acuña, they were pulled over by two Mexican authorities. Pablo's son's truck had an Oklahoma license plate, and that made the authorities suspicious. Pablo's son handed them the registration and his identification, but because the truck was registered to his U.S.-citizen wife, the police concluded that the truck was stolen. After Pablo and his son made many futile attempts to prove that the truck was not stolen, the police demanded that they pay $200 immediately. If the two grieving men did not pay, the officers threatened to throw the bodies of their son/brother and friend off the back of the truck. Pablo pleaded: "Look! We're carrying these bodies. . . ." The policemen interrupted, "No, no, no! [Those registration papers] don't mean shit! If you don't pay us now, we'll throw those bodies to hell off the back!" Pablo wondered, "If they see someone coming with this burden, with two dead bodies, and they still rob them? They're animals." Faced with this disgusting demonstration of human greed, Pablo and his son paid the officers the $200.

Finally, after all he had been through, Pablo was able to return to his home and bury his son where he belonged. His grief did not cease there, however. He described what happened following his return: "One becomes badly disillusioned. You go crazy from those things. Those things eat at you. I wouldn't wish it on anyone. It was an extremely sad thing, like few things, few things." Due to his loss, Pablo didn't even want to walk; his family was traumatized. Problems began to arise due to the stress and the pain. People from the town began to blame Pablo for his son's death. Even though he assured them that he had begged his son not to go, they accused him of lying about the first boy who he thought was his son. They thought Pablo was trying to take advantage of the death of his son. Pablo said he truly believed that the first boy was his son because of the boy's shoes. He had even spent all of his money on a cross and on the funeral for the first boy.

Eventually Pablo was able to move on, although it was clear that his loss affects him to this day. He now lives peacefully with his wife and two daughters in a house he built in Tlacuitapa. "It's important that many people realize that migrating is not so easy. These are serious things."

DOES BORDER ENFORCEMENT AFFECT THE DECISION TO MIGRATE?

Because of the nature of our field data, we cannot test how migrants' responses to evolving U.S. immigration policy have varied over the last twenty years. We can, however, assess the extent to which knowledge and perceptions of border enforcement affect an individual's propensity to migrate.

As in earlier studies of deterrence effects among unauthorized migrants from Tlacuitapa and other migrant-sending communities (Cornelius and Lewis 2007; Cornelius, Fitzgerald, and Lewin Fischer 2007), our dependent variable is the intention to migrate to the United States during the next twelve months. Our independent variables are: (1) respondent believes it is difficult to evade Border Patrol, (2) respondent knows someone who died trying to cross the border, and (3) respondent knows about new U.S. Border Patrol projects (in this instance, the new border fence). Finally, we chose five demographic variables as controls: age, gender, marital status, education, and legal status. The models used a maximum-likelihood logit estimation approach with robust standard errors (table 2.7).

Model 1 considers the impact of basic demographic factors on the interviewee's intent to migrate in the next twelve months. Men were more likely than women to respond affirmatively about their intent to migrate. Documented individuals were more likely than undocumented individuals to respond affirmatively about their intention to migrate. Moreover, the older the individual, the more likely he or she would not respond in the affirmative regarding intent to migrate. These results were all

statistically significant and robust to the inclusion of other variables that
addressed possible impediments to migration, which were specified in
models 2 through 5. Neither marital status nor educational level had any
impact on the interviewee's response regarding intention to migrate. In
models 2 through 5, we consider border enforcement variables that could
influence intent to migrate. There was no statistically significant relationship between the respondent's knowledge about the difficulties of traversing the border and intent to migrate in the coming year.

Table 2.7 Logit Models: Migration Decisions and Perceptions of
Border-Crossing Difficulty/Danger—All Respondents

	Model 1 β	Model 2 β	Model 3 β	Model 4 β	Model 5 β
Difficult to evade Border Patrol		−0.389 (0.376)			−0.382 (.376)
Knows someone who died trying to cross			0.061 (.271)		0.115 (.294)
Has information on Border Patrol projects				−0.055 (.334)	−0.007 (.359)
Male	0.400** (.197)	0.417** (0.207)	0.398** (.197)	.405** (.197)	0.428** (.207)
Age	−0.018* (.009)	−0.020** (0.010)	−0.018** (.009)	−0.018* (.009)	−0.020** (0.010)
Married	−0.027 (.233)	−0.035 (.237)	−0.021 (.234)	−0.014 (.235)	−0.027 (.239)
Education	−0.010 (.034)	−0.021 (.036)	−0.011 (.034)	−0.009 (.034)	−0.021 (.036)
Legal	1.633*** (.285)	1.640*** (.297)	1.634*** (.285)	1.631*** (.285)	1.644*** (.298)
Constant	−0.677 (.448)	−0.185 (.625)	−0.712 (.489)	−0.643 (.500)	−0.271 (.686)
N	588	553	587	587	552
Chi-squared	40.11	39.61	40.04	40.14	39.84

* 90 percent, ** 95 percent, *** 99 percent confidence levels; robust standard
errors in parentheses.

Model 6 considers the impact of basic demographic factors on reported
intent to migrate in the next twelve months among individuals with previous U.S. experience (table 2.8). Documented individuals were more likely

than undocumented individuals to respond affirmatively about their intent to migrate. The older the individual, the more likely he or she would not respond affirmatively on this point. All results were statistically significant and robust to the inclusion of other variables addressing possible impediments to migration, which were specified in models 7 through 10. We found no effect from respondent's age, marital status, or educational level on reported intent to migrate. In models 6 through 10, we consider border enforcement variables that could influence the intent to migrate. There was no statistically significant relationship between a respondent's knowledge about the difficulties of traversing the border and his or her intent to migrate in the coming year. The models used a maximum-likelihood logit estimation approach with robust standard errors.

Table 2.8 Logit Models: Migration Decisions and Perceptions of Border-Crossing Difficulty/Danger—Respondents with Migratory Experience

	Model 6 β	Model 7 β	Model 8 β	Model 9 β	Model 10 β
Difficult to evade Border Patrol		−0.313 (0.501)			−0.292 (.501)
Knows someone who died trying to cross			0.142 (.486)		0.021 (.495)
Has information on Border Patrol projects				0.146 (.685)	0.117 (.691)
Male	0.012 (.356)	0.030 (0.365)	−0.014 (.360)	0.030 (.356)	0.049 (.367)
Age	−0.043** (.017)	−0.044** (0.018)	−0.044*** (.017)	−0.043*** (.017)	−0.045** (0.018)
Married	−0.174 (.421)	−0.124 (.426)	−0.151 (.424)	−0.143 (.424)	−0.091 (.432)
Education	0.025 (.060)	−0.009 (.063)	−0.024 (.060)	0.029 (.060)	0.013 (.063)
Legal	1.465*** (.358)	1.432*** (.363)	1.462*** (.360)	1.465*** (.359)	1.431*** (.365)
Constant	0.800 (.989)	1.171 (1.244)	0.732 (1.141)	0.647 (1.175)	1.000 (1.456)
N	205	196	204	204	195
Chi-squared	28.41	26.59	28.66	28.79	27.17

* 90 percent, ** 95 percent, *** 99 percent confidence levels; robust standard errors in parentheses.

Our model is robust between different types of migrant-sending communities (Tlacuitapa and Tunkás) as well as across time in a single community (Tlacuitapa, 2005 and 2007). In all of these studies, no border enforcement–related variable had any statistically significant effect on a person's intention to go north again. Believing it is difficult to evade the Border Patrol, knowing someone who died while crossing the border, and knowing about Border Patrol projects *did not* deter migrants from crossing clandestinely.

CONCLUSION

When dedicating a new Border Patrol station in Yuma, Arizona, in 2007, President George W. Bush cited a decline in apprehensions along the border as evidence that tighter enforcement was deterring illegal entry attempts: "When you're apprehending fewer people, it means fewer are trying to come across, and fewer are trying to come across because we're deterring people from attempting illegal border crossings in the first place." Border Patrol reports support the president's claim that apprehensions had decreased: from October 2006 through March 2007, apprehensions were down 30 percent from the same period a year prior (Pear 2007). However, as many scholars have argued, a drop in apprehensions does not necessarily imply a drop in illegal entry attempts. We offer the following alternative explanations for the decline:

- Fewer apprehensions means only that fewer migrants are being *caught*. As migrants, guided by coyotes, are crossing via more remote routes in order to decrease the likelihood of apprehension, it should be no surprise that the Border Patrol is not apprehending them. Our findings indicate that virtually all migrants are ultimately gaining entry. Apprehensions are not a good proxy for border enforcement effectiveness; our data show that close to 40 percent of migrants were apprehended at some point in their journey but nearly 100 percent eventually entered the United States.

- Our data also show that return trips to Mexico are on the decline. If migrants are not returning home as frequently as before, they are also making fewer reentries into the United States, further depressing apprehension statistics though not altering the number of undocumented migrants in the United States.

- More crossings may be occurring through legal ports of entry. Some migrants use falsified papers or hide in vehicles to cross through ports of entry, and these methods are believed to carry a lower risk of apprehension.

- Home construction is slowing nationwide in the United States. The fact that there are fewer jobs in construction and related sectors may be discouraging potential migrants from going to the United States.

Based on data we collected in Tlacuitapa, apprehensions appear to have no bearing on whether migrants ultimately succeed in entering the United States. If changes in U.S. policy over the last twenty years have not deterred migrants from crossing, then what have been the actual outcomes of these policies?

Operation Gatekeeper, implemented in 1994, aimed to "significantly increase the ability of the U.S. authorities to control the flow of unauthorized people and goods across the U.S.-Mexico boundary" (Nevins 2002, 4). How has Operation Gatekeeper (and subsequent programs) performed on the objective of increasing U.S. authorities' ability to control unauthorized entries? The stock of undocumented migrants in the United States has almost quadrupled since 1992 as more migrants are entering and then prolonging their stays or choosing not to return to their home country at all *because of* the strengthening of U.S. border enforcement.

If today's policy is not functioning as intended, how effective will new legislation be? In May 2007, the White House and U.S. Senate agreed on a proposal to significantly alter U.S. immigration policy. The bill, which placed heavy weight on education, language, and job skills, offered illegal immigrants a path to legal residency and ultimately to citizenship. For a fee (about $5,000), an illegal immigrant could obtain a Z visa, to be held for up to thirteen years while applying for legal residency (though a head of household would have to return to the home country within eight years to retain the visa). The bill also contained a temporary guestworker visa, the Y visa, to allow migrants to work legally in the United States for two years. Worksite enforcement was emphasized, including tamper-proof identification cards and stringent penalties for employers who hired unauthorized migrants. As "triggers" for implementing the guestworker and legalization provisions, the bill required significant enhancements to border enforcement, including 300 additional miles of physical fencing, 105 electronic surveillance towers, 70 electronic surveillance posts, and an expansion of the Border Patrol to 20,000 agents by the end of 2010.

Though these proposals seemed quite revolutionary, they were flawed at their core. Because the new border infrastructure had to be developed *first*, it could have been a decade before the nation saw any action on Z visas or worksite enforcement. In the meantime, the expanded physical and virtual barriers would exacerbate the funnel effect that has placed thousands of migrants in peril when attempting to cross the border in remote, inhospitable areas. Coyotes would continue to innovate, a variable that seems to have no limit. Their prices would continue to rise, and circular migration would continue to ebb. The twelve million migrants who would theoretically be eligible for Z visas would be accompanied by millions of fellow countrymen who entered the United States illegally after January 1, 2007, the cutoff date for eligibility for the new program.

T. J. Bonner, president of the National Border Patrol Council, does not believe that heavy border enforcement is the solution: "Fences, at best, slow people down. They don't stop people." With respect to the Secure Border Initiative, Bonner claims that new technology can only do so much: cameras can only buy one hundred yards of sight in certain regions due to mountainous terrain, and over 100,000 border agents would be needed to man the equipment and ensure that no migrant crosses. Ultimately, Bonner concludes, "They will come. I don't care what fences or how many Border Patrol agents you put there, they will come!"

References

Bean, F., and B. Lowell. 2007. "Unauthorized Migration." In *The New Americans*, ed. Mary C. Waters and Reed Ueda. Cambridge, MA: Harvard University Press.

Bustamante, Jorge A., Clark W. Reynolds, and Raúl A. Hinojosa Ojeda. 1992. *U.S.-Mexico Relations: Labor Market Interdependence*. Stanford, CA: Stanford University Press.

Chang, Joseph. 2007. "CPB Apprehensions at the Border." Paper presented at the Conference on Unauthorized Migration Deterrence Factors, Arlington, VA, March 8.

Congressional Budget Office. 2006. "Immigration Policy in the United States." February. http://www.cbo.gov/ftpdocs/70xx/doc7051/0228-Immigration.pdf.

Cornelius, Wayne A. 2001. "Death at the Border: Efficacy and Unintended Consequences of US Immigration Control Policy," *Population and Development Review* 27, no. 4: 661–85.

Cornelius, Wayne A., David Fitzgerald, and Pedro Lewin Fischer, eds. 2007. *Mayan Journeys: The New Migration from Yucatán to the United States.* La Jolla, CA: Center for Comparative Immigration Studies, University of California, San Diego.

Cornelius, Wayne A., and Jessa M. Lewis, eds. 2007. *Impacts of Border Enforcement on Mexican Migration: The View from Sending Communities.* La Jolla, CA: Center for Comparative Immigration Studies, University of California, San Diego.

Cornelius, Wayne A., and Idean Salehyan. 2007. "Does Border Enforcement Deter Unauthorized Immigration? The Case of Mexican Migration to the United States of America," *Regulation & Governance* 1: 139–53.

Espenshade, Thomas. 1995. "Using INS Border Apprehension Data to Measure the Flow of Undocumented Migrants Crossing the U.S.-Mexico Frontier," *International Migration Review* 29: 545–65.

Heyman, J. M. 1995. "Putting Power in the Anthropology of Bureaucracy: The Immigration and Naturalization Service at the Mexico–United States Border," *Current Anthropology* 36: 261–87.

Marcelli, Enrico A., and Wayne A. Cornelius. 2001."The Changing Profile of Mexican Migrants to the United States: New Evidence from California and Mexico," *Latin American Research Review* 36, no. 3: 105–31.

Massey, Douglas S., Jorge Durand, and Nolan J. Malone. 2002. *Beyond Smoke and Mirrors: Mexican Immigration in an Era of Economic Integration.* New York: Russell Sage Foundation.

McConnell, Eileen D., and Enrico A. Marcelli. 2007. "Buying into the American Dream? Mexican Immigrants, Legal Status, and Homeownership in Los Angeles County," *Social Science Quarterly* 88, no. 1 (March): 199–221.

Nevins, Joseph. 2002. *Operation Gatekeeper: The Rise of the "Illegal Alien" and the Making of the U.S.-Mexico Boundary.* New York: Routledge.

Orrenius, Pia M. 2004. "The Effect of U.S. Border Enforcement on the Crossing Behavior of Mexican Migrants." In *Crossing the Border: Research from the Mexican Migration Project,* ed. Jorge Durand and Douglas S. Massey. New York: Russell Sage Foundation.

Passel, Jeffrey S. 2007. "Size and Characteristics of the Unauthorized Migrant Population in the U.S." Washington, DC: Pew Hispanic Center, September. http://pewhispanic.org/reports/report.pho?ReportID=61.

Pear, Robert. 2007. "Bush Ties Drop in Illegal Immigration to His Policies," *New York Times*, April 10.

Reyes, Belinda I., Hans P. Johnson, and Richard Van Swearingen. 2002. *Holding the Line? The Effect of Recent Border Build-up on Unauthorized Migration.* San Francisco, CA: Public Policy Institute of California.

Riosmena, Fernando. 2004. "Return versus Settlement among Undocumented Migrants, 1980 to 1996." In *Crossing the Border: Research from the Mexican Migration Project,* ed. Jorge Durand and Douglas S. Massey. New York: Russell Sage Foundation.

Rubio-Goldsmith, Raquel, Melissa McCormick, Daniel Martinez, and Inez M. Duarte. 2006. "The 'Funnel Effect' and Recovered Bodies of Unauthorized Migrants Processed by the Pima County Office of the Medical Examiner, 1990–2005." Tucson, AZ: Binational Migration Institute, University of Arizona.

Singer, Audrey, and Douglas S. Massey. 1998. "The Social Process of Undocumented Border Crossing among Mexican Migrants," *International Migration Review* 32, no. 3 (Fall): 561–92.

Trejo Peña, Alma Paola. 2006. "Repercusiones de la política migratoria estadounidense en el perfil sociodemográfico y las rutas de ingreso y retorno de los migrantes mexicanos, 1993 y 2003." Master's thesis, El Colegio de la Frontera Norte.

Group of undocumented migrants being led by a *coyote* into the Arizona desert.

3 *Coyotaje*: The Structure and Functioning of the People-Smuggling Industry

JEZMÍN FUENTES AND OLIVIA GARCÍA

> *Like I told you, there are a lot of business partners, right? Those who no longer want to work as coyotes, they do the following. But it's hard to get started. You have to get a lot of money together. Once you have around $40,000, you buy your own cars and buy your own people. But if you fail, all the money you put together goes to waste. It's like, if I wanna be the boss, I need to save some money and then look for a client, like "Hey, you all wanna cross over?" And then I am a new boss. You start from the bottom, getting to know everyone, you understand? But when you first start, the truth is, it's a lot of money going into it. I would just see my boss handing out money here and there and there.*—Rodrigo, a 22-year-old former coyote based on the Arizona-Sonora border.[1]

Mexican migrants' reliance on people-smugglers has been observed since the late nineteenth century (Spener 2005, 3). But post-1993 U.S. border enforcement policies have given a huge boost to the people-smuggling industry. What used to be a modestly profitable activity has been transformed into an extremely lucrative one as the number of clients has burgeoned.

The smuggling services offered by individual *coyotes* (people-smugglers) are part of a larger phenomenon known as *coyotaje*. David Spener, one of the few social scientists to study people-smuggling from Mexico to the United States, defines it as "the set of labor migration strategies and practices elaborated by *coyotes* at the behest of and in concert with migrants, migrants' friends and family members, and/or migrants' U.S.

---

1. Rodrigo, originally from Tlacuitapa, was a very valuable informant in our research. He is quoted many times throughout this chapter; in succeeding quotes we identify him simply as Rodrigo.

employers" (2005, 2). The increased need for smuggling services in the post-1993 era has created an infinitely diverse human-smuggling market. In his analysis of the process through which a smuggling deal is arranged, Spener (2001) identified four types of coyotes: *pateros*, local-interior, friends and kin, and border-commercial (also called border-business). For the purposes of this chapter, we focus on the characteristics of local-interior and border-commercial smugglers. Local-interior coyotes are usually experienced migrants who are based in the migrant-sending community, where they are known and trusted by their potential clients (see Fuentes et al. 2007). Border-commercial coyotes, in contrast, are based in the border region. It is believed that they assist the highest proportion of migrants, given the large clientele arriving continuously in the borderlands. The scale of people-smuggling operations also varies. While small-scale smugglers continue to operate in South Texas, for example (Spener 2004), "the border crackdown fueled the emergence of more skilled and sophisticated transnational migrant smuggling groups, creating a more serious organized crime problem along and across the border" (Andreas 2003, 3).

Our study of people-smuggling supports the findings of past research conducted in Tlacuitapa, Jalisco, and Las Ánimas, Zacatecas, in 2005, and in Tunkás, Yucatán, in 2006.[2] Although no socially embedded coyotes were found in Tlacuitapa itself, the town's long history of U.S.-bound migration enables us to study coyotaje in considerable detail. By comparing Tlacuitapa to towns like Tunkás, which has a relatively recent international migration history, we can understand how the use of coyotes evolves over time in migrant-sending communities. We address four main questions: How are coyotaje networks organized? How does a migrant from Tlacuitapa hire a coyote? How have coyotes reacted to heightened border enforcement? And is there a connection between people-smuggling and drug smuggling?

THE ORGANIZATION OF COYOTAJE

> *They give orders. They provide the money. They provide the trucks or the people. . . . They bring people from El Salvador. They already have all their connections from El Salvador, from Honduras, and from different states here in Mexico.*—Rodrigo.

---

2. For the 2005 research in Tlacuitapa and Las Ánimas, see Cornelius and Lewis 2007; for Tunkás in 2006, see Cornelius, Fitzgerald, and Lewin Fischer 2007.

The rise in demand for people-smugglers has fed the development of sophisticated smuggling networks. In the larger of these transnational networks, there is an extensive hierarchy of workers who collaborate to provide smuggling services. Through an elaborate division of labor, the coyotaje network has developed into a quasi-corporation that defies intervention by the U.S. government. As Kaizen and Nonneman observe, coyotaje "usually [takes] place through cooperation between various criminal groups in origin and destination areas, often backed by corrupt government officials and even legitimate businesspeople" (2007, 127–28). Similar to the transnational people-smuggling organizations that operate in Belgium (Kaizen and Nonneman 2007) and China (Chin 1999), large Mexico-based smuggling organizations reflect a highly developed division of labor. The following breakdown of functions and personnel is based on information gathered from one border-based coyote and confirmed by many unauthorized migrants from Tlacuitapa.

At the top of the hierarchy are the bosses—the *patrones* or *socios*, as they are called—who manage the business administration and finances and give orders to those beneath them. As a border-commercial coyote noted, "They just get the money. But if a car gets lost or if we're taken to jail, they go and bail us out—on the Mexican side. In the United States, you can't do that." These "business partners" are in charge of supervising specific regions within Mexico and the United States and ensuring the smooth operation of their smuggling activity. They are the owners of the hotels, safe houses, vehicles, and other smuggling instruments used by their subordinates. These bosses establish contact with and bribe key political figures and law enforcement officers. Patrones in Mexico also maintain close business connections with their counterparts in Central America and Asia, who provide them with the most lucrative smuggling deals.

> The boss tells you, "Go find your helpers. But useful ones. It is up to you who to choose." If you find a dumb ass, then you get a dumb ass. You're the one that hired him.—*Rodrigo.*

The patrones also have the key role of setting the price to charge to migrants. They decide how this money will be divided among their subordinates, and, according to people-smugglers interviewed at the border, they usually keep at least half of the money charged to each migrant. Thus, if migrants are charged $2,000 to cross the border and a group of twenty migrants is crossed successfully, the top boss would reap $20,000 in a single trip. Bosses normally establish their own enterprises with profits they accrue over years of acting as a coyote. Once a boss has established himself as trustworthy, people seek out his or her assistants and the business expands.

The head of a human-smuggling operation in San Diego states he will only cross migrants who are recommended to him. Because he cannot personally cross every person who comes to him, he and other top bosses share their expertise, training others in a variety of ways to cross migrants over the border. The head of the San Diego organization said that he knew the border region like the back of his hand, and he claimed to have photos detailing every part of the borderlands where he conducts his business. The success of a main boss depends directly on how well he has trained his coyotes. He is paid only when migrants are crossed successfully.

The coyotes or *guías* occupy the next level in the hierarchy. They are familiar with the details of Border Patrol operations, such as work shifts, times of aerial surveillance, places where agents are stationed, and the technology in use. Analyzing weak points in U.S. enforcement efforts enables smugglers to devise strategies to evade the Border Patrol and get their human cargo safely to the United States. Coyotes' services range from crossing undocumented male migrants to making *viajes especiales* (special trips) with pregnant women or Chinese and Central American immigrants en route to Southern California. Coyotes move undocumented migrants across the border and hand them over to the person in charge of arranging their transportation within the United States. Migrants are held in safe houses until the smuggling fee is paid in full—in cash. One smuggler we interviewed reported that he receives between $200 and $400 for each migrant he drives through the Arizona sector. Considering that he transports between twelve and seventeen migrants in his truck on each trip, we estimate that this coyote is receiving at least $2,400 per border crossing.

Next in the chain of command are the coyotes' assistants. One to three assistants normally accompany a coyote on a given trip. They report directly to the coyote and are under his direction. Their principal duty is to ensure that the migrants keep together during the journey. Once these "coyotes-in-training" learn to navigate routes by night and have mastered the operations, they are promoted to coyote status.

Working under the assistants are the *chequeadores* and *chequeadores pa'rriba* (lookouts), who signal when it is safe to cross the border and to pass through the various checkpoints within the United States. Chequeadores who work along the border monitor the Border Patrol. Driving slowly along the border and using infrared night-vision scopes provided by the patrón, chequeadores signal the places that Border Patrol vehicles are stationed.[3] They have extensive knowledge of Border Patrol operations, including work shifts.

> There is one chequeador at the checkpoint and one who checks the border. The former is already waiting for me in Yuma. When we arrive, if we go from San Luis to Yuma, that one is ready over there. He is ready for us on the highway, ready to start on the way. That one goes to the first checkpoint. They call him chequeador pa'rriba. The other one is the chequeador for the border.—Rodrigo.

Once a Border Patrol agent ends his shift, the chequeador rushes back to the migrants and signals them to leave. One border-based coyote describes this tactic as follows:

> The chequeador would hide in his truck as stealthy as can be. The roads were already well marked. He would stop his Cherokee and park. And then he would check the area and would go back and check another, and he would stay there searching until he found a Border Patrol vehicle moving out. And the moment it left, he would take off like a demon. Then they placed sensors, but it didn't matter because they didn't work.

---

3. Intensified surveillance by the Border Patrol is matched by the smugglers' careful scrutiny of Border Patrol operations. Because the bosses have provided their smugglers with the same technology that the Border Patrol uses, such as infrared night-vision scopes, the advantage the Border Patrol once had is nullified.

Chequeadores pa'rriba are residents of cities and towns located near smuggling routes. When a smuggler crosses through an area, the local chequeador pa'rriba is called upon to guide the smuggler's car safely across, driving his own car ahead of the vehicle carrying the migrants, generally at night. As Rodrigo described it, "Well, they can't arrest him. He's in his own car. He's not carrying any migrants. He's got a driver license and insurance. Yeah, he gets paid less, but he's only the lookout." Once the human cargo makes it safely across, another chequeador pa'rriba from the neighboring region takes over. This chain of links extends until the migrants reach their destination.

The sole job of the chequeador pa'rriba is to ensure that the vehicles with migrants are not stopped. Chequeadores pa'rriba use cell phones and two-way radios to alert the smuggler if traffic checkpoints along the highway are in service, so that the smuggler can exit the highway and wait for a better time to proceed.

> He [the chequeador pa'rriba] moves ahead. He says, "Wait fifteen, twenty minutes. I'll call you in a bit so that you can come." Then he calls and says, "Come on, it's clear." Then, vrooom. Of course, you have to drive at the speed limit over there. Not too fast or too slow. But sometimes you get bored and you step on it. Some folks want to get there fast, and they speed and that is when they get stopped by the sheriff.

If the car he is guiding is stopped by law enforcement, the chequeador pa'rriba notifies the boss, and calls are made to report the rented car lost or stolen so that the car cannot be used to track the people-smugglers or any individuals who may be involved in money laundering at the car dealership the smugglers used. Of course, smugglers always try to evade law enforcement as best they can.

> We would always run from the police. We would run for a bit, then stand around on the street pretending, so that the police wouldn't catch us. And then we would try and mix in with the people so they didn't know we were coyotes. But the truth is they almost always figure it out. I don't

> know how they do it, but they can tell. They must know
> just by our appearance.—Rodrigo.

Within this division of labor, a participant's share of the proceeds is proportionate to the risk taken. As one moves down the hierarchy, pay and risk both decrease. Chequeadores pa'rriba run little risk of arrest; they drive their own cars and have all necessary legal documents. Hence they are paid much less than coyotes, who may receive $400 for each person they transport from San Luis Río Colorado to Los Angeles.

Cuidanderos (caretakers) are at the bottom of the hierarchy. They are mostly 12- or 13-year-olds whose main job is to distract Border Patrol agents. By locating and removing the tire spikes that the Border Patrol places on suspected transport routes, they also enable a smoother crossing for those higher up in the hierarchy. These participants are paid the least. Even Anglo teenagers sometimes fill this kind of supporting role in people-smuggling. In 2005, smugglers were found to be recruiting teenagers outside of San Diego County high schools. Smugglers would pay the teenagers about $1,500 to drive a vehicle through a legal port of entry; the teen would generally not know whether he or she was crossing drugs or migrants. Teens offer a valuable stream of workers for smuggling organizations. They arouse little suspicion, and if caught, Anglo minors incur far less severe consequences in the legal system than would adult noncitizens. In 2004, only about twelve of some one hundred teenagers apprehended for people-smuggling were prosecuted (Isackson 2005).

> Sometimes they send them [the cuidanderos] ahead so they
> will see where the Border Patrol is. They are youngsters
> really. Twelve, thirteen years old. They send them as bait
> so the Border Patrol will say, "Ah! Got one." The Border
> Patrol only holds them for two, three hours and then lets
> them go.—Rodrigo.

A border-based coyote reported that he had young Anglo women on his payroll. They would pick up migrants and transport them to their destinations in the U.S. interior. As related by our informant, "We had a ton of American women working with us. Young women. Americans.

They're the ones who take the migrants from the border on up." The integration of Anglo teenagers and women into smuggling organizations is further evidence of the ease with which coyotaje operations adapt in response to heightened border enforcement.

People-smuggling networks manage many safe houses along their trafficking routes in the United States. About twelve undocumented migrants are kept in a two- or three-bedroom house. On a typical day, approximately half of the clients are adult men; the rest are women and children. Once clients arrive at a safe house, they telephone family members or friends in the United States to have them pay the balance of the smuggler's fee and to make arrangements to be picked up. If the money owed to the smugglers is not paid within a week or so, the smugglers find ways to encourage payment. As Rodrigo recalled:

> We left them there for a week. If by the end of the week
> they did not pay, we tried to arrange payment directly with
> the person being smuggled. If he couldn't pay, we returned
> him to Mexico. We deported him.

Migrants are closely supervised in the safe houses to ensure that no one escapes without paying for their trip. Rodrigo described what happens if a client gets caught trying to escape:

> We'd finish them. Well, how can I say it so that it doesn't
> sound so bad? First we punch them or point a gun at them
> and force them back inside. The truth is there were times
> that they would get away. My boss would almost die of
> anger when someone would escape.

HIRING A COYOTE

Our study found that fewer Tlacuitapeño migrants are hiring coyotes at the border and more are hiring their coyote before migrating, demonstrating that the expanding web of coyotaje can now advertise its services even in the interior of Mexico, where migration decisions are made. This promotional work is done by *vaquetones*, a term denoting people who are basically idle. The vaquetón's job is to find people who are planning to migrate to the United States without benefit of documents and then recommend these individuals to people-smuggling operations at the border. The main boss of a smuggling organization pays $150 for each customer a vaquetón delivers. Thus, although migrants find their coyotes through people in their hometown, it is really the people-smuggling organizations based at the border that facilitate the crossing into the United States.

Key factors that can affect the outcome of the migrant's border-crossing experience are the way in which the coyote is contracted and whether the coyote is paid before or after the trip. As shown in figure 3.1, migrants from Tlacuitapa generally pay their coyote when they reach their destination; among Tlacuitapeños who crossed between 2000 and the time of our interviews in 2007, 85.6 percent paid their smuggling fee at the end of their journey. Advance payment in full has virtually disappeared post-2000, primarily because migrants know that if they pay before reaching the border, they are less likely to receive assistance with subsequent attempts at entry if they are apprehended on the first try. As David Spener notes, "increased patrolling at the border results in a higher probability of apprehension of migrants," such that "smugglers have to make repeated attempts to get groups through the Border Patrol's lines of defense" (2001, 148). In essence, payment at the end of the trip is a form of insurance, obliging coyotes to deliver migrants to their final U.S. destination if they want to collect their fee.

In Tlacuitapa, we found that there has been a change in the way migrants find smugglers. The majority of Tlacuitapeños who crossed after 2000 reported that they found their coyote through family and friends in their hometown (see figure 3.2).

Even though most Tlacuitapa migrants rely on family and friends in the hometown to help them identify and hire a coyote, ultimately it is U.S.-based family and friends who are the principal source of funds with which to pay the smuggler's fees (see figure 3.3). This is particularly true of the most recent (post-2000) coyote-assisted crossings reported by our interviewees. A coyote based at the U.S.-Mexico border confirms that most of his business is done over the phone with the migrant's family member or friend in the United States who will be paying for the smuggling services. As a result, migrants may be unaware of the actual cost. An illustrative case is a young woman from Jalisco whom we interviewed in Tijuana just hours after she was deported from the United States. When asked how much she was paying her smuggler, she admitted that she had no idea because her family in California had arranged her trip.

Figure 3.1 Modes of Payment for Coyote Services

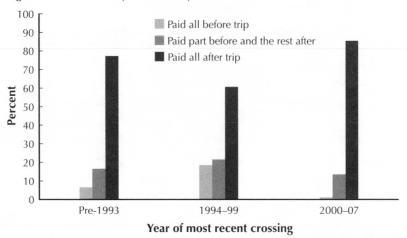

N = 172.

Figure 3.2 Method of Hiring a Coyote

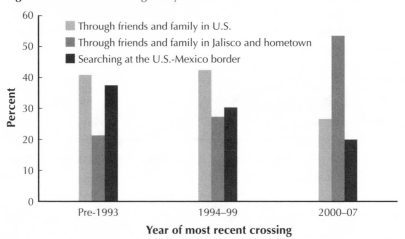

N = 179.

Figure 3.3 Modes of Financing an Undocumented Trip to the United States

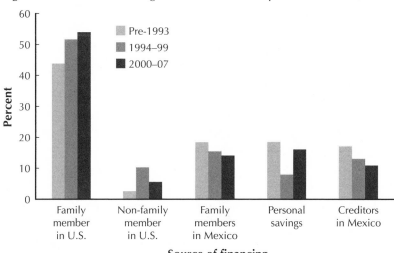

N = 212.

Tlacuitapeños' extensive transborder social networks help explain the differences between their border-crossing experiences and those of migrants from regions of Mexico that lack a tradition of U.S.-bound migration; the latter tend to report a higher incidence of abusive treatment by their coyotes.[4] Only 11.1 percent of the undocumented migrants we interviewed from Tlacuitapa reported abuse from their coyote, and 10.2 percent stated that the coyote had abandoned someone (not necessarily the interviewee) during the trip. These low rates of abuse and abandonment likely reflect the fact that most migrants now have their U.S.-based families pay upon delivery.[5] The clients, and their relatives, must be satisfied with the service. A related advantage stemming from the established networks typical of long-standing sending communities is that the coyotes

4. One exception involves migrants from Tunkás, Yucatán, 11 percent of whom reported abuse (about the same level as found among Tlacuitapeños) even though Tunkás has only recently become a source of migrants to the United States (Kimball, Acosta, and Dames 2007).

5. Reyes, Johnson, and Van Swearingen (2002: 62–63) report that, in contrast to Mexican migrants who have family members who can pay the coyote upon their arrival, "those without connections in the United States had to pay in advance or personally upon arrival. Because these people had to carry money with them, they were more vulnerable to robbery, sometimes by the coyote."

are more likely to have ties to these communities, which gives them a greater stake in ensuring the well-being of migrants from these towns.

THE QUALITY OF COYOTE SERVICES

As reliance on coyotes has increased, smugglers have developed ways to cater to the needs of a more diverse group of migrants. Smuggling "packages" come with a range of prices and options. These packages generally include the trip across the border (on foot or in a vehicle), a stopover at a safe house, and transportation to the ultimate destination. They can also be all-inclusive trips by airplane or "special trips" designed to cater to the needs of pregnant women. In one case, undercover agents in Arizona exposed fourteen travel agents who had arranged for the air transportation of unauthorized migrants within the United States (Preston 2007). Rodrigo described the process through which smugglers "prepare" migrants to be flown to their destination:

> We didn't take people to San Jose by car; we always sent them on a plane. They would pick them up and buy them IDs and everything.

The lack of "socially embedded" coyotes in Tlacuitapa has forced migrants and their families to turn to smugglers in nearby Lagos de Moreno, León, or Aguascalientes. Table 3.1, which was compiled based on interviews with informants in Tlacuitapa and the United States in 2007, describes the steps taken by Tlacuitapeños who hire their coyotes in the Mexican interior and the process by which they successfully enter the United States.

One of the reasons that unauthorized migrants have such high rates of success entering the United States on the same trip to the border is that coyotes offer them unlimited "free tries" (see chapter 2, this volume). Border-based coyotes whom we interviewed in Tijuana confirmed that they will attempt as many crossings as necessary to get the migrant to the destination. According to one border-business coyote: "They're assured that if they get caught, we're going to cross them again. We'll try until we get them in. They know what hotel to go to." This guarantee is most likely linked to the "payment-on-delivery" option now preferred by most families of migrants (figure 3.1). Leaving a migrant on the Mexican side of the border translates into a financial loss for the coyote.

Table 3.1 A Typical Coyote-Assisted Border Crossing for
Migrants from Tlacuitapa

- Once a person makes the decision to migrate, he or she begins asking around town for contact information for coyotes. Typically, a relative or acquaintance will provide a phone number.

- The would-be migrant then calls the number and agrees on a time for a coyote to meet at the migrant's home. Typically the person who attends the meeting at the migrant's house is not the same as the one who received the initial phone call.

- During the meeting at the migrant's home, the deal is made and a fee agreed on. However, at that point the migrant has no idea when he or she will embark on the journey. The migrant must wait for a phone call from the smuggling organization setting a time and place to start the journey.

- In the meantime, the organization is drumming up business in order to fill up the bus that will depart from the area. Smuggling organizations generally use standard tour busses, which hold about sixty passengers. Once the organization has secured enough clients to fill a bus, the migrant receives a phone call telling him/her where and when to board. Typically, busses depart from Lagos de Moreno, approximately 25 kilometers from Tlacuitapa.

- A typical journey to the border involves boarding a bus in Lagos de Moreno and traveling nonstop (except for one or two bathroom breaks) for almost thirty hours to the Arizona border.

- During the bus ride, coyotes only identify themselves if a problem arises. They offer information only when necessary, often use nicknames, and avoid carrying identification. If apprehended by the Border Patrol, coyotes pretend to be migrants, and the migrants do not give them up because they would lose the opportunity to try to cross later with the same organization.

- Once migrants arrive at the border—typically at Agua Prieta, Sonora, for migrants from Tlacuitapa—they are taken to a hotel to shower and rest while awaiting the signal to depart. The hotel is usually owned by the smuggling organization.

- Led by one or two guides, migrants walk anywhere from eighteen to thirty hours through desert areas so remote that they are out of reach of the Border Patrol.

- Migrants are told to bring only a small bottle of water, because anything larger would slow them down. The coyotes instruct the migrants not to use flashlights or light cigarettes, which could reveal their location to the Border Patrol.

Table 3.1 continued on page 92

Table 3.1 continued

- If detained by the Border Patrol, migrants know that they will be released just across the border with Mexico and that they should return to the hotel to await instructions for making another crossing attempt.

- If the initial crossing attempt is unsuccessful, the original guides are replaced, and guides are continually replaced until the migrants are successfully crossed. Migrants report that it is not unusual to try to cross on four different nights with four different guides.

- Migrants walk the entire trip to the outskirts of Douglas, Arizona, where they crouch by the highway as the guide divides them into groups and gives them instructions for catching their pickup vehicles, which are staggered over a few hours to avoid drawing attention to the area.

- Cars rented with fake credit cards are used to pick up the migrants in Douglas. If pursued by the Border Patrol, the coyotes and migrants are prepared to abandon the rented cars, knowing that the smugglers cannot be traced through the rental agency.

- Migrants are taken to Phoenix, Arizona, in large pickup trucks, with as many layers of migrants as possible lying flat on the truck bed "like sardines," as one migrant put it.

- Upon arriving in Phoenix, migrants are taken to a safe house and divided into groups depending on their destination and then transported from the safe house in minivans.

- Coyotes only receive payment once family members have received word from the migrant that he or she has arrived safely. Payment is typically made by family members in the United States or in Tlacuitapa, with the money paid to any "branch" of the smuggling organization.

Source: Interviews with experienced migrants conducted by Jessica Sisco, January 2007.

Migrants reconnecting with their coyotes after being apprehended by the Border Patrol and released just a few yards inside Mexico are a common sight in Tijuana. Their downcast faces and dirty feet make the migrants hard to miss, as does the wrinkled piece of paper they carry with the coyote's phone number. These recent deportees wait in groups for their coyote to pick them up and take them out to try again.

As recently deported migrants wait near the border to be picked up by their coyote, they become prey to vaquetones, who promise them a sure and safe crossing if they switch to a new coyote. However, most migrants are too savvy to take the bait and will wait to be reconnected with their original coyote. Vaquetones have their best success among undocumented migrants who have lived in the United States so long that they have lost their links to their sending community and hence have no option but to hire a coyote without knowing his or her previous history in assisting border crossings.

Rather than halting or even reducing people-smuggling activities, heightened border enforcement has only spurred smugglers to develop new ways of doing business. The boss of a Tijuana-based human-smuggling organization suggested that the Border Patrol's tactical shifts are quixotic. His organization always knows the location of Border Patrol agents, but they never know where his coyotes will be operating. As long as there is demand for his services, this boss noted, his organization will find a way to get migrants across. When asked if the Secure Fence Act of 2006 would make it more difficult to cross undocumented migrants into the United States, he responded: "If they put up a wall, we'll dig more tunnels. When they shut down the tunnels, we'll go by sea." He then declared that the Border Patrol, coyotes, and migrants will continue to play this game of cat and mouse as long as the would-be crossers' "hunger is greater than their fear."

SETTING FEES

> *People-smugglers have a lot of contacts. I think that's why they charge so much. One coyote hands you off to another one, and from him to another. In the past, one coyote would bring us all the way. Not now. Now they send you over there and then over there. . . . It's a chain.*—Lourdes, an unauthorized Tlacuitapa migrant residing in Oklahoma City.

In response to the intensification of enforcement at the border in recent decades, migrants have turned increasingly to coyotes to ensure a safe crossing. Post-2000, the share of Tlacuitapeño migrants who crossed with the help of a coyote rose from the previous level of 71 percent to 93 percent (see chapter 2, this volume). Spener argues that "increased efforts required by smugglers to get migrants through the border region lead them to charge more for their services" (2001, 148). Rising demand has produced rising returns to people-smuggling organizations, and the largest and most successful have invested their profits in efforts to reach a larger pool of customers. Because they have the advantage of size, they have largely been able to set the price for a border crossing (Spener 2001, 148).

Peter Andreas (2001, 116) notes that coyotes' prices depend on "location, the quality of service, and the set of services being purchased." A key factor in determining the price is the migrant's country of origin. Central Americans get charged at least twice as much as Mexicans. And people migrating from further away, as from China, are charged three times the Mexican price for the same service or for a reduced service package. For example, a border-based coyote informed us that Chinese migrants have to pay for their room and board while waiting for an opportune time to cross the border. Spener notes that "larger smuggling rings are free to charge higher prices for their services" (2001, 148). Smuggling organizations whose networks extend across the Americas and further abroad can charge the highest prices, because these organizations provide the most services over the largest area.

Figure 3.4 lists nine coyotes' self-reported prices for three types of border crossing. Not all of the coyotes offer all three methods, which explains why there are no prices for coyotes D, G, and H on certain strategies. In fact, according to the head of a people-smuggling organization based in San Diego, each network of coyotes specializes in certain tactics. His own business concentrates on crossing people through the desert, for the bargain price of $1,600 to $1,800 per migrant.

Another coyote said that a migrant's age and sex may also play a role in determining the crossing fee. We found some evidence that women may be charged more than men when crossing the border on foot. However, one female coyote observed that women sometimes pay some of the fee through sexual favors: "If she puts out, male coyotes give her a discount." The range of prices that one male border-business coyote charges migrants to cross the border on foot along a sector of the Arizona desert appears in table 3.2.

Figure 3.4 Prices Charged by Coyotes in the San Diego–Tijuana Area

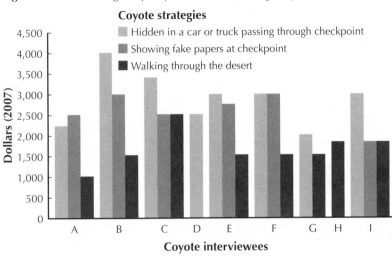

Table 3.2 Prices Charged for Smuggling an Undocumented Person into the United States on Foot through the Arizona Desert (in U.S. dollars)

	From San Luis Río Colorado to . . .		
	Yuma, Arizona	Phoenix or Los Angeles	San Jose, California[a]
Men	$800–1,000	$2,000	$2,500–2,700
Women	$1,500	$2,700	$3,000
Pregnant women	$2,000	$3,500	$3,500
Mother/child (5+yrs) "package"	$2,000	$4,500	$3,000
Mother/baby			$4,000–5,000

Note: The service includes crossing the desert on foot with a coyote, vehicle pickup on the U.S. side, conveyance to a safe house, and transport to the final destination.
[a] May include airfare from a stopover city to San Jose.

When we asked coyotes why women who are not pregnant pay less, one answered: "Well, if they are in good shape and can run, they don't need as much care. But, you know, you really have to take care of pregnant women." The price difference is due, then, primarily to the special attention pregnant women require and their physical limitations, which can affect their speed on the desert crossing. There are also price differences depending on a woman's stage of pregnancy. This same coyote mentioned that mixing pregnant women, especially those in their last trimester, with other migrants slows everyone down and puts the entire group at greater risk.

Some coyotes offer a *viaje especial* or "special trip" for pregnant women who can afford it. One coyote described a viaje especial as follows: "Five pregnant women. You gather them together and take them in a truck." They are not hidden but are seated like regular passengers throughout the entire trip to their destination. Pregnant women pay about $5,000 for a viaje especial, compared to $3,500 charged to a pregnant woman who crosses the border on foot. Although there is a substantial decrease in risk for pregnant women who take "special trips," the high cost of such a crossing can be prohibitive for many migrants.

Figure 3.5 Coyotes' Prices to Traditional versus Nontraditional Destinations

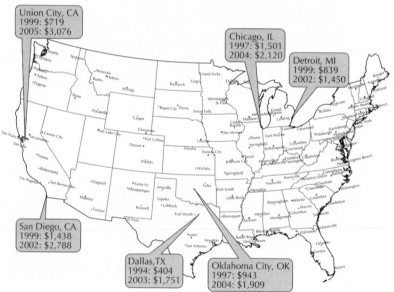

The best "deal" in the people-smuggling business is the price charged to cross children, which serves as an incentive to cross children into the

United States while they are very young. A border-based coyote affirmed that children are the easiest to cross; children can use false documents to enter through a legal port of entry more easily than can adult migrants. The price for crossing a child up to 12 years of age with false documents ranges from $500 to $600.

Another factor accounting for variations in the prices coyotes charge is the number of additional checkpoints to be navigated before reaching the migrant's final destination. A coyote interviewed at the border reported that his set fee for smuggling a migrant across the border at San Ysidro, either with false papers or via a desert crossing, was $1,500. For each checkpoint along the way to the migrant's final destination, he adds $500. Thus migrants going to Los Angeles would pay an added $500 for being passed through the San Onofre checkpoint near Camp Pendleton. Coyotes' fees also vary depending on the migrant's final destination (see figure 3.5).

PEOPLE-SMUGGLING AND DRUGS: THE UNCERTAIN CONNECTION

> *Look, I'm gonna tell you something. Coyotes send people where they know they might get caught. They don't care so much if they get caught. But for smuggling drugs they have some remarkable routes.*—Rodrigo.

Large drug-trafficking organizations that operate along the border sometimes delve into the business of people-smuggling, though the smuggling of people and drugs are not always intertwined. Because drug smugglers already have established networks of individuals in place, they can easily operate people-smuggling enterprises without interference. According to one of our informants, a border-business coyote, his organization bribes the Mexican Federal Police in order to operate freely: "We arrange with the man in charge of the police, and they let you go like nothing. Well, we pay them, $1,000 per trip to the *federales*."

Drug traffickers' extensive repertoire of strategies for evading U.S. law enforcement allows them to add a human-smuggling sideline. Like drug trafficking, people-smuggling is highly profitable, but it carries much less risk. Even though one organization may be involved in both drug trafficking and people-smuggling, drugs and people are rarely combined in one trip. Rather, the two "cargos" go by separate routes, with the drug-smuggling routes being more remote and less likely to be detected. Rodrigo described the rationale behind maintaining the two types of smuggling separate:

> Almost nobody mixes people and drugs. It's not even permitted under their own rules. . . . Because for smuggling drugs they only use *"borregos"* [sheep]. They'll send one or two at a time. They'll put the drugs in small backpacks. One person takes 20 kilos, another takes another 20, and in they go. The same boss has his own people to smuggle drugs, but it's a whole different scheme.—Rodrigo.

While borregos carry backpacks loaded with drugs and cross through the remote desert alone or by twos on foot, people-smugglers use routes that pass much closer to Border Patrol locations and cross large groups. As a border-based coyote noted, "they also use people as bait." That is, the drug smugglers can use their sideline of crossing undocumented migrants to draw law enforcement attention away from their more profitable drug smuggling.

A coyote we interviewed at the San Diego border offered a different view: "Drug smuggling is a very different business, a danger in which you risk your life." Unlike the drug-smuggling business, his organization is not territorial and does not have access to under-border tunnels. When asked about the connection between drug trafficking and people-smuggling, the head of a people-smuggling organization in San Diego claimed that each smuggling organization specializes in either drugs or people, and they do not interfere with each other: "There's no way drug smugglers are going to carry something of so much value through the mountains."

CONCLUSION

Coyotaje is a business that displays almost infinite adaptability. Formerly just an option, a coyote is now a virtual necessity for a clandestine border crossing, and this rising demand for assisted crossings has prompted people-smuggling organizations to adapt quickly to changes in U.S. border enforcement strategy. Whether based at the border or embedded in the sending or receiving community, coyotes are defying all of the Border Patrol's efforts to put them out of business.

To ensure a successful crossing through the U.S.-Mexico border, the people-smuggling industry has developed a complex hierarchical network that can advertise its services far from the border. Paradoxically, people-smuggling networks have become the primary beneficiaries of U.S. immigration policies. Rather than putting people-smugglers out of business, the post-1993 U.S. border buildup has been a bonanza for them. The planned expansion of the Border Patrol to twenty thousand agents and the installation of elaborate electronic surveillance systems and other border enforcement strategies to be implemented over the next five to ten years will only fuel the growth of the transnational people-smuggling businesses that thrive in the U.S.-Mexico borderlands.

References

Andreas, Peter. 2001. "The Transformation of Migrant Smuggling across the U.S.-Mexico Border." In *Global Human Smuggling: Comparative Perspectives*, ed. David J. Kyle and Rey Koslowski. Baltimore, MD: Johns Hopkins University Press.

———. 2003. "A Tale of Two Borders: The U.S.-Mexico and U.S.-Canada Lines after 9/11." Working Paper No. 77. La Jolla, CA: Center for Comparative Immigration Studies, University of California, San Diego. http://ccis.ucsd.edu/PUBLICATIONS/wrkg77.pdf.

Chin, Ko-Lin. 1999. "The Social Organization of Human Smuggling." In *Smuggled Chinese: Clandestine Immigration to the United States*. Philadelphia, PA: Temple University Press.

Cornelius, Wayne A., David Fitzgerald, and Pedro Lewin Fischer, eds. 2007. *Mayan Journeys: The New Migration from Yucatán to the United States*. La Jolla, CA: Center for Comparative Immigration Studies, University of California, San Diego.

Cornelius, Wayne A., and Jessa M. Lewis. 2007. *Impacts of Border Enforcement on Mexican Migration: The View from Sending Communities*. La Jolla, CA: Center for Comparative Immigration Studies, University of California, San Diego.

Fuentes, Jezmín, Henry L'Esperance, Raúl Pérez, and Caitlin White. 2007. "Impacts of U.S. Immigration Policies on Migration Behavior." In *Impacts of Border Enforcement on Mexican Migration: The View from Sending Communities*, ed. Wayne A. Cornelius and Jessa M. Lewis. La Jolla, CA: Center for Comparative Immigration Studies, University of California, San Diego.

Isackson, Amy. 2005. "Teens Used for Smuggling across U.S.-Mexico Border." *All Things Considered*. National Public Radio broadcast, June 2. http://www.npr.org/templates/story/story.php?storyId=4677792.

Kaizen, Julie, and Walter Nonneman. 2007. "Irregular Migration in Belgium and Organized Crime: An Overview," *International Migration* 45: 123–46.

Kimball, Ann, Yesenia Acosta, and Rebecca Dames. 2007. "Impacts of U.S. Immigration Policies on Migration Behavior." In *Mayan Journeys: The New Migration from Yucatán to the United States*, ed. Wayne A. Cornelius, David Fitzgerald, and Pedro Lewin Fischer. La Jolla, CA: Center for Comparative Immigration Studies, University of California, San Diego.

Preston, Julia. 2007. "Travel Agents in Arizona Helped Smuggle Illegal Immigrants by Plane, Authorities Say," *New York Times*, March 31.

Reyes, Belinda I., Hans P. Johnson, and Richard Van Swearingen. 2002. *Holding the Line? The Effect of the Recent Border Build-up on Unauthorized Migration*. San Francisco, CA: Public Policy Institute of California.

Spener, David. 2001. "Smuggling Mexican Migrants through South Texas: Challenges Posed by Operation Rio Grande." In *Global Human Smuggling: Comparative Perspectives*, ed. David J. Kyle and Rey Koslowski. Baltimore, MD: Johns Hopkins University Press.

———. 2004. "Mexican Migrant Smuggling: A Cross-Border Cottage Industry," *Journal of International Migration and Integration* 5, no. 3 (Summer): 308–12.

———. 2005. "Mexican Migration to the United States, 1882–1992: A Long Twentieth Century of Coyotaje." Working Paper No. 124. La Jolla, CA: Center for Comparative Immigration Studies, University of California, San Diego. http://ccis.ucsd.edu/PUBLICATIONS/wrkg124.pdf.

The other wall. (Used by permission of Paul Fell, *Lincoln Journal Star*.)

4 Jumping the Legal Hurdles: Getting Green Cards, Visas, and U.S. Citizenship

LAURA VÁZQUEZ, MARYSOL LUNA GÓMEZ, EMILY LAW, AND KATE VALENTINE

Supporters of strict immigration control argue that undocumented immigrants should "get in line" and wait for proper authorization to enter the United States. According to Congressman John Culberson (R, Texas), "If they want to work here and eventually become citizens, illegal immigrants should go home and reenter our country legally to show they are willing to respect our laws. They need to use the existing visa system and get in line with everyone else" (2007). For many potential migrants, though, legal channels are not a realistic option, so they opt to cross the border clandestinely despite the associated dangers and rising financial costs. Immigrants are shut out of the legal system by immigration laws that restrict the number of visas for less skilled workers and for family reunification. There is a serious mismatch between what the current legal immigration system can provide and the number and kinds of would-be legal immigrants.

Given Tlacuitapa's long migration history, there is the potential for divisions to emerge within the community based on access to the U.S. legal migration system. Many Tlacuitapeños became permanent U.S. residents under special legalization programs enacted during the twentieth century (Barajas et al. 2007). For example, 80-year-old Pedro migrated from 1950 until 1962 through the Bracero Program. When the program ended in 1962, his employer sponsored Pedro for legal permanent residency, a process that Pedro stated was very quick in those days. He later applied for citizenship and then submitted permanent residency applications for his immediate family to join him in the United States. Because he is legalized, he can move freely between Tlacuitapa and the United States, and he now lives part of the year with his family in Mexico and part with relatives in Oklahoma. This is not an unusual case. Many Tlacuitapeños have been able to take advantage of past programs to legalize their status in the United States and petition for documentation for their immediate relatives.

However, for Tlacuitapeños with no legal relatives in the United States and no employer willing to sponsor them, the options for entering the United States are extremely limited. Though the U.S. demand for their labor remains high, only one in five employment-based visas is designated for less skilled workers, and the total number is capped at five thousand per year.[1] Only two categories exist for less skilled workers to obtain temporary immigrant employment visas: H-2A for agricultural workers and H-2B for seasonal workers. Less skilled migrants received only 16 percent of all temporary employment and training visas granted in 2002 (Paral 2005).

For Tlacuitapeños who have an immediate family member who is a legal resident or citizen of the United States, the family-based petition offers another channel for legal immigration. However, this avenue is plagued by extremely long delays. Pilar, a resident of Tlacuitapa, has a sister who is a naturalized U.S. citizen. Pilar filed a family-based petition and has been waiting to be interviewed at the consulate for thirteen years. The only legal option remaining for those with no immediate relatives who are U.S. legal permanent residents or citizens is to navigate the complexities of the legal system in hopes of obtaining a "green card." But today's green card applicants face an agency that is under pressure due to financial shortages, an absence of efforts to innovate, increased security demands, and a difficult organizational transition from the Immigration and Naturalization Service (INS) to the Department of Homeland Security (DHS) (Hsu 2007).

GREEN CARDS

A "green card" (U.S. Permanent Resident Card) is a ten-year visa that allows an immigrant to live and work legally in the United States. A

---

1. The Immigration and Nationality Act allows for 10,000 visas for low-skilled workers. However, the number was reduced temporarily to 5,000 to make visas available for the Nicaraguan and Central American Relief Act of 1997. This reduction will remain in effect as long as necessary to offset adjustments under the 1997 Act (Meissner et al. 2006).

legal permanent resident may join the Armed Forces, own property in the United States, and attend public schools, colleges, and universities.[2] Green card holders may work at any job that does not require U.S. citizenship. Permanent residents are protected by all federal, state, and local laws, and they can vote in local elections where U.S. citizenship is not required (USCIS 2007a). The three main categories under which Tlacuitapeños can apply for legal permanent resident status are employment, special legalization programs, and marriage or family. Though other categories exist, none applies to Tlacuitapa's migrants.

Many people in Tlacuitapa have green cards, reflecting a multigenerational tradition of migration to the United States that dates from the late nineteenth century, when a combination of political unrest, poor economic conditions, and the completion of a railroad connecting Mexico to the United States encouraged migration to *el norte*. The early migrants retained close ties to their home community and encouraged the same among their U.S.-born children through frequent visits to Mexico. Tlacuitapeños who entered the United States during the Bracero Program (1942–1964) continued to migrate to the United States even after the program ended and were often sponsored for residency by their former employers (Cornelius 1976). This widespread participation in the Bracero Program and the migrants' maintenance of close ties with their sending community are important factors defining Tlacuitapa's status as a community with an unusually high migration density. Cornelius's study of nine rural communities in the Los Altos region of Jalisco found that by 1975 Tlacuitapa already displayed exceptionally high emigration rates.

The Immigration Reform and Control Act of 1986 (IRCA) also enabled many Tlacuitapeños to obtain legal status in the United States. IRCA's Legally Authorized Workers (LAW) program granted amnesty to people who had been living in the United States continuously since 1982, and its Special Agricultural Workers (SAW) program legalized farmworkers who had been working for at least ninety days prior to May 1, 1986. Over three million undocumented migrants living in the United States gained legal status under these programs, and approximately 75 percent of these new legal permanent residents were Mexicans (Massey, Durand, and Malone 2002). Because Tlacuitapa was heavily represented among migrants to

---

2. These educational rights are not limited to legal permanent residents.

the United States preceding the 1986 amnesty, a large number of migrants from the town were legalized under IRCA. Of the legalized Tlacuitapeño migrants we interviewed in 2007, 82 percent reported having a green card and 24 percent had obtained their green card through IRCA.[3]

When attempting to apply for amnesty under IRCA, many undocumented migrants had difficulty proving that they had resided in the United States since 1982. Farmworkers, however, found it relatively easy to obtain green cards within the SAW program.

> [The SAW] was so loosely administered, so nebulous in its criteria, and so plagued with opportunities for fakery that it induced many Mexicans who never worked in U.S. agriculture, or even been in the United States, to cross the border in hopes of being legalized through fraudulent means (Kandel 2004, 247).

Migrants who had legalized under the SAW and the LAW provisions spurred an immigration surge as their spouses and children obtained green cards as "amnestied" migrants (Cornelius 1989), and the cumulative number of legal permanent residents rose dramatically after the mid-1980s (see figure 4.1).

Many Tlacuitapeños know how to get a green card. Most of those we interviewed in our 2007 survey (80 percent) had learned about the requirements for obtaining a green card from family and friends, as opposed to the mass media (8 percent) and other sources (figure 4.2). However, they are not all fully confident about their knowledge of the application process. A 22-year-old man who was born in Tlacuitapa and now resides legally in the United States (with a green card) explained that he did not feel confident helping someone else with an immigration application: "No way. . . . I don't want to help. I'll take them to the place but I won't help them fill out the papers."

Most Tlacuitapeños also understand the importance of family contacts and feel that it is important to obtain citizenship in order to sponsor their relatives (see table 4.1). Of those with migration experience, 22 percent reported having applied for a green card for a dependent.

---

3. Sixty-five percent obtained their green card through legalized family members and 10 percent through employer sponsorship following the end of the Bracero Program.

Figure 4.1 Cumulative Number of Tlacuitapeños with
U.S. Legal Permanent Resident Status, 1960–2005

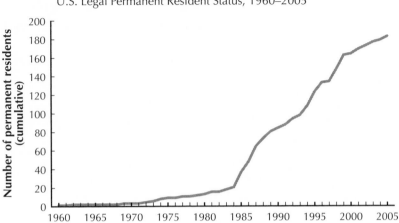

Figure 4.2 Source of Information about Procedure for Obtaining a Green Card

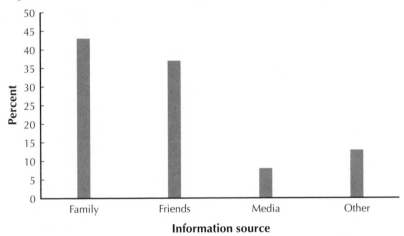

N = 342.

When Tlacuitapeños were asked what it cost to obtain a green card, the median response was US$2,000 (answers ranged from $30 to $20,000). This estimate is not far off the mark. Filing an application for a green card involves more than paying a registration fee. Applicants also pay for their fingerprints to be taken and for medical exams; some elect to hire lawyers to assist with the process (Gilot 2006). In 2007 the United States Citizenship and Immigration Services (USCIS) raised the legal residency application fees significantly; the fee for an individual application (form I-130) rose from $190 to $355; that for the additional I-485 application to register for permanent residence increased from $325 to $930; fingerprinting fees are now $80; a medical exam costs between $140 and $200; four photographs run about $20; and legal fees could be $1,000 or more—running the total cost for applying for an individual green card as high as $2,500 or even more.

Table 4.1 Question: How does one obtain a green card?

By marrying a U.S. citizen	52%
By having a close relative who is a U.S. citizen	52%
Employer sponsorship	27%
Other	16%

N = 362.

Given current wage levels in Tlacuitapa,[4] these fees represent a substantial economic hardship, and their dramatic increase will certainly block the path to legalization for many Tlacuitapeños. When asked why they had not applied for a green card, about 20 percent cited the high cost. Others mentioned lack of knowledge about the process or no job or family waiting in the United States. (A few said they had no economic need to migrate.)

We also asked how long it took to obtain a green card. A third of our respondents thought it would take a year, and 22 percent thought it would take ten years; other answers ranged from one month to fifteen years (figure 4.3). The fact that half of the respondents said it took one or two years to receive a green card reflects how Tlacuitapeños have benefited from legalization programs like IRCA. Many respondents who received green cards during the 1980s were able to legalize much more quickly than applicants today, whose applications are stuck in the USCIS backlog. Table 4.2 shows the different categories under which a person can apply for a green card based on the family-preference category, along with the average time it takes for an application to be processed. Tlacuitapeños' expectations align fairly well with the actual situation on both points.

---

4. The average adult returned migrant worker living in Tlacuitapa makes about US$400 per month; the average worker with no migration history makes approximately $228 per month.

Figure 4.3 Question: How long do you think it takes to get a green card?

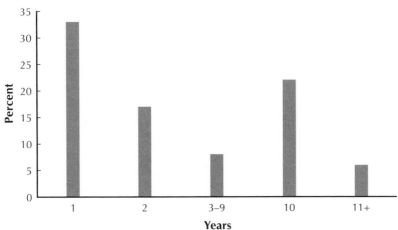

N = 296.

Table 4.2 Green Card Processing Times by Family-Preference Category

Preference Category	Average Wait Time before Application is Reviewed
1st (unmarried sons and daughters of U.S. citizens)	16 years
2A (spouses and children of legal permanent residents)	6 years
2B (unmarried sons and daughters of legal permanent residents)	15 years
3rd (married sons and daughters of U.S. citizens)	19 years
4th (brothers and sisters of adult U.S. citizens)	13 years

Source: U.S. Department of State 2007a.

Tlacuitapeños have less access to employment-sponsored visas than to family-based visas. The U.S. Department of State provides a yearly maximum of 140,000 employment-based permanent resident visas on average, plus any unused family-preference visas from the previous year, to applicants worldwide. Occupation-based green cards tend to go to highly skilled workers, defined as priority workers (H-1B) with extraordinary ability in sciences, arts, education, business, and athletics, or identified as outstanding professors and researchers (USCIS 2007b). There is also a professional category for people with advanced degrees (PhD or Master's) or five years or more of post-baccalaureate experience. The number of employment-based permanent visas available to less skilled workers is capped at 5,000 (see table 4.3), not enough to meet the demands of the U.S. economy. Approximately 350,000 undocumented workers are entering the U.S. workforce each year, and most of them are finding jobs in low-wage service-sector jobs (Meissner et al. 2006).

Table 4.3 Employment-based Visas Issued in FY2005

Visa Type	Number
H-1B, high-skilled workers	65,000 (capped)
H-2A, low-skilled agricultural workers	31,892 (no cap)
H-2B, low-skilled nonagricultural workers	66,000 (capped)
Immigrant visas (EB-3) to low-skilled workers	5,000
Immigrant visas (EB-1 and EB-2) to high-skilled workers	107,328

Source: Office of Immigration Statistics 2006.

In Tlacuitapa, only 9 percent of people who applied for a green card did so under the employment visa category. Because only 5 percent of Tlacuitapeños interviewed in 2007 had more than a high-school education, few could qualify for a professional or H-1B priority employment visa. An employment category that is potentially open to Tlacuitapeños is EB-3, which contains a provision for "other workers," but there is strong competition for these visas and, according to the USCIS, "a petitioner could expect to wait many years before being granted a visa under this category" (USCIS 2007b). To obtain an EB-3 visa, a migrant must have a sponsoring U.S. employer willing to demonstrate that the migrant is vital to the business and that there is no native-born worker available for the position. In effect, employment-based visas are a closed path to legalization for the unskilled workers of Tlacuitapa.

KNOWLEDGE OF CURRENT IMMIGRATION REFORM PROPOSALS

President George W. Bush and some members of the U.S. Congress have supported recent attempts to reform the immigration system. In 2007,

Representatives Jeff Flake (R, Arizona) and Luis Gutierrez (D, Illinois) introduced the STRIVE (Security Through Regularized Immigration and a Vibrant Economy) Act, which calls for an increase in Department of Homeland Security personnel, interior enforcement that addresses crimes committed by aliens, and penalties for employers who hire undocumented persons. The bill's most significant feature, however, is the creation of a new worker "H-2C" visa that allows a path to legalization in two ways: employment-based (employers may file for an H-2C on behalf of the person) and self-petition (the worker may petition for a visa for at least five years) (National Immigration Forum 2007).

Table 4.4 Knowledge of the Bush Immigration Reform Proposal, by Migration Experience

	All Migrants	Documented Migrants	Undocumented Migrants	Potential Migrants
Believed that President Bush's proposal entails a guestworker program	67% (N = 452)	72% (N = 267)	64% (N = 185)	47% (N = 185)
Replied that, if enacted, a guestworker program would influence their decision to migrate to the United States	55% (N = 310)	74% (N = 132)	41% (N = 178)	55% (N = 372)

At the time of our survey, President Bush had proposed a new guestworker program that would allow foreign workers in both the United States and foreign countries to apply for a temporary work visa if they had a job waiting for them in the United States. The visa would expire after a defined period and could be renewed a limited number of times (White House 2007). In our research community, a substantial 64 percent of undocumented migrants and 47 percent of potential migrants (residents of Tlacuitapa with no emigration experience) were aware that Bush's proposal included a guestworker program (see table 4.4). When asked whether a guestworker program would affect their decision to migrate, 41 percent of undocumented experienced migrants and 55 percent of potential migrants affirmed that it would. Some potential migrants who said they would take advantage of a guestworker program may have believed that the program could lead to permanent legal status and family reunification, but for most this does not signify an intention to move to the United States permanently.

TOURIST VISAS

For persons who are ineligible or uninterested in settling permanently in the United States, there are options for temporary admission to work or visit. The United States Citizenship and Immigration Services oversees most aspects of legal immigration to the United States, and the Department of State administers the visa-issuance process. The latter grants nonimmigrant visas to foreign visitors, and an immigration officer at the port of entry makes the final decision as to whether the migrant is allowed to enter the United States. The application process for a tourist visa is conducted through a consular office in the applicant's home country. Tlacuitapeños apply for tourist visas at the consulate in Guadalajara, approximately two hours away by car.

Applicants must first make an appointment at the consular office at least four months in advance of their intended travel date. The appointment must be scheduled via an automated phone system, and the caller is charged a per-minute fee for this call. Second, applicants pay a nonrefundable fee of US$100, whether or not the visa is issued. Finally, they must submit a basic form which, according to information on the consulate's Web site, must be completed on line.

There are also other costs associated with the tourist visa application process over and above those collected by the consulate. Applicants must have a valid Mexican passport (which costs approximately $35). Some Tlacuitapeños request assistance from one of the travel agencies in nearby Lagos de Moreno for the application process and must pay a fee to the agency. Last is the expense of getting to the consulate. A one-way bus ticket from Lagos de Moreno to Guadalajara costs about $14. Thus, for a resident of Tlacuitapa, the total cost of applying for a U.S. tourist visa can easily total over $175, an amount equal to more than half a month's wages for the average nonmigrant Tlacuitapeño.

Some of our informants believed that the visa application process is a money-making scheme operated by the U.S. government through the Guadalajara consulate. A 52-year-old woman who has tried unsuccessfully three times to get a tourist visa, said,

> That's why I say they get a lot of money. Because if you saw, there are thousands and thousands and thousands of people there every day. It's a lot. That's why I say, why are they like that? If they don't plan to give the visa, well, it would be better if they would call the people to whom they are going to give them. Right? And to those they are not, tell them "no."

Once an applicant has paid the fee and secured an appointment at the consulate, he or she must wait to be called for a brief interview with a consular officer. Consular officers are required by immigration law "to view every visa applicant as an *intending immigrant* until the applicant proves otherwise" (U.S. Department of State 2007b; italics added). Therefore, applicants must provide proof of strong ties to their home country and of their intention to return there in order to be granted a tourist visa. On its Web page, the consulate in Guadalajara recommends bringing to the interview various forms of identification (voter card, Social Security card, birth certificate); recent pay stubs; work ID; a letter from the current employer stating title, length of service, and salary; proof of ownership of a business or farm animals; or proof of a pension. These documents do not guarantee that an applicant will receive a visa; consular officers have the final say on the application and there is no appeal process.

Because so many residents of Tlacuitapa have relatives who have settled in the United States, it would seem that tourist visas would be a popular option for visiting family members, especially those who cannot return frequently to their hometown. Yet only 20 percent of adults in Tlacuitapa had applied for any kind of visa to visit the United States; 84 percent of these had requested a tourist visa. One explanation for the low application rate for tourist visas may be the low rate of approval; 60 percent of those who applied for a tourist visa had their applications denied.

More women than men apply for tourist visas, and the majority of applicants are over 50 years of age. Some older women in Tlacuitapa who have adult children in the United States have requested tourist visas in order to visit their family members. One woman, who suffers from a variety of ailments, including poor eyesight, said she is alone in Tlacuitapa, with no one to care for her, so she uses her tourist visa to stay with family members in Washington State. Not all older women are able to obtain a tourist visa to visit relatives in the United States, however. Lucía has been denied a tourist visa three times because she cannot prove that she is not an "intending immigrant." She is not employed in Tlacuitapa and has been unable to demonstrate sufficiently strong ties to her hometown to convince consular officials that she will not remain in the United States. Lucía has spent between $500 and $600 on each application attempt and has decided not to reapply though her children are encouraging her to do so.

The consulate advises applicants to reapply only if their family or economic situation has changed significantly since their previous application, but this advice may not be reaching the public. According to Lucía:

> I arrived [at the consulate] and they asked me what I wanted. And I told him I was going to visit a son I had over there. Well, they asked me what we have here, and I told them we are poor, we have our livestock and nothing else. "No," they told me; they couldn't grant me a visa. About a year later I returned again, and they told me the same thing. And then a little more than a year later, they only asked me a few questions, but they told me "no." That I didn't have the necessary things to go and that they couldn't give me the visa.

Lucía said that her family told her to open a bank account in order to boost the chances that the consulate would grant her a visa, and they sent her money to do so. However, information on the consulate's Web site specifies that recently opened bank accounts do not demonstrate an applicant's economic stake in Mexico.

The majority of Tlacuitapeños who do obtain a tourist visa report that they do not overstay the visa or violate its terms by working in the United States. Of the Tlacuitapeños who had received a tourist visa, 84 percent said they returned when their visa expired, and 85 percent did not work while in the United States. This is in contrast to national-level data that show a high rate of overstaying; according to one estimate, as many as 45 percent of unauthorized migrants residing in the United States in March 2005 had used a temporary, nonimmigrant visa—usually a tourist visa— to enter the United States (Pew Hispanic Center 2006). Tlacuitapeños may be more likely to comply with the terms of their tourist visa than other groups because those who intend to stay in the United States can apply for a family-sponsored immigrant visa thanks to the large number of Tla- cuitapeños already residing there legally.

CITIZENSHIP

Mexicans living in the United States have a very low naturalization rate in comparison with green card holders from other countries. According to the 2000 census, roughly eight million U.S. residents had been born in Mexico, and only 20 percent of them were U.S. citizens (Massey and Bartley 2005). Data collected by the Urban Institute in 2001 showed that only 35 percent of eligible Mexican legal permanent residents applied for U.S. citizenship, compared to an overall rate of 59 percent among resi- dents of all nationalities (Gonzalez 2005). Among legal permanent resi- dents from other countries of origin, the average time between obtaining legal residence and naturalization is eight years, but for Mexicans it is eleven years (Taylor, Torres, and Paral 2006). Thirty percent of green card holders in the United States are of Mexican origin (see figure 4.4), making Mexicans the largest subgroup among legal permanent residents; yet only 8 percent of recently naturalized U.S. citizens are Mexican. This is some- what surprising given the advantages of taking U.S. citizenship: natural- ized U.S. citizens need not apply for a green card renewal every ten years and need not fear deportation or revocation of their legal permanent resident status. Further, they gain the same access to social services as na- tive-born citizens, and it is easier for them to sponsor the immigration of family members still in Mexico (Castañeda 2006). Although Tlacuitapa's status as a developed migrant-sending community helps explain its use of the legal system for green cards and visas, when it comes to citizenship Tlacuitapa is more or less on par with national application levels.

Figure 4.4 U.S. Legal Permanent Residents and Recently Naturalized Citizens, by Region of Origin

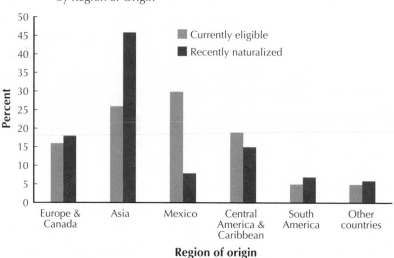

Source: Passel 2005.
Note: Ages 18 and over. Based on March 2004 Current Population Survey.

Various pieces of new legislation dramatically altered U.S. immigration policy in the 1980s and 1990s. IRCA radically changed immigration policy in the 1980s, but it made no changes to existing U.S. citizenship requirements. Therefore, though the number of visa applications soared, citizenship applications initially were not affected. But in 1992, five years after IRCA's passage, the Immigration and Naturalization Service recorded a dramatic nationwide increase in the number of Mexican applicants for citizenship, as legal permanent residents amnestied under IRCA became eligible to apply for citizenship (Migration Policy Institute 2005). In just one year the number of applications rose from 342,269 (1992) to 522,298 (1993), and this upward trend continued through much of the 1990s (Office of Immigration Statistics 2004). The system could not handle the growing number of applications, and a backlog began to build.

While the majority of Tlacuitapeños we interviewed had considered applying for citizenship, only 28 percent of green card holders have actually applied. The two main reasons given for not applying are the language barrier and a general apathy regarding naturalization as a U.S.

citizen. A 34-year-old man who lives in Oklahoma and was interviewed in Tlacuitapa said he had applied for citizenship but failed the test by a single question. Upset by what he perceived as bias on the part of the immigration officer, he has not reapplied. Many legal permanent residents are comfortable with the protections afforded them by their current status and see no reason to naturalize. For example, a 45-year-old native of Tlacuitapa who now resides in California said he has not applied for citizenship because he feels secure with his green card. He stated that he does not have a criminal record and does not see how he could have any problem. Another man from Tlacuitapa, who has lived almost his entire life in California and owns a business there, had not yet applied for citizenship though he stated that he intends to apply. The sense that citizenship is unimportant could stem from the fact that, prior to 1996, there was little difference for most people between being a citizen and being a legal permanent resident. Until that time, a legal permanent resident and a citizen received the same benefits and social services (Castañeda 2006). But in 1996, spurred by immigration opponents who painted IRCA immigrants as a burden on the welfare system,[5] the U.S. Congress passed the Anti-terrorism and Effective Death Penalty Act (AEDPA) and a welfare reform law (PRWORA, the Personal Responsibility and Work Opportunity Reconciliation Act), which severely restricted legal permanent residents' rights and their access to most federal social services.

AEDPA made it much easier to "arrest, detain, and deport non-citizen immigrants by providing for the automatic deportation of immigrants who had committed an 'aggravated felony'" (Migration Policy Institute 2005, 3). Additionally, the definition of "aggravated felony" was expanded to include more petty crimes, and the retroactive nature of these new laws put many legal permanent residents in jeopardy. After the 1996 reforms were enacted, for example, a legal permanent resident who had been convicted twenty years earlier of something as minor as jumping a subway turnstile or painting graffiti could now face deportation (NYSDA 2003).

---

5. Advocates of restricting benefits estimated that PRWORA would save the government billions of dollars by limiting legal immigrants' use of food stamps, Supplemental Security Income, and aid for low income elderly, the blind and the disabled (Castañeda 2006, 87).

PRWORA, meanwhile, denied social services to many noncitizens previously eligible to receive them (USCIS 2007c). A legal permanent resident no longer qualified for Temporary Assistance for Needy Families (TANF), Supplemental Security Income (SSI), food stamps, Medicaid, and the State Children's Health Insurance Program (SCHIP) (Balistreri and Van Hook 2004). States were also given jurisdiction "to bar current legal immigrants from both major federal programs and state programs" (USCIS 2007c). Scholars suggest that these reforms had a huge impact on the number of naturalization applications, at least initially. For example, George Borjas argues that "many immigrants [have] become citizens not because they want to fully participate in the U.S. political and social systems, but because naturalization is required to receive welfare benefits" (2002, 383). The question, then, is whether these restrictive reforms had a long-term impact on the number of citizenship applicants among Mexican legal permanent residents.

Immigration researchers Michael Fix and Jeffrey Passel agree with Borjas that, after the 1996 reforms, the numbers of Mexican legal permanent residents who naturalized increased over their historically low level (Fix and Passel 2002). However, neither national findings nor findings from Tlacuitapa show a long-term relationship between the 1996 reforms and the number of legal permanent residents applying for citizenship (see figures 4.5 and 4.6). Figure 4.5 shows the number of applications for citizenship in five-year increments. While naturalization rates rose in the 1990s, the drop-off in applications beginning in 2001 suggests that the long-term effects of the 1996 reforms on naturalization rates were minimal.

Figure 4.6 shows the number of applicants from Tlacuitapa, which generally parallels the pattern in the nationwide data. In 1997, the year following the implementation of PRWORA and AEDPA, the number of Tlacuitapeños who submitted naturalization applications *fell*. Moreover, Tlacuitapeños did not submit any naturalization applications from 2003 through 2005. High fluctuations in the number of citizenship applications among Tlacuitapeños in the ten years following the passage of the 1996 PRWORA and AEDPA acts suggest that it is unlikely that these legislative changes were the main cause of a long-term increase in the number of citizenship applications.

Figure 4.5 Naturalization Applicants in the United States, 1980–2004

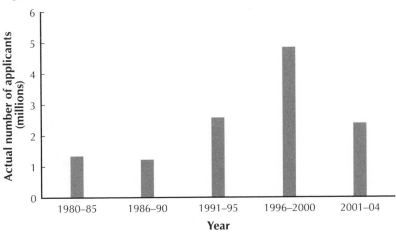

Source: Office of Immigration Statistics 2004.

Figure 4.6 Number of U.S. Naturalization Applicants among Tlacuitapeños, 1980–2004

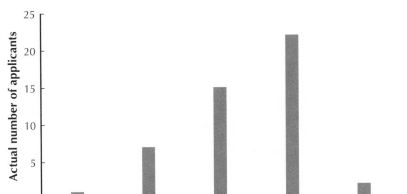

As mentioned earlier, applications for U.S. citizenship began to increase dramatically nationwide in 1992 (the first year that many legal permanent residents were eligible for citizenship after the passage of IRCA), but the first major spike in citizenship applications from Tlacuitapeños did not appear until 1995, when 15.4 percent of eligible Tlacuitapeño legal permanent residents applied for citizenship.[6] Though it could be argued that this increase in applications was a response to the anti-immigrant sentiments epitomized by the passage of Proposition 187 in California in 1994, an alternative explanation for the increased number of applications is the Citizenship USA program (CUSA). CUSA was created in 1995 to reduce the backlog that began to accumulate after the 1992 boom in applications for naturalization. By the mid-1990s, the wait time for processing a citizenship application was three years (Migration Policy Institute 2005). Though CUSA was extremely successful in reducing processing times, its success was overshadowed by scandal when it was discovered that many applicants who had been given citizenship had criminal records and should not have received approval.[7] In response, the INS implemented new safeguards for background checks to ensure against a similar situation in the future. This led to a decrease in the number of citizenship applications processed, and the backlog began mounting once again (Migration Policy Institute 2005).

Figure 4.7 shows the number of Tlacuitapeños who received U.S. citizenship between 1977 and 2007. There was a naturalization bubble throughout the 1990s, which reflects the short-term combined effects of IRCA, AEDPA, PRWORA, and CUSA. Each of these programs affected citizenship applications over the short term, as the data make clear, but what is not evident is any long-term success these legislative measures may have achieved.

In 2006, the U.S. Citizenship and Immigration Services, formerly the INS, began a pilot program with a "testing process that is standardized, fair, and meaningful" (USCIS 2006). The written and history portions of the test were made more difficult, and USCIS also increased the application fee (as of July 2007) from $400 to $675, including fingerprinting. In contrast to the CUSA program, this new pilot program appears to charge more but offer no additional benefits. In anticipation of the changes to come with the new pilot program, there was a spike in the number of

---

6. An "eligible" Tlacuitapeño is a legal permanent resident who has been living in the United States for five consecutive years.

7. Nearly 20 percent of the 1.05 million people naturalized in 1995 failed the required background check (Cox 1997).

applications for naturalization in 2006, as 18 percent of Tlacuitapeños with green cards applied for citizenship.

Figure 4.7 Number of Tlacuitapeños Who Received U.S. Citizenship, 1977–2007

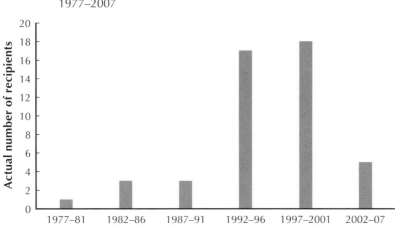

Our research in Tlacuitapa suggests that naturalization applications are ultimately tied to an individual's sense of cultural identity. Although 68 percent of Tlacuitapeños have considered applying for citizenship, only 28 percent of U.S. legal permanent residents from Tlacuitapa have gone through the application process. Similarly, of those who were considering naturalizing in 2007, 33 percent responded that citizenship was not important to them, despite the impacts of the restrictive legislation of the 1990s. As Alejandra Castañeda suggests, "for some migrants [naturalizing] is a choice that implies an analysis of their loyalties, their identity, as well as their practical needs, and the position they hold in the United States" (2006, 99). This insight may help explain why, historically, Mexican naturalization rates, even in a deeply rooted migrant community like Tlacuitapa, have remained so volatile.

CONCLUSION

Tlacuitapa's extensive migration history has helped shape a community in which many members have green cards or are U.S. citizens. Numerous

Tlacuitapeños seized the various opportunities to legalize their status that appeared during the twentieth century. Yet, of the migrants we interviewed in 2007, 58 percent stated that they made their most recent trip to the United States without legal authorization, a figure that speaks to the inaccessibility of the legal migration system for those leaving for the United States today. For these Tlacuitapeños, legal migration is not an option, due to the shortage of employment visas and the caps on family-sponsored visas. Even those who envision only a short visit find it difficult to obtain a tourist visa. Placing the burden on the applicants to prove they are not "intending immigrants" and the absence of a clear checklist of requirements make the tourist visa process subjective and difficult to comprehend. It is for these reasons that many Tlacuitapeños opt to migrate without documents. "Waiting in line" is simply not an alternative.

Advocates on both sides of the immigration debate are hopeful that reforms can be implemented soon. One proposal involves de-emphasizing the current family-based immigration system to focus on a points system that would favor highly educated and skilled immigrants. Under such a plan, residents of Tlacuitapa would face an even more restrictive immigration system. A move away from family-reunification immigration would have a strong impact in Tlacuitapa, where the best route to permanent resident status is through a family member. As an immigrant who participated in a rally in Washington, DC, in support of comprehensive immigration reform expressed it: "We work hard, we pay taxes and have kept a clean record, but we have absolutely no way to become legal" (Constable 2007).

References

Balistreri, Kelley, and Jennifer Van Hook. 2004. "The More Things Change the More They Stay the Same: Mexican Naturalization before and after Welfare Reform," *International Migration Review* 38, no. 1 (Spring): 113–30.

Barajas, Yesenia, James Besada, Elizabeth Valdez-Suiter, and Caitlin White. 2007. "Profiles of the Research Communities." In *Impacts of Border Enforcement on Mexican Migration: The View from Sending Communities*, ed. Wayne A. Cornelius and Jessa M. Lewis. La Jolla, CA: Center for Comparative Immigration Studies, University of California, San Diego.

Borjas, George. 2002. "Welfare Reform and Immigration." In *The New World of Welfare*, ed. R. Blank and R. Haskins. Washington, DC: Brookings Institution Press.

Castañeda, Alejandra. 2006. *The Politics of Citizenship of Mexican Migrants*. New York: LFB Scholarly Publishing.

Constable, Pamela. 2007. "Rally Draws Thousands of Immigrants to Capitol," *Washington Post*, June 3.

Cornelius, Wayne A. 1976. "Out-migration from Rural Mexican Communities." In *The Dynamics of Migration: International Migration*. Washington, DC: Smithsonian Institution.

————. 1989. "Impacts of the 1986 U.S. Immigration Law on Emigration from Rural Mexican Sending Communities," *Population and Development Review* 15, no. 4: 689–705.

Cox, Christopher. 1997. "Damage from 'Citizenship USA' [INS] Can Never Be Undone," *House Policy Committee Policy Perspective. Justice Denied.* http://www.justicedenied.net/INSCorruption_01.htm.

Culberson, John. 2007. "Illegal Immigrants Need to Get in Line with Everyone Else." http://blog.thehill.com/2007/05/21/illegal-immigrants-need-to-get-in-line-with-everyone-else-rep-john-culberson.

Fix, Michael, and David Passel. 2002. "The Scope and Impact of Welfare Reform's Immigrant Provisions." Discussion Paper. Washington, DC: Urban Institute.

Gilot, Louie. 2006. "Citizenship, Residency Filing Fees May Double in April. Immigrants Encouraged to File Early to Avoid Higher Costs," *El Paso Times*, December 13.

Gonzalez, Daniel. 2005. "Mexican Migrants Slow to Seek U.S. Citizenship," *Arizona Republic*, March 29.

Hsu, Spencer S. 2007. "Immigration Agency Mired in Inefficiency," *Washington Post*, May 28.

Kandel, William A. 2004. "A Profile of Mexican Workers in U.S. Agriculture." In *Crossing the Border: Research from the Mexican Migration Project*, ed. Jorge Durand and Douglas Massey. New York: Russell Sage Foundation.

Massey, Douglas S., and Katherine Bartley. 2005. "The Changing Legal Status Distribution of Immigrants: A Caution," *International Migration Review* 39, no. 2: 469–84.

Massey, Douglas, Jorge Durand, and Nolan J. Malone. 2002. *Beyond Smoke and Mirrors: Mexican Immigration in an Era of Economic Integration*. New York: Russell Sage Foundation.

Meissner, Doris, Deborah W. Meyers, Demetrios G. Papademetriou, and Michael Fix. 2006. *Immigration and America's Future: A New Chapter.* Washington, DC: Migration Policy Institute.

Migration Policy Institute. 2005. "Backlogs in Immigration Processing Persist," *Immigration Facts* 10 (June). http://www.migrationpolicy.org/pubs/Jernegan_Fact_Sheet_June_2005.pdf.

National Immigration Forum. 2007. "Strive Act at a Glance." http://www.immigrationforum.org/documents/PolicyWire/Legislation/110/STRIVE_Glance.pdf. Accessed April 15, 2007.

NYSDA Immigrant Defense Project. 2003. "Alert for Lawful Permanent Residents with Criminal Records Considering Applying for United States Citizenship." New York State Defenders Association. http://www.nysda.org/NYSDA_Resources/Immigrant_Defense_Project/03_CitizensAlert.pdf.

Office of Immigration Statistics. 2004. "G-22.2 Adjudication Summary Report and G-22.3 Naturalization Summary Report." Washington, DC: U.S. Department of Homeland Security, November.

———. 2006. "Yearbook of Immigration Statistics: 2005." Washington, DC: Office of Immigration Statistics, U.S. Department of Homeland Security.

Paral, Rob. 2005. "No Way In: U.S. Immigration Policy Leaves Few Legal Options for Mexican Workers." Washington, DC: Immigration Policy Center, American Immigration Law Foundation.

Passel, Jeffrey S. 2005. "Naturalization Trends and Opportunities: A Focus on Mexicans." Washington, DC: Pew Hispanic Center, September.

Pew Hispanic Center. 2006. "Modes of Entry for the Unauthorized Migrant Population." Washington, DC: The Center, May 22.

Taylor, D. Garth, Maria de los Angeles Torres, and Rob Paral. 2006. "The Naturalization Trail: Mexican Nationality and U.S. Citizenship." Notre Dame, IN: Institute for Latino Studies, University of Notre Dame.

USCIS (U.S. Citizenship and Immigration Services). 2006. "USCIS Naturalization Test Redesign: Fact Sheet." Washington, DC: U.S. Department of Homeland Security. www.uscis.gov.

———. 2007a. "Now That You Are a Permanent Resident." Washington, DC: U.S. Department of Homeland Security. http://www.uscis.gov/portal/site/uscis/menuitem.5af9bb95919f35e66f614176543f6d1a/?vgnextoid=fe17e6b0eb13d010VgnVCM10000048f3d6a1RCRD&vgnextchannel=4f719c7755cb9010VgnVCM10000045f3d6a1RCRD.

————. 2007b. "Immigration through Employment." Washington, DC: U.S. Department of Homeland Security. http://www.uscis.gov/portal/site/uscis/menuitem.5af9bb95919f35e66f614176543f6d1a/?vgnextoid=840961 38f898d010VgnVCM10000048f3d6a1RCRD&vgnextchannel=4f719c7755c b9010VgnVCM10000045f3d6a1RCRD.

————. 2007c. "Historical Immigration and Naturalization Legislation: Legislation from 1981–1996." Washington, DC: U.S. Department of Homeland Security. http://www.uscis.gov/files/nativedocuments/Legislation%20 from%201981-1996.pdf.

U.S. Department of State. 2007a. *Visa Bulletin* 105, no. 8 (May). http://travel.state.gov/visa/frvi/bulletin/bulletin_3219.html.

————. 2007b. "Visa Denials." http://travel.state.gov/visa/frvi/denials/denials_1361.html.

White House. 2007. "Fact Sheet: Fair and Secure Immigration Reform." http://www.whitehouse.gov/news/releases/2004/01/20040107-1.html.

Mole factory owned and operated by the Amézquita family since the 1970s.

5 Development in a Remittance Economy: What Options Are Viable?

ALEJANDRO MACÍAS, PETER NICHOLS, ERIC DÍAZ, AND
ANDREA FRENKEL

> *Sometimes those who return from the United States have a big impact. People here can't buy trucks; they can't buy whatever they want. Then a norteño drives into town in a truck, dressed well, with his stereo system. And the other guy says, "I need to go," even though he has a job here. He says, "I'm going up there." The point is, this town no longer sees migration as a necessity; it sees it as a tradition. Here, you turn 17 and it's, "Let's go north!"*—Gustavo, a 54-year-old returned migrant from Tlacuitapa.

Lack of economic opportunity is often the determining factor in the decision to migrate. When analysts evaluate the effect of international migration, they look closely at whether such migration promotes or impedes the development of the economic opportunity structure in the sending community. Though most of the literature poses a binary choice—migration either helps or hinders—we demonstrate that in Tlacuitapa migration can both help and hinder the local economy.

Many scholars have posited that U.S.-bound migration fosters economic dependence to the point that the economy of the sending community could not survive independent of migration. Further, they argue that U.S. earnings are not invested in job-creating activities or infrastructure, but are directed instead to the purchase of consumer goods for the household, a use of remittances that constitutes a drag on local development. Moreover, as a town's residents go north, they deplete the local labor market.

In contrast, other scholars assert that international migration exerts a positive impact on development in rural sending areas. These experts highlight the fact that the astonishing amounts of money migrant workers send home to support their families in Mexico translate into greater household autonomy and preserve rural livelihoods in sending communities (Jones 1995, 1–3). It is the productive channeling of remittances and what remittances are doing to increase community independence that matter most to those who see a benefit from migration. The more independent a population becomes and the less it "needs" migration, the more positive will be the effect of migration in that community.

Yet most researchers are reluctant to categorize migration definitively as having either a positive or a negative impact on development. This is especially true because they "use different units of analysis (individual, family, state, region, etc.), study different parts of the world, and come from different disciplines (anthropology, political science, sociology, economics)" (Jones 1995, 3).

In this chapter we set the help-or-hinder approach to migration and development to one side by posing a pivotal question framed by de Haas (2005): "Under what conditions are migration and development more positively correlated than under others?" We highlight the areas in Tlacuitapa that have benefited or suffered as a result of migration, and we discuss other economic options. We begin by analyzing the economic opportunity structure in Tlacuitapa, focusing especially on the town's agricultural sector. We examine remittances as a resource for productive investment, evaluate their actual local economic impact, and consider the potential role of collective remittances. The investment climate in Tlacuitapa is assessed through case studies of local businesses and through profiles of migrants who invest in their hometown.

THE LOCAL OPPORTUNITY STRUCTURE

U.S.-bound migration from Tlacuitapa is rooted in a local economic opportunity structure that residents, especially older residents, view as very restricted. Overall, 59 percent of the town's residents felt one had to leave Tlacuitapa in order to "get ahead." Interestingly, younger Tlacuitapeños, both with and without U.S. migration experience, were less likely to feel that economic mobility was blocked if one remained in the town (see table 5.1), with no statistically significant differences between U.S.-based and Mexico-based respondents. An intriguing question is, why do youths view the local opportunity structure differently than their elders, especially given Tlacuitapa's pervasive "culture of migration," which seems to drive people *al norte*? If the next generation is more optimistic about economic prospects in Tlacuitapa, what evidence or experience is the basis for this mind-set?

Table 5.1 Can a Young Person Progress in Life without Leaving Tlacuitapa?

	Migrants				Nonmigrants			
Age	<20	20–29	30–39	40+	<20	20–29	30–39	40+
YES. Can progress without leaving Tlacuitapa	69.2%	40.3%	31.3%	33.5%	53.6%	45.3%	41.1%	41.2%
NO. Must leave Tlacuitapa in order to progress	30.8%	59.7%	68.8%	66.5%	46.4%	54.7%	58.9%	58.8%
N	396				444			

The differences in responses by age group have much to do with a respondent's economic experience. Economic activity correlates positively with age; that is, as one grows older, one should, on average, also gain in economic activity. With more economic activity comes the acquisition of work experience. Thus we hypothesize that the differences in economic perceptions have more to do with experience than with age. Yet, due to the extremely positive relationship between experience and age, a respondent's age will tell us roughly how many years of experience he or she has as a worker.

Seventy percent of the town's population between the ages of 15 and 20 are working for wages and are therefore considered economically active. Yet, even with some work experience, young people are still quite optimistic about their economic prospects in Tlacuitapa, which would seem to counter the argument that optimism fades quickly with actual experience of the local economic opportunity structure. However, only 9 percent of respondents in this age group are married; because most do not face the pressing need to provide for a family, their perception of the local economy may still be somewhat naive. Until these adolescents gain more practical experience with the job market, the local economy, and family responsibilities in general, their responses are hard to interpret. Another factor affecting young people's perceptions is the recent capitalization in the region. A new shoe factory, increasing dairy production, and even the presence of the Internet could potentially influence these youths to stay. And even if migration is the path they choose, their migration may be more investment-oriented, that is, migration aimed specifically at accumulating capital to invest in or near their hometown.

Tlacuitapa's youth attend the local public primary school. Because many families depend on their children's help at home and in the fields,[1] the government has instituted two class schedules—from 8 a.m. to 1 p.m. and from 11 a.m. to 4 p.m.—to allow families to maintain their household economy while also keeping their sons and daughters in school. Chuy, an 11-year-old sixth grader, is typical. Arriving home one afternoon, he dropped his schoolbag on the couch and began plucking a chicken. Chuy's family prepares chickens for sale in the town's plaza, a business that involves Chuy and the other two children still living at home; two older sons work in San Jose, California, at a restaurant operated by other migrants from Tlacuitapa.

Chuy's older brother, 16-year-old Raúl, is no longer in school; he tends to the family's animals and helps his father throughout the day. However, even if there were no economic demands on him, Raúl, like all young people over 14 years of age in Tlacuitapa, does not have the option of continuing his education, because there is no local high school. Migrant parents consistently mention the absence of educational opportunities for their children as a strong factor in their decision to migrate. Laura, a 49-year-old prospective migrant who is applying for her green card, explained:

> The reason we want to go [to the United States], it's not because we want to live there. It's to work, to give our children an education, so they live well. If we could work here, if we could give our children an education here, we wouldn't want to go.

---

1. Young people typically assist with household tasks like cooking and cleaning and with farm chores such as unloading livestock feed and milking cows.

There is an option, however, for local children who want to continue their education. A *tele-secundaria* (distance learning school) was established in 1967 to deliver up to a ninth-grade education to youths from ages 12 to 15 (grades 7 to 9) in their hometown. Lectures are transmitted into the classroom via satellite, and this core information is then supplemented and reinforced by classroom teachers. Many communities throughout Mexico that are too small to meet state requirements for a fully staffed public school depend on this government program.

After leaving the public education system, young adults in Tlacuitapa have few economically productive options. Capitalization of dairy farming has made it one of the few profitable businesses in Tlacuitapa, and owners of dairy cows often hire workers from the town for wages. But other work in the local agricultural sector, which includes raising small livestock and growing corn and beans, is oriented toward household consumption and is therefore unpaid. For example, most families keep cows, chickens, and goats to provide for their daily food needs. As seen below, our survey revealed a local labor market that is dominated by economically inactive people, especially housewives, who make up 82 percent of the economically inactive respondents (see figure 5.1).

Figure 5.1 Employment of Tlacuitapeños, by Sector

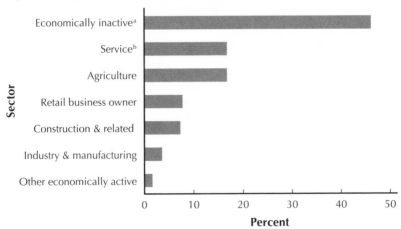

N = 659.
[a] Includes housewives, students, and retired persons.
[b] Includes both professional and nonprofessional services.

Some residents create employment for themselves by establishing small businesses, but these rarely employ people from outside the network of family and friends. Such local entrepreneurial endeavors include a carpentry shop, corner store, restaurant, cantina, butcher shop, bakery, two furniture stores, and a *mole* factory. Certain businesses, such as furniture stores and cantinas, exist primarily to cater to returning migrants and their families during the town's annual fiestas.

THE AGRICULTURAL ECONOMY

Raising livestock and growing crops are the most important economic activities in Unión de San Antonio (the *municipio* in which Tlacuitapa is located), and they involved 31 percent of respondents who indicated in our January 2007 survey in Tlacuitapa that they were actively employed.[2] Thirty-six percent reported that they or their family own land, and 39 percent of those who have migrated to the United States said they had worked in agriculture before emigrating. Thirty-five percent of the land in Unión de San Antonio is dedicated to agricultural purposes, and 42 percent is used for raising beef cattle or dairy cows (INEGI n.d.). Seventy-three percent of the land is privately owned; 16 percent belongs to an ejido.

In Unión de San Antonio—indeed, throughout most of the Los Altos region—most crops are grown for livestock feed. However, crop productivity is poor in Tlacuitapa, partly because of its shallow, sandy soils (Macías 1990, 18–19) and also because of scarce and irregular rainfall. The rainy season is short, and the poor soil cannot absorb or retain much water when the rains do arrive. Overgrazing has exacerbated the problem by exposing the nutrient-poor soils to erosion.

Productivity levels can be brought up with irrigation; in the case of seed corn, for example, irrigated land produced an average of 4.66 tons per hectare in 2005, while rainfed land yielded only 1.5 tons per hectare. But there is little irrigated land available, not because there is no water (there is substantial underground water) but because of the expense

2. This actually represents a decline from 2005, when 39 percent of respondents said they were engaged in agricultural or livestock-related activities (see Cantú, Shaiq, and Urdanivia 2007), but it is consistent with 2005 census data for the municipality.

of extracting it and maintaining and operating an irrigation system, especially given the region's high energy costs.

Another impediment to irrigated agriculture in Tlacuitapa is the failure to make use of the La Maroma reservoir (also known as El Caracol). This reservoir, which can hold twenty million cubic meters of water, was initially part of the hacienda of San Antonio (now the community of San Antonio de la Garza). The 1937 land reform that created Tlacuitapa's ejido left the reservoir in the hands of the former hacienda owners, and the family has not filled the reservoir since then, claiming that they use the land to grow wheat (though no wheat is grown there currently). According to local residents, if the reservoir were filled, it could provide water for all ejido land around Tlacuitapa and thereby improve the region's agricultural productivity.

The combination of poor soils and lack of water leads farmers to cultivate crops with low resale value, such as seed corn. And with prices for corn falling (a drop of 24 percent between 1999 and 2005) and production costs rising, Tlacuitapa's agricultural sector is being severely stressed.

Livestock-Raising and Dairy Farming

Livestock-raising has been a key activity in Los Altos since the colonial period, and dairy farming has been the region's most important agricultural activity since 1943, when the Nestlé Corporation established itself in Lagos de Moreno. Since then, various joint projects between the government and makers of dairy products have promoted milk production in Los Altos (Rodríguez Gómez 1996, 357).

Given Tlacuitapa's location in one of Mexico's most important milk-producing areas, it is not surprising that many local residents are engaged in some aspect of dairy farming. In 2005, 62 percent of Tlacuitapeños working in agriculture reported owning cows, even though dairy production was on the decline statewide due to a variety of factors (see figure 5.2). Foremost among them is the fact that the agricultural economy in Los Altos is composed of small family enterprises. In Tlacuitapa, the average number of cows per farmer is nineteen, and most farmers have only five animals. Forty-one percent of respondents in a CCIS survey conducted in 2005 had no more than five cows, and only 9 percent had fifty or more (see figure 5.3).

Figure 5.2 Milk Production in Jalisco, 1995–2006

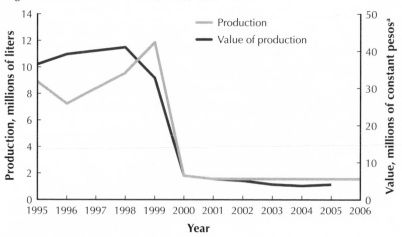

Source: SAGARPA, various years.
[a] Deflated with the national currency index (December 2003 = 100).

Figure 5.3 Dairy Cows per Farmer in Tlacuitapa

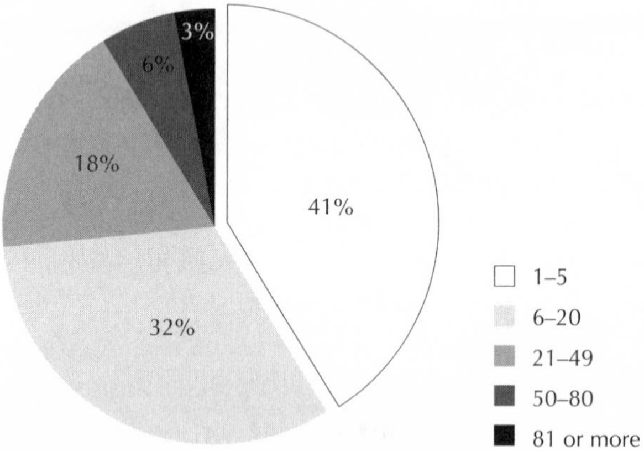

Source: Mexican Migration Field Research and Training Program survey, 2005
N = 68 producers.

Small-scale farmers in Tlacuitapa, and in Mexico generally, have suffered many economic setbacks over the past two decades. Only a few have been able to meet the changing production requirements that increasing globalization demands, including greater efficiency and attention to quality.

The current crisis in dairy farming in Tlacuitapa stems from changes in the Mexican economy, including Mexico's entry into the General Agreement on Tariffs and Trade (GATT) in 1986 and the North American Free Trade Agreement (NAFTA) in 1994. Under these agreements, the dairy market has been deregulated, subsidies have ended, credits have been reduced and interest rates raised, and there has been a liberalization of the importation of dairy products. In addition, an overvalued peso and reduced import tariffs—in combination with rising domestic production costs, diminishing subsidies, and reduced agribusiness capacity—have converged to make imported dairy products cheaper than domestic ones and have turned Mexico into the world's number-one importer of powdered milk (Rodríguez Gómez 1996, 353; 1998, 42).

Falling milk prices (see figure 5.4) and escalating production costs, primarily for feed and electricity, have not gone unnoticed among Tlacuitapa's farmers. According to Carlos, one of the town's small dairy farmers:

> All I know is that about nine or ten years ago, the bulk of the feed cost 27 pesos and milk cost anywhere between 2 and 2.20 pesos. And we're now at the point that feed costs 100 pesos or more and milk is at around 3 pesos.

Figure 5.4 Average Price Paid to Producer per Liter of Milk in Jalisco, 1981–2005, with 1995–2005 Data for Unión de San Antonio (in 2003 pesos)

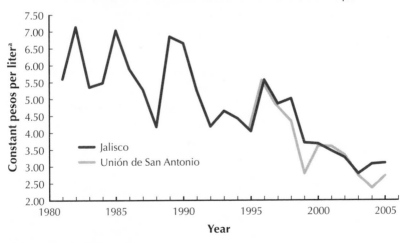

Source: SIAP, various years.
[a] Deflated with the national producer price index (December 2003 = 100).

Rafael, another Tlacuitapeño dairy farmer, explained how high electricity costs frustrate farmers' efforts to modernize production:

> If the government helped me out, I could make it. Electrical power is so expensive; I need a government subsidy for that. If I can't earn enough to cover costs, I'm not going to make the effort. We're paying 3,000 or 4,000 pesos every month for electricity, in addition to paying our workers and for the operation of the *termos* [holding tanks].

The physical and macro-economic conditions that make small-scale dairy farming economically unproductive are exacerbated by increasing demands on the part of the agribusinesses that buy the milk. For example, dairy processors in Los Altos[3] now require farmers to refrigerate their milk, a relatively new condition for purchase.

When the refrigeration requirement was instituted in the early 1990s, farmers across Los Altos banded together to purchase refrigeration tanks. Thanks to these collective investments and the Ranchero Tanks Program (through which agribusinesses loan refrigeration tanks to groups of farmers), nearly 73 percent of small and midsize dairy producers in the region had access to cooling and refrigeration systems by the late 1990s (Rodríguez Gómez 1998, 52). However, the demands of agribusinesses did not end with the refrigeration tank issue, and it is the small and midsize producers who have had the most difficulty complying with the latest wave of requirements. As Rafael recalled:

> Around 1998, a group of us, about forty people, started working with Sello Rojo so they could lend us a tank. After about three years of working together, they began asking for other things so that the milk could go directly from the cow to the tank. They asked us to begin processing milk on the farm, but our little ranch had no electricity, so this meant a great expense, in addition to the need to dig a well. They offered help to lower the prices, but it still cost too

3. These include Nestlé, Lechera Guadalajara, Parmalat, Yoplait, Alpura, La Concordia, Lácteos Deshidratados de México, and Alprodel, among others (Cervantes, Santoyo, and Álvarez 2001, 169).

much and at that time we couldn't afford the expense, so
they stopped doing business with us.

Some dairy farmers like Rafael, who were initially put out of business by
such demands, continued to organize with others and eventually bought
collective tanks. Others, like Guadalupe, a dairy farmer from San Antonio de la Garza, bought their own individual tanks with help from the
agribusinesses.[4]

Tlacuitapa also has three termos, which small-scale farmers use to
hold and refrigerate their milk until it is picked up and delivered to the
processing plant. For many dairy farmers in Tlacuitapa, the termo is the
usual stop for milk on its way to market, despite the fact that the push
for refrigeration tanks was intended to eliminate this intermediate step
between farmers and agribusinesses.

On the upside, however, the termos allow agribusinesses to monitor
milk quality more closely to discourage local farmers from "baptizing"
their milk, that is, diluting it with water. This practice originated when
farmers' input costs began ballooning at a time of falling milk prices. To
compensate for the escalating prices for forage, small producers continue
"baptizing" their product to increase utility levels. As Carlos explained:

> People don't know what to do anymore. If you water down
> the milk, you won't make enough; but if you don't water
> it, you're even worse off. They [the milk processors] should
> pay more; the price of fodder should come down. But we
> should punish those who water their milk. If I produce
> good milk, then they should pay me a good price. But if
> half of the producers water their milk or deliver it dirty, the
> rest of us lose as well.

Despite higher production costs, low prices paid to the producer, and
escalating demands from agroindustries, a few small-scale milk producers have been able to persevere in Tlacuitapa. Several factors help explain
the resilience of this sector. One is the embeddedness of the cattle industry
in general and milk production in particular in Los Altos. Many residents

---

4. An individual tank holds approximately 1,000 liters of milk; a collective tank can
hold more than 5,000 liters.

have inherited land and cattle or, seeing few economic alternatives, have purchased them, and cattle continue to represent a relatively safe source of income, even in hard times, as Rafael noted:

> It's our tradition. Our parents had cattle before we were born, and we are continuing that tradition. Besides, there's no other work here. So we have a little ranch and cows. We don't have much, but we do what we have to in order to survive, even reducing ourselves to the lowest living standards. In the past, maybe you ate meat once or twice a week; now you just eat it once or not at all. That's how we get by.

Furthermore, farmers worldwide typically have various sources of income, which allows them to continue a productive activity that otherwise would not be economically viable. This is true of small-scale dairy producers in Tlacuitapa, who also obtain income by selling yearling calves, piglets, eggs, and meat, by growing their own feed crops, and by operating small businesses or renting out their agricultural equipment. And finally, many producers are able to supplement their incomes with remittances sent by family members who have migrated to the United States.

Sixty-five percent of the people interviewed in our 2007 survey in Tlacuitapa and San Antonio de la Garza reported that they sometimes receive money from the United States, and 79 percent of those who migrated reported remitting part of their income. Although only a small proportion of this money is invested directly in milk production (9 percent of remittance recipients and 14 percent of remittance senders indicated that the money was put to this use), it nevertheless constitutes an important supplement to other family income.

Today's remittances are not the only instance of money from the United States going to support dairy farming in Tlacuitapa. Many Tlacuitapeños, including Carlos and Rafael, migrated to the United States in their early years and used the money earned there to buy land or purchase cows. Clearly, money that Tlacuitapa's migrants earn in the United States ends up supporting milk production at home, directly or indirectly, thereby enabling many small dairy farmers to survive despite the odds.

According to Alarcón (1995, 40), remittances now fill the role previously occupied by the discontinued credits the Mexican government formerly provided to the nation's small farmers.

New Productive Projects in Agriculture

Despite the chronic agricultural crisis in Tlacuitapa, some government-sponsored projects are trying to increase production in this sector. One of these has involved building a greenhouse for growing grains, fruits, vegetables, and flowers. The project is based on the Support to Rural Investment Projects program (PAPIR) financed by Mexico's Ministry of Agriculture. Tlacuitapeños' access to it was facilitated by two prominent members of the community: Román, who has served as municipal delegate for Tlacuitapa and commissioner of the ejido, and his wife, Beatriz, formerly the councilor for Tlacuitapa on the Unión de San Antonio city council.

The greenhouse was constructed in 2006, with 70 percent of the cost paid by PAPIR and 30 percent by the partners. In its first season, November 2006–January 2007, the greenhouse was used to grow cherry tomatoes for sale regionally. Plans for the second season were to cultivate tomatoes and onions, to bring in additional partners, and to link up with other greenhouses to improve marketing.

Although the greenhouse has only created employment for its partners, it does present an option for making local agriculture more profitable. Upcoming years will reveal whether other Tlacuitapeños follow the model of greenhouse agriculture and whether this will create enough local employment to affect out-migration.

REMITTANCES AND LOCAL DEVELOPMENT

As local agricultural production has declined, the migration economy has gained importance for Tlacuitapa. In this section we discuss economically productive and unproductive uses of remittances, which in 2006 totaled some US$23 billion, or 3.6 percent of Mexico's GDP. We explore several basic questions about remittances in Tlacuitapa: Who remits and how? What are remittances used for? Is this use economically productive? What connection, if any, exists between remittances, investment, and development?

Remittance Sending

Roughly two-thirds of Tlacuitapeño migrants currently living in the United States send money to their home community on a regular basis, remitting US$393 per month on average, or about $4,700 per year. We initially estimated that Tlacuitapa received roughly $773,000 in remittances each year, or about $1,340 per resident. However, because our survey was not totally inclusive of the population of Tlacuitapeños living in the United States, we used other survey data to calculate a more precise population size based on the median ratio of number of siblings currently residing in the United States to the total number of siblings. The weighted sample led us to more than double our original estimate of remittances to Tlacuitapa to $1.6 million per year, raising the per capita inflow to just over $2,770.

The fact that the typical U.S.-based migrant from Tlacuitapa is able to remit nearly $5,000 while earning only about $23,000 per year, or just above the poverty line for a U.S. family, is truly astounding. By working in the United States and remitting a part of their earnings to family in Mexico, migrants are able to raise their families out of poverty, and this appears to be the primary force driving the decision to migrate.

Tlacuitapeño migrants send remittances via various channels. The most common is electronic transfers, as through Western Union or MoneyGram. Nearly two-thirds of migrants choose this method because of its relative speed and ease (see figure 5.5).

A Sustainable Flow?

Some of our most suggestive findings relate to the stability of remittance flows. DeSipio (2002) suggests that as migrants assimilate in the United States, they will cease to remit money. Several recent surveys accord with DeSipio's findings. For example, Marcelli and Lowell (2005) used data from a 2000 survey of undocumented Mexican migrants in Los Angeles to assess the impacts of assimilation on remittance behavior. They found that remitting is negatively correlated with traditional assimilation factors (education, years in the United States)[5] but positively correlated with attendance at community meetings. When we asked non-remitting Tlacuitapeño migrants why they did not send money home, 61 percent

5. For example, non-remitters averaged 18 years in the United States, while remitters averaged only 13.9 (Marcelli and Lowell 2005).

responded that they had no family left in Mexico to receive the money.[6] This suggests that whole-family migration may provide a better explanation than assimilation for a decrease in remittances.[7]

Figure 5.5 How Migrants Remit Funds

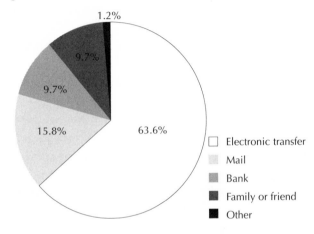

N = 330.

Another factor that could affect the long-term potential of remittances to maintain a social safety net in migrant-sending communities is the behavior of migrants' U.S.-born children. Our data suggest that the second generation continues to send money back to the parents' hometown. Though our sample of U.S.-born interviewees is too small for rigorous analysis, it is worth noting that fifteen of our twenty-nine U.S.-born respondents regularly send money to a relative in Tlacuitapa. Additionally, eleven respondents had sent money for a public work in the town, presumably through the informal hometown association discussed later in this chapter.

Uses of Remittances

Many migration scholars have examined how remittances are spent in the home community (see, for example, Taylor 1999; Binford 2003; Cohen,

---

6. See chapter 1, this volume, for a discussion of the decline of circular migration and the rise of whole families migrating to the United States.

7. Whole-family migration is a trend that has been spurred in part by increased U.S. border enforcement; see chapter 2 in this volume and Cornelius 2007: 3–5.

Jones, and Conway 2005; Taylor and Mora 2006). If these funds are spent solely on consumption, we would expect relatively little impact on the local economy, especially if most of the goods are purchased outside of the hometown. However, if remittances are directed to productive ends, such as education and investment, we would expect a larger impact on overall development. Early research on this topic reached fairly negative conclusions, finding that remittances generally were spent on basic consumer goods. However, even though most remittances in Tlacuitapa do go toward sustaining family members remaining in Mexico, some portion is directed to community projects and small-scale investments, as discussed later in the chapter.

Unfortunately, survey responses may not be accurate indicators of the role of remittances in household expenditures. Taylor (1999) argues that instead of asking recipients how they spend remittances, we should use household income and expenditure data to compare remittance recipients and equivalent households that do not receive remittances. Several authors have followed his prescription (see, for example, Adams 2005; Taylor and Mora 2006) and found that households that receive remittances spend less on consumption and more on investment and education than was evident in the early studies. These findings fit well into the new paradigm for understanding migration, development, and remittances, which holds that migration provides capital to developing nations and should spur development or at least ameliorate the worst effects of poverty (Cohen, Jones, and Conway 2005). Additionally, this paradigm reassesses the impact of consumption spending, arguing that although benefits may not accrue directly to migrants and their families, additional consumption spending may create a climate for future investment and development (Taylor 1999).

In our analysis, we interpret responses about how remittances are spent as suggestive of how remittances are perceived: do senders and receivers view remittances as funds to be invested or simply as money to pay for daily necessities? Our data suggest that most senders and receivers feel that remittances should be used solely or primarily for basic sustenance (80 percent of senders, 75 percent of receivers), including health-related expenditures (34 percent of senders, 23 percent of receivers) and clothing (15 percent of senders, 27 percent of receivers) (see figures 5.6

and 5.7). Most Tlacuitapeños do not see remittances as a source of capital for investment; this is even true of those who have used money earned in the United States for investment purposes. However, our results may underrepresent the use of remittances for investment. By asking respondents to report *regular* or *monthly* remittance uses and to rank their top three, we may well have missed one-time remittance uses, such as might be needed to start a business.

Figure 5.6 Remittance Use as Reported by Senders

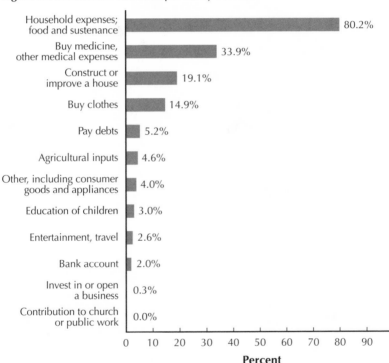

N = 303.

Remittance senders often assume that remittance receivers are spending the money differently than they actually are, with more money than anticipated going for clothes and entertainment. Senders and receivers agree, however, that the biggest need is to maintain the household and provide basic necessities, supporting our assertion that Tlacuitapeño migrants are reactive migrants (seeking money to sustain themselves and their families) rather than proactive migrants (seeking money to invest in their hometown). Only 2 percent of remitters expected recipients to deposit the money in a Mexican bank account, which reflects the low proportion of respondents who have a bank account in Mexico (15 percent) and the fact that virtually all the money that is remitted is needed to cover day-to-day expenses.

Figure 5.7 Remittance Use as Reported by Recipients

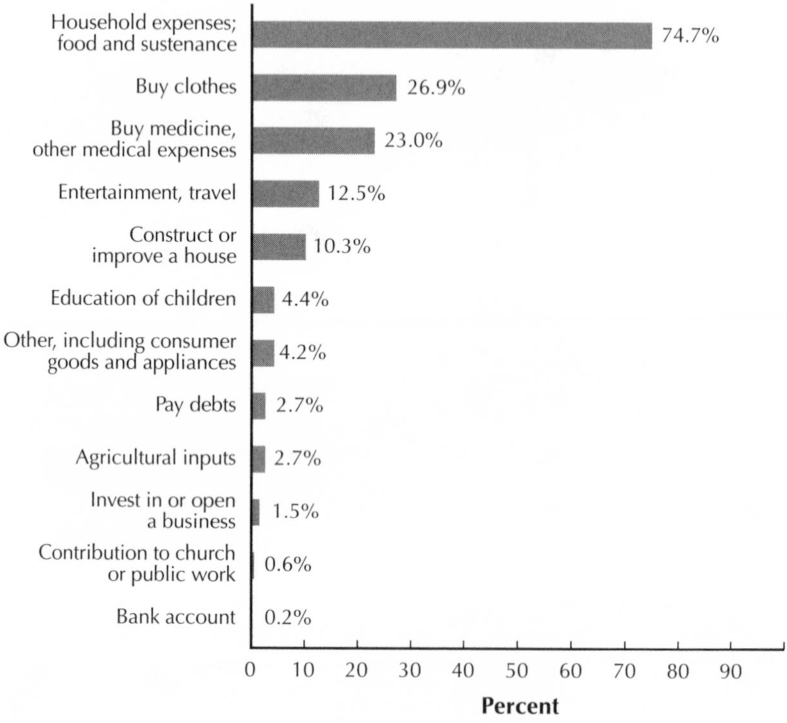

N = 526.

Location of Remittance Use

To fully understand the local economic impact of remittances, we need to know *where* remittances are spent (see figure 5.8). Many residents of Tlacuitapa do much of their shopping in nearby Lagos de Moreno or Unión de San Antonio (both about 30 minutes away by car), suggesting that the multiplier effect in Tlacuitapa may be minimal. In fact, over half of every dollar received in Tlacuitapa is spent in these neighboring towns, which have stronger economies and perhaps more competitive prices and greater selection.

Figure 5.8 Location of Remittance Expenditures

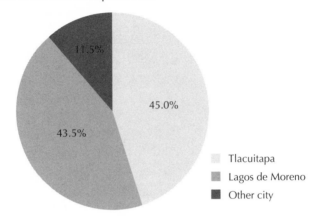

45.0%

43.5%

11.5%

Tlacuitapa
Lagos de Moreno
Other city

N = 840.

Moreover, in addition to remittances, migrants also bring significant amounts of money with them when they return from the United States, whether permanently or for a short visit. We estimate that returning migrants brought US$296,000 to Tlacuitapa in 2007 in the form of pocket transfers. Anecdotally, our team observed that many of the large expenditures that returned migrants made during the annual fiestas consisted of goods bought outside the hometown. These included wedding dresses, floral arrangements, and rentals of bands and carnival rides. Returning migrants also reported giving 37 percent of the money they brought from the United States as gifts to Tlacuitapa-based family and friends.

We also found that shopping outside of Tlacuitapa was positively correlated with wealth. Shopping outside of Tlacuitapa requires transportation; however, 74 percent of Tlacuitapeños own a car or truck and therefore can opt to shop outside the town. To provide an alternative source of information about a respondent's or household's wealth, we created a wealth index based on the self-reporting of goods the household owns, assigning 1 point each for a television and stereo, 2 points for a refrigerator, and 4 points each for a computer, washing machine, and car, with a maximum score of 16. Someone scoring at the top of the wealth index would own all of the above-mentioned items, while someone at the low end might own only a television or a radio. We then compared the scores on our wealth index with the location in which remittances were spent (see table 5.2).

Table 5.2 Shopping Location, by Family Wealth

Wealth Index Score	Shop in Tlacuitapa	Shop outside Tlacuitapa
0–4	70.3%	29.7%
5–8	51.0%	49.0%
9–12	43.5%	56.5%
13–16	33.8%	66.2%
N	357	426

Clearly, the remittances and pocket transfers entering Tlacuitapa are raising local residents' quality of life. Nevertheless, the sustained or multiplier effect of this money is what matters most for the future development and strengthening of the local economy. Unfortunately, our data suggest that the lion's share of these remittances seems to be escaping to other towns.

Collective Remittances

How can remitters ensure that their hard-earned money remains in the hometown? Do they care where the money is spent and whether their towns develop? Is it the responsibility of local government to promote local development or the role of private investors to bring competitive businesses to the town? Surprisingly, Mexican migrants across the United States are making coordinated communal efforts to use remittances to develop their hometowns.

Collective remittances are "bundled" remittances sent by a group of migrants to finance a public project of some sort in their hometown. Often these projects are organized by the church in the migrant-sending community, as is the case in Tlacuitapa. One finding from our survey is the high proportion of Tlacuitapeño migrants (43 percent) who report contributing to a public project in Mexico. This is especially surprising because Tlacuitapa does not have a hometown association (HTA), which is the usual infrastructure through which collective remittances are organized. Yet the town has successfully solicited money for a number of church-sponsored projects from Tlacuitapeño communities in Oklahoma City and in Union City, California, largely thanks to the strong migrant networks in the receiving communities and their close ties with their hometown.

Over the years, migrants have financed the building of two bridges, a basketball court, funeral parlor, new church, and a set of bells for the church in Tlacuitapa. One of the bridges links San Antonio de la Garza with Tlacuitapa. The other, named Puente Morelos in honor of the parish priest who was instrumental in soliciting government aid and migrant donations for the project, was built in 2006. This sturdy cement bridge is adorned with lampposts, benches, and a plaque reading; "Works that bring progress, a joint effort of the people and the government. Task completed." It appears, then, that Tlacuitapeños have created an informal organization that is accomplishing many of the objectives of a formal HTA.

In Oklahoma City, migrant families from Tlacuitapa talked about their responsibilities at the local parish in the United States. According to these migrants, each month a few couples are assigned to visit the home of every family from their hometown and collect money for their U.S. church and community. Occasionally, the priest in the receiving community contacts the priest in Tlacuitapa to organize a collection for a hometown project. At these times, the visiting couples ask their migrant neighbors for donations for the specific project in Mexico. Visiting the Tlacuitapeño families is fairly easy because Tlacuitapa's migrants often live close together in the receiving community and attend the same church, a proximity that helps support communal ties, religious customs, and social networks, and also provides the environment for effective collective remittances.

By definition, hometown associations draw together people from the same migrant-sending town, allowing them to preserve social identities and communal relationships, and to ease the settlement process in a foreign society (Orozco 2000). To this point, the informal HTAs that Tlacuitapeño migrants have established in Oklahoma City and Union City have done just that. The structure of these informal HTAs resembles that of the more formally organized groups studied by Orozco and others. There are monthly dues for collections managed by the church and local members, but the migrants are limited to communicating and coordinating with the hometown parish priest. Though Tlacuitapa would seem to have high social capital, little of the economic capital derived from collective remittances is actually being used for local development.

Most of the collective remittances from Tlacuitapa's informal HTA are focused on improving the church, funding public projects headed by the church, and sustaining the town's religious festivals. When studying a similar HTA in Los Angeles, Leticia Hernández Vega (2006) referred to it as an informal HTA in a primitive state due to the lack of economically productive goals (such as job creation). Following this reasoning, in order for a town to reach the next level of development through remittances from hometown associations, it must shift its focus to the town's infrastructure. Although Tlacuitapa has already met its basic infrastructure needs (it has a well, electricity, and telephone lines), there is room for improvement. For example, only one in ten Tlacuitapeños owns a computer, and the municipal offices lack public Internet access, something that the informal HTA could remedy.

Who Invests in the Hometown?

What factors determine who invests in the local community? To better understand the economic consequences of migration for the sending community, we compare the characteristics of people who have invested and have not invested in a business in Tlacuitapa (see table 5.3). More than one in five Tlacuitapeños (22 percent) reported that they had invested in a business.

Investors are older than non-investors, and a higher percentage of them are male. Fewer than half of both groups have sent money home for a public project in Tlacuitapa, but considering that some respondents had never been to the United States, the percentages are relatively high, confirming the presence of an informal HTA and the church's success in collecting money for public projects.

Notably, Tlacuitapeño investors with U.S. migration experience tended to have substantially shorter stays in the United States than non-investors with migration experience, probably because the investor group migrated with the specific intent to earn just enough for a given investment in their hometown. We found anecdotal evidence that many people who had invested in agriculture or cattle had gone to the United States for short periods to earn enough money to purchase the equipment and cattle needed to support them through the next year, repeating the cycle year after year. These agricultural investors had no intention of remaining in the United States; rather, they used money earned there to support a small business that was not sustainable on its own.

Table 5.3 Characteristics of Investors and Non-Investors in Tlacuitapa

	Investor	Non-Investor
Age (years)	46	32
Male	53.2%	43.6%
Has U.S. migration experience	47.3%	54.8%
Average length of U.S. residence[a]	41 months	58 months
Average years of education	6	6
Has contributed to public works in Tlacuitapa	38.8%	42.9%
Has sent remittances[a]	92.5%	76.2%
Has received remittances	68.3%	66.4%
Invested in business with money earned in United States[a]	100%	0%
Would locate new business in Lagos de Moreno	76.6%	70.0%
Has bank account in Mexico	36.7%	10.3%
Has bank account in United States[a]	15.6%	45.6%
Wants to retire in Tlacuitapa	84.1%	71.4%
N	129	631

[a] Among respondents with U.S. migration experience. Respondents who reported investing only in the United States were excluded.

All Tlacuitapeño investors with U.S. migration experience report that they used money earned in the United States to invest in a business. However, a majority of both investors and non-investors said that if they were to start a new business, they would locate it in Lagos de Moreno.

This is consistent with our finding that Tlacuitapa is not viewed as a good investment location and that remittances on the whole are not being invested there. While many Tlacuitapa residents do not want to leave their hometown, they do not feel that its economy is strong enough to support a business. Nor is investing in the United States much of an option, primarily because of legal obstacles and migrants' strong ties to their hometown and region. Lagos de Moreno has the advantage of proximity to Tlacuitapa, and its economy is much more developed.

Interestingly, not everyone who had invested in a business with money earned in the United States considered that business to be their principal job. For example, 23 percent of them self-identified primarily as housewives; these may be women who view themselves as investors because their husbands have put money into agriculture or a business though they themselves have no income to invest. Also, 22 percent of Tlacuitapeño investors reported that they work in agriculture. While they consider agriculture to be a business, it is clearly quite different from owning a shop or other business wherein town residents and returned migrants might spend their money locally.

Case Studies in Migrant Entrepreneurship

Case studies of entrepreneurship in migrant-sending areas are rare in the literature. We hope the following discussion of how a few local businesses were started, what they entail, whether they were established with money earned in the United States, and how successful they have been will contribute to a better understanding of how the local economy of a migrant-sending community functions and what challenges local business owners face.

Francisco's Carpentry Shop

Francisco worked in construction in the United States for three years, earning money to take back home. He invested some of it in a small carpentry shop in Tlacuitapa, where he makes chairs, tables, closets, staircases, and doors. Most of his customers are migrants who are improving their homes in Mexico. Francisco started his business a few years ago but got no work for the first three or four months. Once he landed his first job, however, referrals sufficed to provide him with a steady flow of clients.

Francisco decided to establish his business in Tlacuitapa because he knows and loves the town and because costs are lower there than in a larger city. He works in a house owned by an uncle who is presently in the United States, which significantly lowers Francisco's costs. He says that, though he earns little, he feels at home and is with his family. Even though wages are better in the United States, "it's not worth it because most of the money stays there anyway." Francisco prefers to earn less and have a lower cost of living in Tlacuitapa.

Francisco employs his brother and one other young man, paying them each about 600 pesos a week, which he says is low but all he can afford. The young man usually works part-time; Francisco's brother sets his own work schedule. When business is good, Francisco works up to twelve hours a day and nets 1,200 pesos a week after paying his costs, including salaries.

Francisco pays for his inputs in cash, preferring not to purchase on credit or to borrow from a credit union or bank. "You can't mess around with banks and loans because they can leave you in ruin." He feels that his business is profitable and he wants to expand it. He has made some improvements but sees room for more, even possibly branching out to Unión de San Antonio. He has applied for a government grant of 72,000 pesos to purchase the machinery that would allow him to expand (he would contribute 8,000 pesos) and when interviewed was still waiting to hear whether he would receive the money. If he receives the funds and keeps his business going for three years thereafter, the machines become the property of his business, but if he closes before three years have passed he would owe the full purchase price of the machines. When applying for the program he was asked to sign a document stating that he would not participate in any other aid program. So even though he recently learned of another program that would help him purchase discounted products, he could not take part in it. He has not received any support from the municipal government and noted that the government programs that help businesses obtain inputs and machinery at discounted prices are not available in Tlacuitapa.

When asked how he sees the investment climate of Tlacuitapa, Francisco said that most people are not willing to assume the risks associated with starting a business:

> You don't see that kind of ambition. The people don't dare
> risk losing money. But when I started to work, I went three or
> four months with no work. And yet there I was . . . holding on.
> And then I started to get work and things started to improve.

According to Francisco, there is the potential for businesses in Tlacuitapa to be successful if people are willing to invest the money, time,
and energy required, as his business has demonstrated. Francisco's case
suggests that investing remittances in the local economy could be a way
to improve the town and to slow migration. However, Francisco's customers are migrants, so if migration stops or if migrants no longer return
to their hometown, there would be little need for a carpenter. The same
logic applies to many other businesses in the town.

Laura's Clothing Factory

Laura is the owner of a small clothing factory. She established the business five years ago but worked without pay for the first three years in
order to get the business up and running. Before establishing her factory,
Laura was one of twenty-five people who took a three-month course in
dressmaking offered by a group that came from Mexico City. Some of
those who took the course asked the governor for sewing machines so
they could open a dress shop; he complied, and the president later gave
them additional machines.

In the beginning, the shop specialized in making dresses only and employed all twenty-five women who had taken the sewing course. Over
time, however, many of the women, discouraged by the long hours and
low pay, left to care for their families. Laura explained:

> Of the twenty-five, only my aunt and I remained. They start-
> ed to leave because it was three years of work, work, work.
> No pay or anything. . . . Everything we earned was reinvest-
> ed. We went three years without pay. Three years working
> seemingly for nothing. But we were also gaining experience.

Laura persisted in hopes that the business would eventually succeed, and
she branched into other types of clothing. Though she sometimes thought
of closing the shop, she did not have any other work options. This was
prior to the establishment of the shoe factory, discussed below.

Eventually, Laura and her aunt received an order from Guadalajara for five thousand pairs of pants for school uniforms, to be completed within three months. They hired extra women workers and finished the job in a month and a half. The next year they got the same order. The first year they had to pay for the fabric in advance, but the following year they were able to purchase the material on credit and repay the loan once they had collected payment for their work. They netted 50,000 pesos profit the second year and hope to secure the same order again. They have received orders for pants from other companies and individuals as well, and they also make pants that they themselves sell outside of Tlacuitapa. Even so, the work is still not constant.

Laura and her aunt, who are partners in the business, have six women employees, including Laura's mother and sister. They earn about 400 pesos for a week and a half of work: piece rate for the factory orders and by the day when they take clothes to sell outside the town. Although they received some sewing machines from the government, they have purchased two more and hope to purchase a third, very expensive machine, which would make their work process more efficient.

Unlike Francisco's undertaking, Laura's small business was not started with remittances but with the help of the government. Though her startup costs were high, her business seems to be growing and is employing others from the town.

The Athletic Shoe Factory

A shoe factory that opened on the outskirts of Tlacuitapa three years ago exemplifies the type of large-scale employment that Tlacuitapa needs. We spoke with the factory supervisor, Carlos Trejo, and with Víctor, the plant manager; both were born in Tlacuitapa and both received undergraduate degrees at the University of Guadalajara, the former in information technology and the latter in communications.

The factory is a subsidiary of a shoe factory in San Francisco del Rincón, Guanajuato, that sells tennis shoes throughout Mexico. The precut materials come to Tlacuitapa from the main factory (the Tlacuitapa factory does not have the machines for cutting the component pieces), where the shoes are assembled and then shipped. The factory owners in San Francisco decided to locate a factory in Tlacuitapa because of the ample labor supply and the lack of businesses that might compete for local workers.

The factory employs between seventy and eighty workers. About 70 percent of them are women, mostly young girls between the ages of 15 and 20, though a few older women work there as well. Most have only a middle school education.

There are two areas in the factory: sewing and assembly. Pay varies with the difficulty of the task, from a low of 2 pesos to a high of 20 pesos per item. Workers can train in more difficult tasks as time permits, and thus are able to rise in position and income. The factory produces between 4,000 and 4,500 pairs of shoes per week. Workers earn an average of 400 pesos per week, and the most productive can earn up to 2,000 pesos a week. The job is year-round, but the busiest months are November and December. The work schedule is 8 a.m. to 5:30 p.m. Monday through Friday, and 8 a.m. to 1 p.m. Saturday, with a breakfast break from 11 to 11:30 a.m. and a 15-minute break at 4 p.m. There is no lunch break. Workers receive about two weeks off during the year.

Work at the shoe factory can be very strenuous. Most workers stand all day and come in contact with strong chemicals. However, Trejo says that work conditions are good and that if workers get tired, they can sit for a minute, and if they feel sick, they can visit the town clinic next door.

Though the shoe factory offers a much-needed local alternative to work in agriculture, it is not growing as fast as it could and it has high turnover. Two years ago, the factory employed fifty people (Cantú, Shaiq, and Urdanivia 2007). Though it now employs about eighty, Carlos Trejo said that the factory is not meeting production quotas and needs more workers. The low wages and difficult working conditions probably account for the factory's difficulty in retaining its employees, though Trejo attributes the high turnover rate to irresponsibility on the part of the workers. He said that the younger girls often simply do not come back from vacation and that women leave when they marry, not necessarily because the husband does not want them to work but because the women feel their place is in the home. He also suggested that women do not need to work because their fathers and husbands support them: "They lack the commitment to say, 'I'm going to work because I want to, and I'm going to continue working for some time.'"

The high rotation of workers is costly. It takes time to train new workers, and having a lot of new employees brings productivity down. According to Trejo, at any given time most of the factory's workers are still in training. When asked if he would consider raising salaries in order to lower turnover and training costs, Víctor responded: "It is not the pay but the mindset of the people . . . their way of thinking. There are people here who earn very little but others who earn a lot." Because workers are paid by the piece, Víctor alleges, if they earn less, it is because they do not want to work hard. The factory occasionally gives bonuses to motivate workers to higher levels of productivity, but Víctor does not believe that low salaries are the explanation for the high number of workers who leave the factory.

The shoe factory would like to hire more men because, according to Trejo, the fact that they have families to support makes them better workers and less likely to quit. Currently there are ten men working in the factory. According to Trejo, men sometimes think that sewing is women's work, but he notes that the main factory in San Francisco employs mostly men. Trejo explains the shortage of male workers in the Tlacuitapa factory by noting that all of the local men have gone north.

Two years ago the factory established a paid three-month training program for boys about to leave middle school to prepare them for a transition directly into the factory. About ten boys enter the training program each year, but only two or three end up working in the factory. Trejo claims that the factory is not losing these younger boys to migration, given that young men usually leave for the United States at an older age. Rather, these youngsters are choosing to work with their families in agriculture, demonstrating that work in the factory is not a sufficiently attractive option.

In contrast to the managers' view of conditions at the factory, the workers we interviewed complained about the difficult and dangerous working conditions. Two women said that they are paid very little, too little for the work that they are doing and the danger posed by the chemicals to which they are exposed.

The shoe factory is one of the most successful businesses in Tlacuitapa. Furthermore, because it does not depend on money from the United States, it offers a good model for growth. Unfortunately, such businesses set up operations in rural towns to take advantage of an abundant and low-cost labor force, paying wages that are too low to deter workers from migrating.

The Mole *Factory*

The *mole* factory was established in the 1970s by the Amézquita family to sell homemade mole at the annual fiestas.[8] Their mole proved very popular, and family matriarch María Dolores Amézquita was often asked to cater family events and social functions. When she died in 2001, other family members continued the business, preparing a total of nearly 6,000 kilos per year in two batches. The process takes about fifteen days, beginning with the roasting and peeling of the chiles and ending with packaging for market. Three generations of Amézquitas are involved in the family business, including nephews and grandsons who live in California but help make and package the mole when they are in Tlacuitapa for the end-of-year celebrations.

The key to the viability of the Amézquitas' business is its basis in social and family networks. It depends largely on the unpaid work of family members and neighbors; the mole factory has very few wage workers. Most of the ingredients are bought wholesale in Guadalajara and delivered at cost by family members, and the product labels are made by a friend at a discounted price. The chile is purchased from growers in Aguascalientes who have ties with Tlacuitapa through marriage.

The Amézquitas sell their mole in three presentations: 300 grams (which serves about six people and costs 30 pesos wholesale), 600 grams (59 pesos), and 900 grams (88 pesos). The jars are distributed mainly in stores in Lagos de Moreno, León, and other towns in the region, and are also sold from a family-owned locale in Tlacuitapa. Locals and visitors have carried this product as far away as Europe. For example, a Swiss industrialist who moved to Lagos de Moreno to work at Nestlé buys mole to take to his family in Switzerland. So extensive is the fame of the Amézquita mole that when the company's founder died, newspapers in Lagos de Moreno ran articles for five days stating their hope that the company and product would continue.

The company's main impediment to growth is restricted demand. Though the product is clearly popular, increasing demand would involve enlisting a wider distribution network, and the family has been reticent

---

8. *Mole* is a thick paste of ground nuts, chocolate, chiles, cinnamon, and multiple other ingredients, that is usually diluted with broth and served with chicken or pork. The dish is associated with festive occasions.

to turn marketing responsibility over to people outside of their cohort of family and friends. According to family members, "we prefer selling in small quantities with people we know, so we won't get robbed."

CONCLUSION

Migration of its townspeople to the United States yields a substantial in-flow of dollars to Tlacuitapa's local economy. However, these remittances are not being directed to the kinds of productive ends that would give the town economic independence. Even though remittances have supported the creation of some small businesses, Tlacuitapa's small customer base limits the number of small businesses that can be viable. Moreover, the town's customer base is unstable, fluctuating as migrants come and go or— as is increasingly common—as migrants go and stay in the United States.

Further, the migrants who do return, especially for the annual fiestas, spend most of their money in the larger towns around Tlacuitapa; and even within Tlacuitapa, many of the merchants selling goods during the fiestas are from out of town. Thus, even the busiest and most economically active months do not suffice to carry local business through the rest of the year, forcing much of the population to rely on remittances. Nothing much seems to have changed in Tlacuitapa since the late 1980s, when Cornelius observed: "One of the ironies of U.S.-bound emigration from these communities is that it has probably done more to fuel entrepreneurship in nearby Mexican urban centers, and perhaps even in the United States, than in the source communities themselves" (1990, 16). Because people do not view Tlacuitapa as a good investment site, money earned in the United States is often used to start businesses in larger locales. Nevertheless, even though migration has not created a platform for self-sustaining economic development, it has put in place a vital social safety net for Tlacuitape-ños who remain in the town. Migrants' remittances have brought a higher standard of living and quality of life than would exist without migration.

Remittances are a good shock absorber, offsetting the instability inherent in local agriculture and dairy farming. Even though remittances are not jump-starting the establishment of new businesses in Tlacuitapa, they provide a cushion for the townspeople, in some sense standing in place of an absent government support program. For this reason, migration will likely continue as a means for sustaining economic well-being in Tlacuitapa.

References

Adams, Richard H., Jr. 2005. "Remittances, Household Expenditure and Investment in Guatemala." World Bank Policy Research Working Paper No. 3532. Washington, DC: World Bank.

Alarcón, Rafael. 1995. "Transnational Communities, Regional Development, and the Future of Mexican Immigration," *Berkeley Planning Journal* 10: 36–54.

Binford, Leigh. 2003. "Migrant Remittances and (Under)Development in Mexico," *Critique of Anthropology* 23, no. 3: 305–36.

Cantú, Brisella, Fawad Shaiq, and Anjanette Urdanivia. 2007. "Migration and Local Development." In *Impacts of Border Enforcement on Mexican Migration: The View from Sending Communities*, ed. Wayne A. Cornelius and Jessa M. Lewis. La Jolla, CA: Center for Comparative Immigration Studies, University of California, San Diego.

Cervantes, Fernando, Horacio Santoyo, and Adolfo Álvarez. 2001. "Gestión de la calidad y desarrollo desigual en la cadena de lácteos en los Altos de Jalisco," *Problemas de Desarrollo* 32, no. 127 (October–December): 163–87.

Cohen, Jeffrey, Richard Jones, and Dennis Conway. 2005. "Why Remittances Shouldn't Be Blamed for Rural Underdevelopment in Mexico: A Collective Response to Leigh Binford," *Critique of Anthropology* 25, no. 1: 87–96.

Cornelius, Wayne A. 1990. *Labor Migration to the United States: Development Outcomes and Alternatives in Mexican Sending Communities.* La Jolla, CA: Center for U.S.-Mexican Studies, University of California, San Diego.

———. 2007. "Introduction: Does Border Enforcement Deter Unauthorized Immigration?" In *Impacts of Border Enforcement on Mexican Migration: The View from Sending Communities*, ed. Wayne A. Cornelius and Jessa M. Lewis. La Jolla, CA: Center for Comparative Immigration Studies, University of California, San Diego.

de Haas, Hein. 2005. "International Migration, Remittances and Development: Myths and Facts," *Third World Quarterly* 26, no. 8: 1269–84.

DeSipio, Louis. 2002. "Sending Money Home . . . For Now: Remittances and Immigrant Adaptation in the United States." In *Sending Money Home: Hispanic Remittances and Community Development*, ed. Rodolfo de la Garza and Brian Lowell. New York: Rowman and Littlefield.

Hernández Vega, Leticia. 2006. "¿De aquí p'a allá o de allá p'a acá? Clubes de migrantes jaliscienses: promoción estratégica de capital social y desarrollo," *Migraciones Internacionales* 3, no. 4 (July–December): 1–8.

INEGI (Instituto Nacional de Estadística, Geografía e Informática). n.d. "Superficie total por distrito de desarrollo rural y municipio según uso del suelo y vegetación (Período de observación de 2002 a 2005)." Mexico: Dirección General de Contabilidad Nacional y Estadísticas Económicas; Dirección General Adjunta de Estadísticas Económicas; Dirección Estadística del Sector Primario, INEGI.

Jones, Richard C. 1995. *Ambivalent Journey: U.S. Migration and Economic Mobility in North-Central Mexico*. Tucson, AZ: University of Arizona Press.

Macías, Juan Manuel. 1990. "Caracterización regional de los Altos de Jalisco." In *Política y región: Los Altos de Jalisco*, ed. Jorge Alonso and Juan García de Quevedo. Mexico: CIESAS.

Marcelli, Enrico A., and B. Lindsay Lowell. 2005. "Transnational Twist: Pecuniary Remittances and the Socioeconomic Integration of Authorized and Unauthorized Mexican Immigrants in Los Angeles County," *International Migration Review* 39, no. 1: 69–102.

Orozco, Manuel. 2000. "Latino Hometown Associations as Agents of Development in Latin America." IAD/TRPI Working Paper. Washington, DC: Inter-American Dialogue.

Rodríguez Gómez, Guadalupe. 1996. "Los Altos de Jalisco: las paradojas de la apertura comercial entre los ganaderos de leche." In *La sociedad mexicana frente al nuevo milenio. Vol. I. La inserción de la agricultura mexicana en la economía mundial*, ed. Sara Lara and Michelle Chauvet. Mexico: INAH, Casa abierta al tiempo, UNAM, and Plaza y Valdés.

———. 1998. "La apertura comercial y la actividad lechera en México." In *Los rejuegos del poder: globalización y cadenas agroindustriales de la leche en occidente*, ed. Guadalupe Rodríguez Gómez and Patricia Chombo. Mexico: CIESAS.

SAGARPA (Secretaría de Agricultura, Ganadería, Desarrollo Rural, Pesca y Alimentación). Various years. *Anuarios estadísticos de producción pecuaria*. Mexico: SAGARPA, Delegación Jalisco.

SIAP (Servicio de Información Agroalimentaria y Pesquera). Various years. *Estadísticas de Producción Agrícola y Pecuaria*. Mexico: SIAP.

Taylor, J. Edward. 1999. "The New Economics of Labour Migration and the Role of Remittances in the Migration Process," *International Migration* 37, no. 1: 63–88.

Taylor, J. Edward, and Jorge Mora. 2006. "Does Migration Reshape Expenditures in Rural Households? Evidence from Mexico." World Bank Policy Research Working Paper 3842. Washington, DC: World Bank.

A U.S.-based migrant returned for the town's annual festival, 2007.

6 Outsiders in Their Own Hometown? The Process of Dissimilation

JAVIER SERRANO, KIMBERLY DODGE, GENEVIEVE HERNÁNDEZ, AND ERICA VALENCIA

> I adore Mexico. But as much as I love Mexico, I love the United States, too. For me, my life is also there. So that is why I tell you I am divided in two countries. I feel they are mine, both of them.—María de la Luz López Cárdenas, 47-year-old Mexican-born U.S. citizen.

Migration's economic impacts on sending communities are clearly visible in improvements to infrastructure and housing. Migration's cultural impacts, meanwhile, generally find expression in changes in clothing styles, consumption patterns, and attitudes. The "culture of migration"—sometimes termed the "migrant syndrome" or "norteñización"—also involves such a deep embedding of migration in the life of a community that young people grow up expecting to leave (Massey 1999; Reichert 1981; Alarcón 1992). Most cultural approaches to the study of migration focus on the negatives, such as returned migrants' "recklessness" or lack of respect for local customs, along with surges in crime rates and drug use. In this chapter we seek to evaluate the kinds of cultural differences that arise between migrants and nonmigrants in terms of self-identity, attitudes, and behaviors, as well as the way that these perceived differences influence opinions and guide interactions within the town. In order to explain how these differences develop among groups that remain connected despite international migration, we situate our analysis in a discussion of the related processes of assimilation and dissimilation.

Dissimilation is the flip side of its better-known complement, assimilation. Both concepts are used to explain changes that emerge when people leave their home countries and adapt to host societies. For the purposes of our study, we view the process of dissimilation as encompassing the ways in which migrants become different, or dissimilar, from those who remain in the sending community. Though dissimilation has been variously described as the process by which one cultural group splits into two or by which later generations of immigrants become increasingly dissimilar from the first generation (Yinger 1981; Brubaker 2001), we find that dissimilation is also useful for understanding the cultural cleavages that develop between migrants and nonmigrants within sending communities (Jiménez and Fitzgerald 2007). Whereas assimilation shows how migrant populations become integrated into a host society by shedding characteristics of their home countries, dissimilation shows how migrants become different from nonmigrant members of their hometowns in their behaviors, beliefs, and self-perceptions.

In his discussion of assimilation, Milton Gordon identifies several variables that can be used to clarify how an immigrant's behaviors and beliefs change during the process of adapting to the host society. Of particular relevance to our study of Tlacuitapa are cultural or behavioral assimilation (acculturation), marital assimilation (amalgamation), attitude receptional assimilation, and behavior receptional assimilation. Acculturation occurs when immigrants change their cultural behaviors to those of the host country. Amalgamation happens when members of the immigrant group and the host society intermarry. Attitude receptional assimilation and behavior receptional assimilation occur when immigrants no longer experience discrimination or prejudice from members of the host society (Gordon 1964, 70–71).[1] These same variables are useful for understanding the process of dissimilation when using the home community as the reference.

In order to evaluate dissimilation within our research population, we compared the responses of migrants and nonmigrants to questions regarding church attendance, out-marriage, group identification, U.S. naturalization and dual nationality, cultural changes, plans for retirement, and political interests and participation. Our analysis focused on differences within migrant groups to determine if specific characteristics—gender,

---

1. The other variables of assimilation identified by Gordon are structural assimilation, identificational assimilation, and civic assimilation (Gordon 1964).

age, time spent in the United States, and place of residence—lead to a greater degree of dissimilation.

Our research was conducted primarily in Tlacuitapa during the annual fiesta in December 2007, which was attended by significant numbers of returned migrants. Using the contacts we established in the sending community, we then conducted additional research in two major receiving communities—Union City, California, and Oklahoma City—and did telephone interviews with migrants in other U.S. communities. Thus our data on migrant opinions reflect a migrant population that continues to be in contact with the home community, either through return visits or through sustained relationships with community members. Migrants who have little contact with people in their hometown are not included in our research population. Our research methodology constitutes a tough test of our hypothesis that significant differences develop between migrant and nonmigrant populations in terms of their attitudes and behaviors. The differences we uncovered within our sample of community members lead us to surmise that migrants who no longer maintain contact with people living in Mexico will represent even more extreme examples of dissimilation.

The growing differences between migrants and nonmigrants also reflect efforts to create "container societies" in both the sending and the receiving country that span the two nation-states. By restricting migrants' ability to move across international borders and limiting their social inclusion and participation, the United States and Mexico are contributing to the differences between migrants and nonmigrants (Waldinger and Fitzgerald 2004). Migrants cannot fully assimilate into the host society, nor can they dissimilate entirely from their home country. For this reason, even though adaptation to U.S. society is changing their beliefs and practices, many migrants seek to maintain ties with their home communities. However, we found that even migrants who are strongly connected to Tlacuitapa do diverge in many ways from community members who remain in Mexico.

Further, through their ties to their home communities, migrants transmit "social remittances"—ideas, behaviors, identities, and social capital obtained in the host country. These social remittances are a "local-level, migration driven form of cultural diffusion" (Levitt 1998, 926). Through migrants' transmission of social remittances, the process of dissimilation effects changes among nonmigrants. Our analysis shows that the attitudes, behaviors, and beliefs of migrants and nonmigrants from Tlacuitapa already reflect this process of dissimilation. As out-migration from the town continues, differences between migrants and nonmigrants will continue to grow and the town increasingly will be transformed by new ideas and practices.

OPINIONS, ATTITUDES, AND BEHAVIORS OF MIGRANTS AND NONMIGRANTS: DATA ANALYSIS

Community Ties

The migrants we interviewed expressed a strong desire to return to Tlacuitapa upon retirement.[2] Sixty-eight percent of migrants currently based in the United States indicated that they would like to retire in Tlacuitapa; another 8 percent expressed a desire to retire elsewhere in Mexico. Only 24 percent intended to retire in the United States. The strong desire to return to the home community reflects migrants' sentimental connection with their *patria chica*—literally, their "little homeland," usually the village or town of birth (Radcliffe and Westwood 1996). Despite the changes they experience as a result of migration to the United States, migrants remain determined to return to their home communities (Alarcón 1992, 315). Sara, a schoolteacher in Tlacuitapa, indicated that many people "have the idea that when they quit working in the United States, they are going to come back to Tlacuitapa. And they arrange their homes in Tlacuitapa so that they are comfortable when they return."

However, our observations in Tlacuitapa suggest that this desire is increasingly unlikely to be fulfilled. In January 2007, 181 houses stood empty in Tlacuitapa; 97 of these were owned by persons residing in the United States. While some of the migrants had made improvements to their homes, speaking to their desire to return to Tlacuitapa to reside permanently, many other houses owned by migrants were empty of furniture and other belongings. If we look at past occupancy data, our current findings suggest that returning to Tlacuitapa upon retirement is more a hope than a reality. In 1995 there were only 36 unoccupied houses; by 2005 the number had increased to 138. The 181 empty houses we counted

---

2. N = 225.

in 2007 suggest that retirement in Tlacuitapa has become less of an option because longer stays in the United States, legalization, and U.S.-born children are tying migrants ever more tightly to their host society. Beatriz recently returned to Tlacuitapa permanently after living in the United States for fifty years. Though she always intended to return to her mother's hometown, she feels she would not have been able to retire in Tlacuitapa if she had children:

> Well, there are many people my age, many of those of us who left as children for the United States, who are now also retired. And they come and stay here for three or four months, but then they have to return because they have children and grandchildren over there. It is not as easy for them as for me.

The desire to retire in Tlacuitapa is an example of the "myth of return." As Bolognani observes of Pakistanis living in Britain, "No matter how much it is cherished and thought about, the return rarely took place permanently when the person was alive" (Bolognani 2007, 64). Beatriz's experience demonstrates how a steadily held connection to the hometown helps migrants manage the challenges of transnational life: "When you are in the United States, even though you live well and have everything you want, you still have the nostalgia, always, of 'my town, my people, my culture, my self.'" Though retirement in Tlacuitapa may have become a less realistic choice for migrants, it remains a comforting, reassuring thought. Believing that return is possible helps migrants live in the host country while maintaining sentimental connections to the home country.

Political Participation

In the 2005 study that CCIS conducted in Tlacuitapa, Jalisco, and Las Ánimas, Zacatecas, the researchers asked members of the research communities about their intention to vote in the 2006 Mexican presidential election, and nearly 50 percent of the U.S.-based migrants responded that they did plan to vote in that election (Chiu and Gutiérrez 2007, 153). To evaluate the actual level of political participation among Tlacuitapeño migrants, we asked them in 2007 whether they had voted in 2006, if they had a voting credential, and whether they returned to Mexico to vote or cast their ballot by mail. Of U.S.-based migrants, 41 percent had a voting credential.[3] However, only 9 percent of migrants currently residing in the United States[4] indicated that they had voted in the 2006 elections, and only 1 of the 143 migrants currently residing in the United States said he had voted by mail.[5] This is consistent with low voter turnout among all Mexicans living in the United States: three million of the approximately ten million Mexicans in the United States were eligible to vote in the 2006 Mexican elections, but only 57,000, or 0.5 percent, tried to register, and fewer than 33,000 actually voted (IFE 2007).

Figure 6.1 Primary Political Interests of U.S.-based and Mexico-based Migrants from Tlacuitapa, 2007

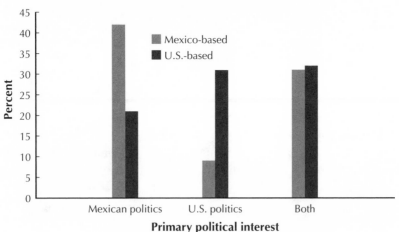

N = 378.

In order to clarify how migration modified political interests, we asked all adults with U.S. migration experience whether they were more interested in Mexican politics, U.S. politics, or both equally (see figure 6.1). Thirty-one percent of migrant respondents reported an equal interest in U.S. and Mexican politics. Nearly the same number (30 percent)

---

3. N = 143.
4. We used migrants' residence in January 2007 as a proxy for their residence at the time of the July 2006 elections.
5. N = 155.

reported that Mexican politics was their primary interest, and slightly fewer (23 percent) reported a primary interest in U.S. politics.[6] Migrants from Tlacuitapa appear to be primarily interested in the politics of the country where they reside, given that they are most likely to affect their daily lives. Forty-two percent of Mexico-based migrants express a primary interest in Mexican politics, compared to only 21 percent of U.S.-based migrants. On the other hand, 31 percent of U.S.-based migrants indicated a primary interest in U.S. politics, compared to only 9 percent of Mexico-based migrants.[7]

Logistic regressions of these data showed that certain characteristics increased the probability of an interest in U.S. politics. The dependent variable for table 6.1 is the place of primary political interest, where the categories are U.S. politics, Mexican politics, and the politics of both countries. The model demonstrates the probability of interest in U.S. and binational politics relative to an interest in Mexican politics, which is the category omitted from the regression.

Migrants who had spent more time in the United States and legal migrants were significantly more likely to indicate an interest in U.S. politics. Each additional year that a migrant spent in the United States increased the probability of a primary interest in U.S. politics by approximately 5 percent. Similarly, each additional year increased the probability of an interest in both U.S. and Mexican politics by approximately 4 percent. A legal migrant was more than twice as likely to report an interest in U.S. politics as in Mexican politics. The fact that legal migrants and migrants who have spent considerable time in the United States are less likely to show a primary interest in Mexican politics is indicative of their shifting priorities from issues in Mexico to those in the United States.

The shift in priorities is also evident in migrants' retirement plans; the place where a migrant intends to retire is significantly and positively correlated with his or her interest in the politics of that place. Migrants who stated that they intend to retire in the United States were more than seven times more likely to report an interest in U.S. politics than in Mexican politics.

---

6. N = 425. Seventeen percent responded that they had no interest in the politics of either country.

7. N = 378.

Table 6.1 Multinomial Logit Model for Political Interests of Migrants from Tlacuitapa (coefficients are reported as the odds ratio)

	Interest in U.S. Politics		Binational Interest in Politics	
	I	II	I	II
Years in U.S.	**1.047** **(.024)**	1.034 (.027)	**1.041** **(.024)**	**1.053** **(.026)**
Age	1.000 (.015)	1.010 (.021)	1.002 (.018)	1.008 (.022)
Male	1.377 (.638)	**4.863** **(2.989)**	**3.113** **(1.765)**	1.627 (.734)
Education	**0.944** **(.055)**	1.131 (.089)	**1.099** **(.072)**	0.965 (.064)
U.S. hourly wage	1.016 (.018)	1.016 (.022)	1.015 (.016)	1.001 (.025)
Legal migrant	**2.352** **(.919)**	**6.503** **(3.192)**	**6.874** **(3.028)**	1.859 (.753)
Discrimination in U.S.		0.491 (.264)		0.575 (.252)
Retirement in U.S.		**7.669** **(5.283)**		**3.747** **(2.381)**
Pseudo R^2	.1062	.1574	.1062	.1574
$p > \chi^2(.)$	.0001	.000	.0001	.000
N	222	211	222	211

Note: Reference category is interest in Mexican politics. Robust standard errors reported.
 90%, 95% 99% confidence levels.

Men from Tlacuitapa are more likely to express an interest in binational politics than in Mexican politics alone. This finding is contrary to other studies that suggest that men are more focused on the home country because they expect their stay in the United States to be temporary and want to maintain their privileged status relative to women in the home community (Jones-Correa 1998, 181). Our finding that men are more likely than women to be interested in both U.S. and binational politics is likely due to the fact that men tend to migrate before their wives and children and hence have spent more time in the United States.

Contrary to expectations, the perception of discrimination against Mexicans in the United States was not a significant predictor of migrant interest in either U.S. or binational politics. Thus our data suggest that racialization in the United States is not a factor driving interest in cross-border politics. This is consistent with Bloemraad's finding in Canada that racial marginalization is a weak predictor of transnational political activity (2004, 418). Although the notion that racialization forces migrants to deny their ties with their home country is prevalent in the transnationalism literature (Glick Schiller 1999, 109), this perceived discrimination is not a significant factor in determining political preferences among migrants from Tlacuitapa.

We also asked migrants about their participation in the marches in support of migrants that took place across the United States on May 1, 2006, to gauge their reaction to the U.S. political climate on the issue of immigration.[8] Forty-six percent of our U.S.-based respondents said they participated in the marches.[9] Since 80 percent of migrants believe there is substantial discrimination against Mexicans in the United States,[10] participation in these marches may have provided them with a concrete way to challenge this discrimination.

Religious Activities and Attitudes about Marriage

A recent national-level study by the Pew Hispanic Center (2007) found an increased level of secularization among immigrant Hispanics in the United States. Sixty-five percent of Latinos who now identify as secular previously followed a different religious tradition; 39 percent of them had been Catholic. To determine whether this trend held true for migrants from Tlacuitapa, which is located in the overwhelmingly Catholic and conservative region of Los Altos de Jalisco (Fábregas 1986), we asked respondents how many times they attended Mass in the last month. The median for both migrants and nonmigrants was four times, or once a week.[11] However, 17 percent of migrants reported that they did not attend church at all in the past month, compared to only 8 percent of nonmigrants.

---

8. These marches, organized by immigrant rights groups and attended mainly by Latinos, highlighted the economic power of immigrants and called for comprehensive immigration reform to put illegal immigrants on the path to citizenship (Stolberg 2006).

9. N = 225.

10. N = 395.

11. N = 854.

While migrants were slightly more likely not to attend church services at all, most migrants appear to maintain their religious practices.

A logistic regression on monthly attendance at Mass showed several significant predictors of religiosity among migrants (see table 6.2). As would be expected, older people attended Mass more often. Surprisingly, wealthier and more educated Tlacuitapeños attended Mass more frequently than did their counterparts. The most important finding for our interests is that migration experience was negatively correlated with religiosity, though the effect was minimal. Each additional year spent in the United States was associated with a 1 percent decrease in church attendance. These data do not allow us to determine if more secular Tlacuitapeños are more likely to migrate in the first place, but priests in Mexico have long blamed exposure to the United States for undermining migrants' faith (Fitzgerald 2005). These results are consistent with the hypothesis that the more time a migrant spends in the United States, the more likely he or she is to adopt behaviors or beliefs that differ from those that prevail among nonmigrants in the home community.

Table 6.2 Multinomial Logit Model for Migrants' Attendance at Mass, Tlacuitapa 2007

Years in U.S.	**−.008*** **(.003)**
Age	**.009***** **(.003)**
Male	−.346 (.059)
Education	**.004***** **(.01)**
Married	−.227 (.076)
Wealth	**.024**** **(.010)**
Pseudo R²	.0902
$p > \chi^2(.)$	.0001
N	675

Robust standard errors reported.
* 90%, ** 95% *** 99% confidence levels.

In order to measure the town's openness to outsiders, informants were asked whether they found it acceptable for a community member to marry someone not from either the town or Mexico. Nearly everyone— migrants and nonmigrants alike—believed this to be acceptable. When asked whether it was acceptable for a community member to marry someone from outside the town, 97 percent of nonmigrants and 96 percent of migrants responded that they would have no objection.[12] With regard to marrying someone from outside Mexico, the responses remained almost the same: 94 percent of nonmigrants and 93 percent of migrants are open to such an alliance.[13] Though we do not have precise figures on the number of community members that marry someone from outside of their hometown or country, we observed many cases of migrants who had married U.S. citizens, both Anglo and Latino.

This tolerance toward marrying outside of one's community or ethnic group is consistent with other studies of Mexican intermarriage. For example, in Ameca, Jalisco, marriage to someone from another ethnic or racial background may "confe[r] great prestige to the family of origin" and leads community members to adapt their rituals to those with other customs (Durand 1998, 219). Durand attributes the recent increase in such tolerance to a "fatalistic acceptance of the fact that . . . intermarried couples will probably remain outside the community and construct their lives in the United States" (1998, 220). This tolerance within migrant communities again reflects the new behaviors and beliefs—social remittances—that migrants develop in the United States and bring back to the home communities, where they change perspectives among nonmigrants as well.

Attitudes about Culture

Both migrants and nonmigrants expressed ambivalence about the effects of U.S. culture and U.S.-bound migration on Tlacuitapa and on Mexico as a whole. Forty-one percent of nonmigrants, but only 33 percent of migrants, said that foreign books, films, and music harm Mexican culture.[14] Women were more likely to report that U.S. influence is detrimental to Mexican culture. When asked if migration has hurt customs and way of

12. $N = 846; p = .191.$
13. $N = 848; p = .423.$
14. $N = 369; p = .00.$

life in Tlacuitapa, 49 percent of migrants and 58 percent of nonmigrants responded that migration has indeed been detrimental.[15] Nonmigrants were more likely to see exposure to the United States as harmful to their immediate community than to see it harming Mexico as a whole, suggesting that nonmigrants care more about the negative impacts they encounter daily in their community of high out-migration than about abstract notions of culture on the national level. Interestingly, a 2006 poll found that a majority of Mexicans perceive U.S. cultural influences to have a negative impact on Mexico (Zogby and Rubio 2006, 15).

Identity

Both migrants and nonmigrants say they identify strongly with people from their hometown. Eighty-seven percent of nonmigrants and 88 percent of migrants identified strongly with being Tlacuitapeño (see figure 6.2),[16] underscoring the local solidarity of both groups. The majority of nonmigrants (79 percent) and migrants (86 percent) also identified strongly with people from Jalisco.[17] Similarly, when asked about their identification as Mexicans, 90 percent of migrants and 87 percent of nonmigrants identified highly as Mexican.[18] In short, the majority of nonmigrants and migrants identify at the local level as Tlacuitapeños, at the state level as Jaliscienses, and at the national level as Mexicans.

Beyond these identifications, however, there are key differences between migrants and nonmigrants. Changing attitudes toward affiliations are noticeable when we consider how migrants and nonmigrants perceive themselves in terms of a Latin American identity. When asked if they strongly identified as Latin American, 51 percent of migrants, but only 28 percent of nonmigrants, said they did identify strongly with that group.[19] When considering Latino identity, the gap is even larger: 66 percent of migrants identify as Latino, compared to only 31 percent of nonmigrants.[20] Given that Latino is a U.S. usage, it is remarkable that even a third of nonmigrants said they strongly identified with Latinos, offering

15. N = 822; p = .008.
16. N = 842; p = .461.
17. N = 843; p = .004.
18. N = 844; p = .109.
19. N = 811; p = .000.
20. N = 786; p = .000.

further evidence that attitudes formed by migrants in the United States are spreading into their home communities in Mexico.

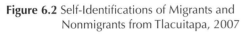

Figure 6.2 Self-Identifications of Migrants and Nonmigrants from Tlacuitapa, 2007

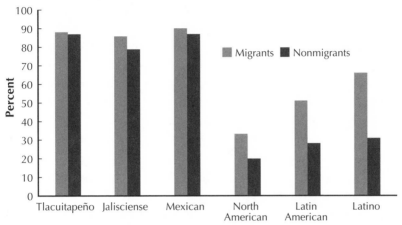

N = 781–842.

Similarly, a 2006 CCIS study in Tunkás, Yucatán, showed that a large percentage of Tunkaseño migrants began to identify as Latin American after living in the United States (Cornelius, Fitzgerald, and Lewin Fischer 2007, 14). When migrants first arrive, they fall into the category of Latin American immigrant, which includes individuals from many countries. This "reclassification" may well be leading Mexican immigrants as a whole to identify not only as Mexican but also as Latin American and Latino—part of a process of re-racialization that De Genova (2005, 199) used in his study of Mexicans in Chicago to describe how U.S. society handles and labels this group of individuals as well as the ways in which the labeled groups use the title to define themselves.

Migrants are also more likely than nonmigrants to identify as North American, though individuals who identify as such form a minority in both groups. Thirty-three percent of migrants, compared to 21 percent of nonmigrants, identified as North American.[21] These data contrast with those

---

21. N = 783; p = .000.

from a 2006 study on attitudes in Mexico, which found that 43 percent of Mexican respondents felt Mexico was more a part of North America than of Latin America (Zogby and Rubio 2006, 18). Mexicans as a whole are more likely than individuals in Tlacuitapa to identify as North American. This difference between Tlacuitapa and the rest of Mexico may stem from their differential contact with *"norteamericanos,"* a term generally applied to U.S. Anglos rather than to people from the North American continent more generally (which also includes both Canadians and Mexicans). The direct contact that many Tlacuitapeños have with *norteamericanos* in the United States may lead them to identify less with that group, given that it overlays the distinction between immigrants and natives.

Interestingly, though most migrants are reluctant to self-identify as North American, they do identify with the U.S. states and towns in which they reside. When migrants were asked whether they identified with the U.S. state where they currently reside, 57 percent responded that they identified strongly with the people of that state.[22] When asked about their identification with the town or city in which they reside, the percentage of migrants who so identify rises to 68 percent.[23] One possible explanation for this high rate of identification with the U.S. states and cities where migrants reside relates to the connections established through social networks of migration. In many cases these social networks provide the resources that facilitate the transition from one country to another. Many migrants from Tlacuitapa migrate to Union City, California, and Oklahoma City, where migrants know each other by name, and brothers and sisters, cousins, aunts and uncles, and in-laws all live within a three-block radius of each other. A sense of community is created that makes the migrants feel welcome and established. The large numbers of Tlacuitapeños in these cities means they can identify with the local receiving community while avoiding the negative stigma attached to identifying with the United States as a whole, which to some would imply a rejection of Mexico.

Dual Nationality and Naturalization

Large majorities of both migrants and nonmigrants—93 and 86 percent, respectively—favor the Mexican law permitting dual nationality (9

---

22. N = 378.
23. N = 381.

percent of migrants said they held dual nationality).[24] Yet nonmigrants are twice as likely as migrants to oppose dual nationality. When asked about their attitudes toward those who become naturalized U.S. citizens, 88 percent of migrants and 80 percent of nonmigrants held a positive view (see figure 6.3). Seven percent of migrants held a negative view of those who became U.S. citizens, compared to 14 percent of nonmigrants.[25] Though nonmigrants were twice as likely as migrants to hold a negative view on this point, this perception is clearly a minority view in both groups. The relative openness to dual nationality and naturalization may relate to Tlacuitapa's long experience with migration to the United States and its deeply rooted culture of out-migration.

Figure 6.3 Migrant and Nonmigrant Attitudes toward Naturalization

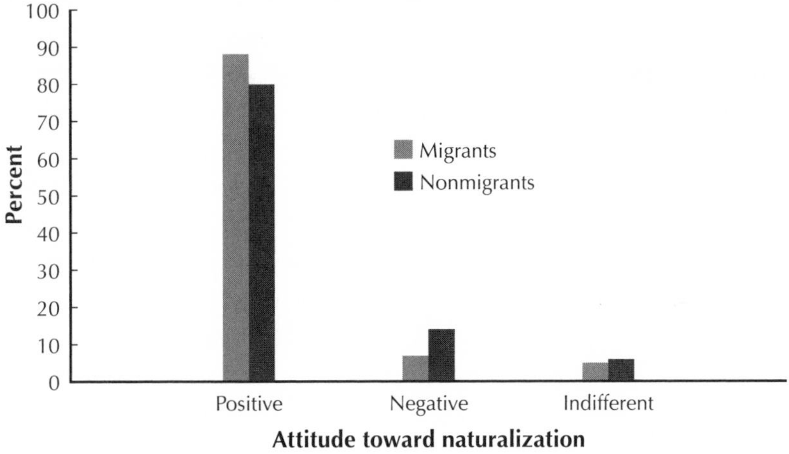

$N = 843; p = .004.$

Dissimilation and Norteño Identity

Our observations in Tlacuitapa indicated that migrants are often labeled *"norteños"* (northerners) when they return to their home community. The use of this label differentiates migrants from nonmigrants and can cause the former to be viewed as outsiders in their own communities, where their distinct physical and ideological characteristics are clearly evident.

---

24. $N = 798; p = .001.$
25. $N = 843; p = .004.$

Migrants often carry U.S. dollars, adopt different styles of dress, and project more "liberal" attitudes. For example, an elementary schoolteacher in Tlacuitapa claims that people have adopted "liberal lifestyles," which include vices such as drug usage and *cholismo*. Angélica, who teaches catechism in Tlacuitapa, mentioned that migrants no longer practice their religion once they leave the community. This perception of migrants as socially liberal creates a division within the community that can lead to the migrants' social exclusion.

José Arturo, an experienced migrant currently living in the United States, expressed a common opinion of norteños even among many people with migration experience: "When they return, they feel they are better than everyone else, better than the ones who stayed." His comment implies an underlying negative sentiment held mutually by nonmigrants and norteños. The process of dissimilation creates noticeable differences that can strain relationships. José Arturo recalls a childhood friend who went to the United States before he did. When the friend returned, José Arturo thought he was very *presumido* (conceited and arrogant), which caused the two former friends to go their separate ways.

It is to be expected that the distinctions we found between migrants and nonmigrants in Tlacuitapa will be even more visible in the next generation—that is, between the migrants' U.S.-born children and people who remained in the home community. Marily, a 23-year-old U.S.-born resident of Tlacuitapa, said that she was shunned when she first arrived in the town ten years ago, because of her inability to speak Spanish. Although many members of the second generation may identify as Mexican, when they return to their parents' hometown for the annual fiesta, they soon realize that they are more American than they thought. Through the process of dissimilation, many children of migrants find it hard to identify with any one culture—either that of their parents' hometown or that of the United States. Primitivo, a 20-year-old U.S. citizen by birth, said he feels "neither fully Mexican nor fully American." When Marily was asked how she identifies, she responded:

> You don't find the answer for either of the two questions, if
> you are Mexican or American. As you think about it, and as
> you try to find an answer, you realize there is none. I think
> that this question will continue to puzzle us for the rest of
> our lives. I will never find the answer because there will

> always be the question, "Who are you?" As much as I try to
> answer this question, I will never find the answer because
> we are part American and Mexican. . . . Our blood tells us
> one thing, and our nationality another.

Marily and Primitivo's responses demonstrate their colliding ethnic and national identities. The second generation often finds itself "caught between two worlds," struggling to define who they are and where they fit in, since they are both American and Mexican (Yinger 1981, 254). The salience of their identities often changes depending on location. As Marily explained: "When I am in the United States, I am American, but when I am here, I am Mexican." This fluidity of identity—and its limitations when tensions develop between migrants and nonmigrants—demonstrates the challenges that Tlacuitapeños and their children face in defining themselves in ways that are recognized by their peers.

CONCLUSION

Dissimilation is a subtle process that is gradually changing several domains of social life in Tlacuitapa. The culture of migration has permeated the community, and migration to the United States continues to increase. The cultural effects of migration are apparent in the ideas, attitudes, and behaviors of both migrants and nonmigrants due to the strong ties that many migrants maintain with their home community and transmit to it through social remittances. There are small degrees of difference in some social domains, and large degrees of difference in others. Specifically, we note considerable differences in migrants' political interests and their notions of identity. Migrants residing primarily in the United States tended to express a primary interest in U.S. politics or binational politics. These preferences are especially prevalent among legal migrants and migrants who have spent more time in the United States. Migrants are more likely to identify with the larger Latino/Latin American community. Further, we observe a less drastic but still significant decline in religiosity among migrants.

As our study shows, dissimilation is a gradual process that takes place by degrees across multiple social domains. Because of migrants' cross-border ties to their sending communities, these changes may be less evident when their hometowns have also been changed by new ideas and behaviors. Studying dissimilation within a community like Tlacuitapa, where migration has continued over many decades, uncovers both the changes that migrants undergo as individuals and the ways in which their social remittances alter their home communities. As out-migration to the United States continues, we expect that migrants' social remittances will make it more difficult to distinguish changes in behaviors, attitudes, and culture within sending communities. Because dissimilation is gradual, as the culture of migration continues to embed itself in sending communities like Tlacuitapa, cultural differences among migrants and nonmigrants may also gradually diminish.

References

Alarcón, Rafael. 1992. "*Norteñización*: Self-Perpetuating Migration from a Mexican Town." In *U.S.-Mexico Relations: Labor Market Interdependence*, ed. Jorge A. Bustamante, Clark W. Reynolds, and Raúl A. Hinojosa Ojeda. Stanford, CA: Stanford University Press.

Bloemraad, Irene. 2004. "Who Claims Dual Citizenship? The Limits of Postnationalism, the Possibilities of Transnationalism, and the Persistence of Traditional Citizenship," *International Migration Review* 38: 389–426.

Bolognani, Marta. 2007. "The Myth of Return: Dismissal, Survival or Revival? A Bradford Example of Transnationalism as a Political Instrument," *Journal of Ethnic and Migration Studies* 33: 59–76.

Brubaker, Rogers. 2001. "The Return of Assimilation? Changing Perspectives on Immigration and Its Sequels in France, Germany, and the United States," *Ethnic and Racial Studies* 24: 531–48.

Chiu, William, and Marisol Raquel Gutiérrez. 2007. "Migration and Political Involvement." In *Impacts of Border Enforcement on Mexican Migration: The View from Sending Communities*, ed. Wayne A. Cornelius and Jessa M. Lewis. La Jolla, CA: Center for Comparative Immigration Studies, University of California, San Diego.

Cornelius, Wayne A., David Fitzgerald, and Pedro Lewin Fischer, eds. 2007. *Mayan Journeys: The New Migration from Yucatán to the United States*. La Jolla, CA: Center for Comparative Immigration Studies, University of California, San Diego.

De Genova, Nicholas. 2005. *Working the Boundaries: Race, Space, and "Illegality" in Mexican Chicago*. Durham, NC: Duke University Press.

Durand, Jorge. 1998. "Migration and Integration: Intermarriages among Mexicans and Non-Mexicans in the United States." In *Crossings: Mexican Immigration in Interdisciplinary Perspectives*, ed. Marcelo M. Suárez-Orozco. Cambridge, MA: Harvard University Press.

Fábregas, Andrés. 1986. *La formación histórica de una región: Los Altos de Jalisco*. México, DF: Centro de Investigaciones y Estudios Superiores en Antropología Social.

Fitzgerald, David. 2005. "A Nation of Emigrants? Statecraft, Church-Building, and Nationalism in Mexican Migrant Source Communities." PhD dissertation, University of California, Los Angeles.

Glick Schiller, Nina. 1999. "Transmigrants and Nation-States: Something Old and Something New in the U.S. Immigrant Experience." In *The Handbook of International Migration: The American Experience*, ed. Charles Hirschman, Philip Kasinitz, and Josh DeWind. New York: Russell Sage Foundation.

Gordon, Milton M. 1964. *Assimilation in American Life*. New York: Oxford University Press.

IFE (Instituto Federal Electoral). 2007. "Voto de los mexicanos residentes en el extranjero: elecciones federales 2006." Mexico: IFE.

Jiménez, Tomás R., and David Fitzgerald. 2007. "Mexican Assimilation: A Temporal and Spatial Reorientation," *Du Bois Review* 4, no. 2: 337–54.

Jones-Correa, Michael. 1998. *Between Two Nations: The Political Predicament of Latinos in New York City*. Ithaca, NY: Cornell University Press.

Levitt, Peggy. 1998. "Social Remittances: Migration Driven, Local-Level Forms of Cultural Diffusion," *International Migration Review* 32: 926–48.

Massey, Douglas S. 1999. "Why Does Immigration Occur? A Theoretical Synthesis." In *The Handbook of International Migration: The American Experience*, ed. Charles Hirschman, Philip Kasinitz, and Josh DeWind. New York: Russell Sage Foundation.

Pew Hispanic Center. 2007. "Changing Faiths: Latinos and the Transformation of American Religion." http://pewhispanic.org/files/reports/75.pdf.

Radcliffe, Sarah, and Sallie Westwood. 1996. *Remaking the Nation: Place, Identity and Politics in Latin America*. London: Routledge.

Reichert, Joshua. 1981. "The Migrant Syndrome: Seasonal U.S. Wage Labor and Rural Development in Central Mexico," *Human Organization* 40: 56–66.

Stolberg, Sheryl Gay. 2006. "After Immigration Protests, Goal Is Still Elusive," *New York Times*, May 3.

Waldinger, Roger, and David Fitzgerald. 2004. "Transnationalism in Question," *American Journal of Sociology* 109: 1177–94.

Yinger, J. Milton. 1981. "Toward a Theory of Assimilation and Dissimilation," *Ethnic and Racial Studies* 4: 249–64.

Zogby, John, and Luis Rubio. 2006. "How We See Each Other." The CIDAC-Zogby International Survey of Attitudes in Mexico and the United States of America, March 19.

The proprietor of a corner store sheds a tear for her brother, an undocumented migrant living in the United States for several years, who can no longer visit her due to tighter border enforcement. "He's a prisoner in the United States," she says.

7 Families in Transition: Migration and Gender Dynamics in Sending and Receiving Communities

LEAH MUSE-ORLINOFF, JESSICA CÓRDOVA, LOURDES DEL CARMEN ANGULO, MOHAN KANUNGO, AND RUTH RODRÍGUEZ

When you arrive in Tlacuitapa for the winter fiestas, you may not immediately understand why the town is sometimes called *el pueblo sin hombres* (the town without men). The plaza, the cantinas, and the cockfighting arena are full of recently returned *norteños*—migrant men and women who spent months working in the United States and saving for this holiday. However, as the fiestas come to a close, homes are boarded up and the plaza empties. The few men who remain are mostly older and idle, and the women whose husbands have migrated to the United States once again assume their normal routine of being both mother and father to their children.

For men whose wives and children live in Tlacuitapa, the visits home are tinged with the bittersweet knowledge that another long separation is imminent. For unmarried young women, it is an opportunity to catch the eye of one of the unmarried norteño men, some of whom are openly looking for a wife. Finally, the Tlacuitapeño men and women who have not migrated observe and react to the ways in which migration is changing their family and friends, and they wait with both impatience and dread for the fiestas to end and the migrants to depart.

This chapter explores how migration perpetuates and challenges gender roles and how men and women live the migration experience differently. We look at both the individual and the family, and consider how men and women experience the migration process across its multiple facets—the decision to leave, courtship and marriage, and incorporation into the labor force. In this study, gender is not merely one more dichotomous variable (is the migrant a man?), an approach that is consistent with calls from scholars in the gender and migration fields to utilize a more comprehensive and sophisticated approach to studying how gender affects migration and how migration affects gender roles (see, for example, Donato et al. 2006).

CONCEPTUALIZING GENDER IN MIGRATION STUDIES

Gender both influences and is shaped by migration patterns (Hondagneu-Sotelo 1994: 2).[1] Migration is a dynamic process of geographical and cultural upheaval and redefinition, and it challenges assumptions about men's and women's roles in the family and community. Gender affects who migrates, how they migrate, and what happens once they arrive in the receiving community. Gender also shapes experiences of the non-migrant members of the community who are left behind by family and friends.

Early studies of gender and migration focused primarily on the experiences of women, neglecting to consider how migration affects gender for men (Donato et al. 2006; Hondagneu-Sotelo 1994, 2003; Kanaiaupuni 2000). This chapter addresses that shortcoming by including the experiences of both male and female migrants and analyzing how migration differs for men and women.

Much of the migration literature has been similarly one sided, focusing on migrants in destination communities and ignoring migration's impacts on communities of origin.[2] International migrants remain important to the development and maintenance of their communities of origin through their remittances, the social mores and norms they bring with

---

1. It is important to distinguish between gender and sex when considering how roles within the family change as a result of migration. Whereas sex refers to the biological or physical differences between men and women, gender refers to the values, expectations, and roles we ascribe to particular sexes. Gender is neither fixed nor innate; rather, it is fluid and evolves depending on an individual's economic, social, and political contexts (González-López 2005; Donato et al. 2006). For our analysis, gender encompasses both men's and women's decision making, behavior, identity, expectations, and values. Gender roles and expectations are reinforced in the micro (individual/family), meso (community), and macro (state) levels (Oishi 2002: 8). Individual relationships, familial expectations, community institutions, and state policies all play a role in shaping gender roles, especially when it comes to migration (Kanaiaupuni 2000: 1312).

2. For a focus on sending communities, see Cornelius and Lewis 2007.

them when they return, or their notable absence in the community (see, for example, Levitt 2001; Smith 2006; Hirsch 2003). For this reason, we also examine gender dynamics in both the sending and receiving communities.

METHODOLOGY

Our analyses are based on data collected in Tlacuitapa and San Antonio de la Garza in 2007 using survey instruments and semi-structured interviews.[3] Quantitative studies of U.S.-based Mexican immigrants and their sending communities traditionally utilize a head-of-household methodology (see, for example, Cornelius and Lewis 2007; Cornelius, Fitzgerald, and Lewin Fischer 2007). We chose instead to employ a more inclusive sample. Expanding the research scope to include all adults nets a broader range of experiences and attitudes, especially across generational or age groups.

A more inclusive sampling approach also counteracts the ways in which traditional head-of-household research has largely ignored the experiences of women or included inaccurate descriptions provided by male heads of household. Because men are usually considered the de facto household head, regardless of who is the main earner or decision maker, a head-of-household research design fails to capture women's experiences and insights.

THE GENDERED LANDSCAPE OF TLACUITAPA

Spaces have gender-specific identities, and men and women experience public spaces differently. Jennifer Hirsch argues that the "street" and the "home" carry connotations, respectively, of masculinity and femininity in Mexico. Men are outdoors because they have to support the household, while women are expected to remain in the home and focus on cooking, cleaning, and family caretaking (Hirsch 2003: 99–100). This sociohistorical division of space is very evident in Tlacuitapa.

For example, although Tlacuitapa's cantinas do not explicitly exclude women, it is clear that women are not welcome in these exclusively masculine spaces. One local woman mentioned that she had never set foot

---

3. This analysis draws on data from 861 respondents from Tlacuitapa and San Antonio de la Garza—407 migrants and 454 nonmigrants.

inside a local bar and did not know what went on at the cantinas. Across the plaza, the owners of the cockfighting arena encourage women to attend the fights by waiving the entrance fee. Yet women's presence there does not mean that this is a place of gender egalitarianism; indeed, the *palenque* is a theater of hypermasculinity, focused as it is on the masculine ideals of strength and competition.

The local beauty contest paints a patriarchal relationship connecting ideals of masculinity and femininity with migration. In their dress and makeup, the contest participants portray a desirable woman as delicate and well cared for. This also implies a certain social class and youthfulness, a woman whose body has not been worn down by fieldwork or childbearing.[4] The contestants ride on the late-model trucks favored by prosperous male migrants, the ultimate symbol of male migrant success.

Table 7.1 Masculinity Indices for Tlacuitapa, San Antonio de la Garza, Unión de San Antonio, and Jalisco

Locality	Masculinity Index, Ages 15–65	Masculinity Index, All Ages
Tlacuitapa (population 1,264)	70.7	74.5
San Antonio de la Garza (population 506)	63.3	86.4
Unión de San Antonio (population 15,484)	77.7	87.0
Jalisco (population 6,752,113)	90.8	94.4

Source: INEGI 2005.

In addition to the gendered nature of public space in Tlacuitapa, the city as a whole reflects the changes that migration has brought to gender dynamics. Because many men leave at a relatively young age, there are many more women than men in the town. Of the interviewees whose data are included in our analysis, 459 are female and 396 are male.[5] These

4. An additional beauty queen was crowned in 2007: Miss Tlacuitapa de la Tercera Edad de USA (an older migrant woman), further illustrating the ties between migration and gender.
5. The average age for respondents was 36 years, and 67 percent of respondents are or have been married.

demographics are consistent with Tlacuitapa's long history as a migrant-sending community. Table 7.1 presents the masculinity indices (the number of men per 100 women) for Tlacuitapa, San Antonio de la Garza, the *municipio* of Unión de San Antonio (which encompasses both towns), and the state of Jalisco. According to these indices, for every 100 women between the ages of 15 and 65 in Tlacuitapa, there are only 71 men in the same age range; the number is even lower in San Antonio de la Garza.

GENDERED MIGRATION STRATEGIES: BREADWINNERS AND TIED MOVERS

Migration creates a power imbalance between men and women within households in both the sending and receiving communities. Much of the imbalance stems from men's greater relative autonomy in terms of the migration decision. Much of the literature asserts that men migrate for financial or labor reasons, while women migrate for family reunification. For instance, Mincer (2003) posits women as "tied movers," "secondary migrants," and "associational migrants." Other scholars have expanded on this view or retooled the definition of tied movers to avoid depicting women as passive actors in the migration process (Blau and Kahn 2006; Cerrutti and Massey 2001; Pedraza 1991; Curran and Rivero-Fuentes 2003). This chapter utilizes the "tied movers" theory as expanded by Blau and Kahn (2006), which allows for autonomous decision making among women but recognizes that women's decisions are constrained by gendered social norms about the migration process.

The concept of social acceptability also informs much of the literature on gender and migration. For example, Oishi's (2002) analysis indicates that social attitudes about female migrants have a greater impact than economic need on women's migratory choices.[6] Confirming that social acceptability is a major consideration in women's decisions to migrate, Kanaiaupuni (2000) documents how women are less likely to migrate for employment opportunities if they will be considered less virtuous as a result.

Pierrette Hondagneu-Sotelo (1994) describes various patterns of family migration, two of which apply to the Tlacuitapa case: family stage

---

6. In Bangladesh, for example, independent women migrants are perceived as "loose" and unmarriageable. By contrast, women in the Philippines are encouraged by the state to go abroad (Oishi 2002).

migration and individual migration. Family stage migration occurs when one or two family members migrate first and the rest of the family follows later. Traditionally, males are the first to migrate. After spending some time in the United States, unmarried male migrants commonly return to Tlacuitapa to look for a spouse. Others marry first and then migrate. In both types of family stage migration, male migrants express the hope that their wives and children will eventually join them in the United States. Family-stage-migration strategies reflect men's ability to act autonomously when deciding to migrate, and they underscore their gendered role as family "provider." Further, family-stage-migration patterns reinforce the belief that caring for children and older relatives is women's work. This is consistent with the research of Hirsch (2003: 187) and Kanaiaupuni (2000), who found that women are less likely to migrate during their reproductive years, while men, especially married men, are more likely to migrate at a young age.

Family stage migration is the most common strategy among Tlacuitapeños, demonstrating that men and women from Tlacuitapa migrate for different reasons. Men are more likely to cite better salaries and labor opportunities as their primary motivation for migration (35.7 percent of men, versus only 8.5 percent of women). Women, on the other hand, most frequently cite family reunification as their reason for migrating. The typical pattern among Tlacuitapa migrants is as follows: A man leaves to work in the United States for a number of years and returns at some point (typically during the town's fiestas in December and January) to find a wife. After the couple has lived apart for some time while the husband obtains legal entry papers for the wife or saves enough money to pay a people-smuggler,[7] the wife joins her husband in the United States.

This migration pattern means that women are far more likely than male migrants to be married at the time of their first migration: 52 percent of first-time female migrants were married, compared to only 15 percent of first-time male migrants. Another indication that men migrate first is

---

7. Because men typically migrate first, they often must borrow money from friends and family members to cover the cost of migrating (Hondagneu-Sotelo 1994). Women migrants generally have husbands who are financially stable enough to have secured visas or green cards for their wives. Therefore, women are less likely to borrow money to finance their trip.

the age at first migration: 32.1 years for women, 21.1 for men.[8] Finally, men report spending more time in the United States (an average of eight years, versus three years for women).

Several women told us that marriage was the factor that prompted them to contemplate migrating. When asked about her migration plans before marriage, María responded that she had none: "I never would have left." Yet as soon as she married, María migrated to be with her husband. Like many other female migrants, María began working in the United States; she obtained a childcare license and began earning an income. Though she earned considerably less than her husband, this was not a concern because her main focus continued to be maintaining the family unit. Although she may have been reluctant to leave Mexico, María considered preserving her family's unity worth the sacrifice.

Whereas men are encouraged to migrate individually, women are essentially forbidden from doing so. María Guadalupe recounted the limited migration opportunities for women, noting that many fathers who could have obtained legal entry documents for their daughters did not do so because they saw no need for women to migrate:

> Before, parents wouldn't allow their daughters to go to the United States. But now, if a girl wants to go and she can stay with relatives who are already there, her parents will help her. But before, no. It didn't occur to them that tomorrow or the next day a woman might want to go to the United States. They would say, "why do they need to go north?" And now these young women are anxious to go. But how?—since their fathers never bothered about papers for them, just because they were girls.

Migration, especially undocumented or solo migration, is considered more perilous for women. Women are three times more likely than men to die of exposure when crossing through the desert (Rubio-Goldsmith et al. 2006). Curran and Rivero-Fuentes (2003) found that would-be migrant women from rural Mexico also depend more heavily on family ties and networks, which decreases the likelihood of independent migration. Data from Tlacuitapa are consistent with these findings; in Tlacuitapa,

---

8. This average is based only on respondents who migrated after the age of 15.

women's migration is almost universally contingent on social and family networks and prior migration by men. In other words, men have more autonomy than women to choose when, with whom, and under what conditions they migrate.

AMOR A LARGA DISTANCIA: LONG-DISTANCE LOVE

The ways in which Tlacuitapeños develop and maintain relationships reflect how migration affects the balance of power between men and women. From courtship to transnational marriages, migration shapes men's and women's expectations of and for the opposite gender.

Dando la vuelta is a courting ritual of long standing in Mexico. In it, small groups of single women walk counterclockwise around the center of the town plaza while unmarried men stand on the outside. When a man is attracted to one of the women, he showers her with confetti and asks if he can walk with her. If the attraction is mutual, the woman accepts and the two walk around the plaza for the rest of the evening. This formalized encounter played a significant role for older generations, when courting out of public view was considered highly inappropriate. Today, however, young couples enjoy substantially more freedom, even though strong expectations about proper behavior toward the opposite sex remain in place.

Courting is not the only aspect of dating to have changed; women now enjoy considerable power to initiate relationships, a change seen throughout Mexico. Hirsch (2003), Chant (1994), Hondagneu-Sotelo (1994), and Arias and Mummert (1987) find that women are experiencing more freedom in their relationships with men. Moreover, marriages in Mexico are becoming more egalitarian and companionate as a result of increased education, greater female incorporation into the workforce, and social remittances brought by returning migrants (Levitt 2001). Tlacuitapeños have noticed the difference. A 68-year-old man talked about the changes he has seen:

> Yes, things have changed a lot. Now women are the ones in control in everything. . . . They do what they want . . . they go out when they want. It used to be that the man was "macho." Whatever the man said, but not anymore.

He went on to add that women are adopting behaviors that were previously associated with men. This is evident not only among married couples but also among young people more generally:

> When I was a young boy, I went to see my girlfriend and we would talk through a crack in the wall. Now the girls go to see the guy at his house; they go look for him wherever they want.

This respondent also pointed out that migration changes men's behavior as well: "The men are changed, less macho. They do whatever the woman orders, what the woman says and everything." These observations reflect a common perception in Tlacuitapa that women now have more agency to initiate relationships. And because migration is a principal mechanism for upward mobility in Tlacuitapa, many women choose to begin relationships with migrant men.

Indeed, for both men and women looking for a spouse, a potential partner's migration experience or willingness to migrate is a major consideration. Material possessions such as cars and clothes are signs of economic success that count to one's advantage. When asked how living in the United States affects his options for dating in Tlacuitapa, Chava, a young man born in Tlacuitapa and now living in the United States, commented:

> If a fellow is coming from the United States, it's easier. He has a truck, and women say, "wow, he's doing well for himself." It's easier to start a relationship. But if you're from here, well, they already know how you live.

Chava's statement illustrates how economic success is tied to men's sense of masculinity. This is particularly the case for migrant men (see also Hondagneu-Sotelo 1994), who are eager to show off their pickup trucks and ATVs.[9]

---

9. While these displays of wealth have the potential to attract suitors and impress local residents, some Tlacuitapeños are dubious of such flaunting of economic status. For example, an older male migrant commented on the late-model trucks seen about town during the fiesta, remarking that the trucks' owners "can't fool him," because he knows these vehicles were bought mostly on credit.

Some male migrants prefer to date women from Tlacuitapa and come to the annual fiestas specifically to find a wife, a search that is facilitated by the many dances, weddings, and *quinceañeras* (girls' 15-year birthday celebrations) that enable people to encounter members of the opposite sex.[10] Several people told us that they met their spouses during the fiestas; María del Rosario met her husband at the recent fiestas and was planning to migrate to join him in the United States as soon as she received her papers. Jesús, a U.S.-based migrant, had been married but was now divorced. He admitted to being in Tlacuitapa during the winter fiestas in no small part to find a girlfriend or wife. Other respondents told stories of couples in Tlacuitapa who split up during the fiestas to see if either could land a U.S.-based spouse.[11]

Such "spouse shopping" in Tlacuitapa reflects a preference for women willing to play a gendered role as "traditional" homemaker and caretaker, a preference clearly expressed in a male migrant's exhortation to the women in our research team not to "Americanize" the town's women. An impromptu focus group of four migrant men also elicited the men's partiality for women born and raised in Tlacuitapa and their feeling that American women are "too liberated" and less inclined to accept a stay-at-home role.[12]

Yet spouse shopping is a two-way process. A man must take care to represent himself to the available women as a good match. Marriage to a male migrant can be a woman's ticket to upward mobility (Reichert 1982; Hirsch 2003), either through the remittances the man sends home or through the woman's own migration and incorporation into the U.S. workforce. While such upward mobility can lead to greater female empowerment and more egalitarian marriages, the fact that a woman's socioeconomic status is generally contingent on a male's migration decision

10. Many Tlacuitapeños said that the winter fiestas are for single people, while summer is the time for families to return.
11. If neither one meets a new partner, they get back together after the fiestas.
12. The inverse of the migrant men's preference for Mexican women is the disapproval among Mexican women and their families of certain practices that U.S.-raised men bring to Tlacuitapa. For instance, Pedro, a young man born and raised in the United States, came to Tlacuitapa for the fiestas and initiated a friendship with a young woman there. One night, Pedro got drunk and was very rambunctious. The girl's father disapproved of Pedro's *falta de respeto* (disrespect) for his daughter and forbade Pedro to talk to her, highlighting the fact that cultural norms are to be preserved by females and males alike even after migration.

indicates that women continue to experience less autonomy than men in Tlacuitapa.

Once a couple has decided to marry, the U.S.-based migrant must save enough money to pay for a wedding and to bring his wife to the United States. Men borrow from family members for a wedding or hold joint ceremonies with friends or relatives to share costs. Most people marry in Tlacuitapa because it is more economical and practical than a U.S. wedding. Weddings often take place during the winter fiestas, when families are together. It is also easier to procure a visa or green card for a spouse if the couple marries in Tlacuitapa. However, obtaining documents is a complicated process, and many years may pass before a couple is able to reunite in the United States.

Because of family stage migration, prolonged separations are common in Tlacuitapa. Families sometimes spend a decade or more apart while the husband pursues legal residency for his wife and Mexico-born children.[13] Javier, a migrant working in Oklahoma, has been trying for nine years to obtain documents for his wife and daughter to join him there.

Such long separations take their toll on couples and families, despite efforts to maintain close contact. Javier commented that he telephones his wife constantly, yet frequent communication does not cure loneliness. Javier said he often sits alone in his apartment drinking on weekends, because socializing with others makes him miss his wife.

Women whose husbands are living in the United States have additional concerns. Alejandra discussed the difficulty of parenting her four children on her own. In particular, she said that it is hard as her sons grow older, since there are "things that he [their father] can talk to them about that I just don't understand as well." And María described her anxiety after her husband decided to make another trip to the United States:

> Many couples are living like that [apart]; they're used to it. But more than anything, it drives them further apart. The men are alone over there, so they begin to see other women, they begin to neglect their obligations, and they see that the men over there are with other women. That leads to the breakdown of the family.

---

13. Some couples wait to have children until they are settled in the United States.

Spousal separation increases the likelihood of marital infidelity. Tla-cuitapeños disagreed about whether men on their own in the United States tend to have affairs. Some, mainly older men, indicated that it is very common for men to develop romantic relationships in the United States and that there is an unspoken code among the men that "what happens in the United States stays in the United States." Others, primarily younger men and women, said that having a *"casa chica"* (a second wife and sometimes a second family) used to be common, but no longer.

> My husband told me about three married men, now legally divorced, and they go around dating women here [in the United States]. They are free and enjoying themselves. They left their wives and children, and now they are starting a new life here. If it were not for migration to the United States, this would not have happened.

Male migrants are not as closely monitored on their behavior in the United States as they would be in their religiously conservative hometowns. Nevertheless, they are not entirely free from social constraints. The extensive social networks among migrants in the United States and the ease with which people can contact their *paisanos* in Mexico mean that news of adulterous behavior can quickly reach wives back home.

TOWARD A QUANTITATIVE MODEL OF PATRIARCHAL MARRIAGE

Hirsch (2003) and Hondagneu-Sotelo (1994) found that marriages typically become more egalitarian following migration; when one or both spouses migrate, husbands contribute more to housework, wives experience more autonomy and contribute financially to the household, and the couple moves toward a more companionate relationship.[14] However, these scholars based their work on qualitative interviews with small, nonrandom samples, and it remains to be seen whether these findings hold when using quantitative modeling with samples representative of

---

14. They, along with Chant (1994), also find that marriages in Mexico are becoming more companionate. That is, social and economic changes in Mexico are modifying the gendered norms for husbands and wives, who are now more likely to view each other as friends as well as partners, and are more likely to collaborate on responsibilities such as housework, childrearing, wage earning, and financial decision making.

an entire community. This section builds on the existing literature by presenting survey data comparing migrant and nonmigrant attitudes toward patriarchal marriage. Given Hirsch's and Hondagneu-Sotelo's findings, our expectation was that migrants would have less patriarchal attitudes than nonmigrants. However, controlling for basic demographic factors, we found that migrants are significantly more likely than their nonmigrant counterparts to express attitudes accepting of patriarchal marriage. In light of the way male migrants return to Tlacuitapa expressly to find a "traditional" wife, both male and female migrants may be adopting more traditionally gendered roles within their marriages.

The survey administered in Tlacuitapa in 2007 included three indicators of attitudes toward patriarchal marriage: a wife's obligation to obey her husband, a wife's obligation to have sexual relations with her husband even if she does not wish it, and a husband's right to strike his wife. The responses on these three points are shown in figure 7.1.

Figure 7.1 Acceptance of Patriarchal Marriage among Migrants and Nonmigrants

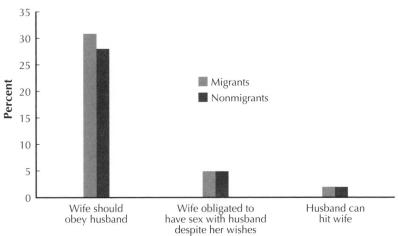

The question about a wife's duty to obey her husband garnered the most affirmative answers: 24 percent of nonmigrants and 33 percent of migrants. Both groups were significantly less likely to accept a wife's

obligation to have sexual relations against her will or to accept domestic violence; approximately 5 percent of both groups responded affirmatively on the former point and some 2 percent on the latter. The difference between migrant and nonmigrant attitudes on the first measure is significant—and in direct contradiction to the work of Hirsch and Hondagneu-Sotelo.

To test our finding further and to control for conflating factors, such as the fact that migrants are more likely to be men, we created a dichotomous variable indicating categorical disapproval (answered "no" to all three questions about patriarchal marriage) or categorical acceptance (answered "yes" to at least one of the three questions). Using the dichotomous variable, the difference in attitudes between migrants and nonmigrants becomes starker: 57 percent of migrants indicate that some level of patriarchal marriage is acceptable, compared to only 43 percent of nonmigrants (figure 7.2).

Figure 7.2 Dichotomized Measure of Acceptability of Patriarchal Marriage among Migrants and Nonmigrants

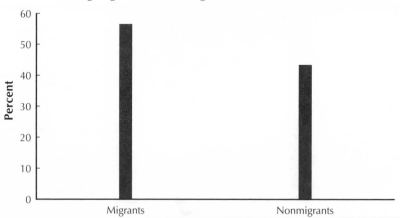

Some form of patriarchal marriage is acceptable

A binomial logit regression further tests how migration to the United States and other pertinent demographic factors correlate with respondents' attitudes toward patriarchal marriage. The dependent variable is the dichotomized "acceptance of patriarchal marriage" variable described above. Independent variables include age, age-squared, education, level of religiosity (measured by how many times respondents indicated they had attended church services the previous month), whether the respondent earned a salary, gender, a measure of family wealth,[15] and whether the couple had at least one U.S.-born child.[16] Results for the regression are presented in table 7.2.

Table 7.2 Odds Ratio of Acceptance of Patriarchal Marriage

Dependent Variable	Odds Ratio (standard error)
Age	.98 (.05)
Age-squared	1.00 (.00)
Migrant	**1.73* (.44)**
Years of education	**.87** (.03)**
Religiosity	1.03 (.14)
Married	1.25 (.37)
Wage earner	.77 (.20)
Female	.67 (.17)
Wealth	**.93* (.03)**
U.S.-born children	.71 (.22)
Pseudo R^2	**.07***
N	505

Reference category: 0 (patriarchal marriage is never acceptable).
* $p < .05$; ** $p < .01$; *** $p < .001$.

Consistent with initial expectations, education decreases acceptance of patriarchal marriage: every additional year of education results in a 13 percent decrease in the likelihood that a respondent will indicate

---

15. The wealth variable was created by weighting responses indicating ownership of durable goods and home appliances in Tlacuitapa. For a more detailed description of how this measure was derived, see chapter 5, this volume.

16. Hirsch locates female empowerment in having U.S.-born children because women who give birth in the United States have greater opportunities and obligations to engage with U.S. bureaucracies, including the health-care system, public school system, and, in some cases, social welfare agencies. These dealings with institutions frequently require women to navigate public transportation systems and to acquire some English skills, which in turn lead to greater confidence in their ability to deal with institutions (Hirsch 2003: 32, 34, 188).

acceptance of patriarchal marriage. These findings accord with studies by Hobcraft (1993), Mehra (1997), Dexter, LeVine, and Velasco (1998), and Parker and Pederzini (1999), who have demonstrated that increased education leads to increases in female empowerment and more gender-egalitarian attitudes.

Arias and Mummert (1987), Hondagneu-Sotelo (1994), and Hirsch (2003) find that when Mexican women enter the labor force, regardless of their migration experience, marriages become more egalitarian. In contrast to these findings and contrary to our initial hypothesis, there is no difference in the likelihood that wage-earning respondents will be accepting of patriarchal marriage. On the other hand, wealth is a significant predictor of respondents' attitudes toward patriarchal marriage. Increases in wealth decrease the acceptance of patriarchal marriage, indicating that wealthier families have more egalitarian marriages. That is, women's increasing autonomy as wage earners has a weaker impact on attitudes about patriarchal marriage than does the family's overall socioeconomic status.

In contrast to Hirsch's 2003 study, which suggests that having U.S.-born children tends to give Mexican migrant women more power in their marriages (see note 16), our data show no significant difference in attitudes toward patriarchal marriage between respondents with and without U.S.-born children. In like manner, age, marital status, and religiosity do not alter the likelihood of respondents' acceptance of patriarchal marriage in any statistically significant way.

Migration history, on the other hand, is a very significant predictor of respondents' attitudes toward patriarchal marriage. Even when controlling for demographic and employment variables, migrants are 73 percent more likely than nonmigrants to indicate that some level of patriarchy is acceptable in marriage.

These results directly contradict the findings of Hirsch and Hondagneu-Sotelo. One possible explanation is the gendered dynamic of migration from Tlacuitapa to the United States. As discussed above, male migrants who return to Tlacuitapa in search of a spouse may be marrying women who are more willing to fulfill the role of homemaker and caretaker, suggesting that these women may be more accepting of patriarchal marriage norms.

Another explanation is that both male and female migrants may glorify what they view as a "traditional" Mexican marriage, and in doing so create roles for husbands and wives that are more extremely gendered in the United States than those in Mexico. This dynamic, known as the "museumization effect" (Das Gupta 1997) of out-migration, describes a pattern whereby migrants assume that attitudes or behaviors in their sending communities remain unchanged from the time of their initial migration, not cognizant of the profound changes that may be occurring in the sending community. In the context of gender relations and patriarchal marriages, migrants may believe that the traditional, patriarchal form of marriage of their parents and grandparents continues to be the norm in Tlacuitapa, and they may feel they are maintaining a tradition that has in fact diminished significantly (Wiest 1973; Chant 1994; Hirsch 2003).

Yet despite these findings, respondents in Tlacuitapa indicated that migrant men are perceived as being less macho than their nonmigrant counterparts and that the marriages of migrants are more egalitarian than those of people who do not leave the home community. Hirsch's work on migrants from Degollado, a town not far from Tlacuitapa, can help explain this paradox. Migrant men must present themselves as "modern" in order to find a spouse; they must be willing to accept the new model of companionate marriage that has become the norm in Mexico. Men do not go around declaiming their desire for a woman willing to do housework and obey her husband. Rather, they say they are looking for a *pareja*, a partner (Hirsch 2003: 145–47), even though their underlying attitudes toward gender roles and marital paradigms indicate strongly gendered and patriarchal assumptions about what marriage should be like.

GENDERED JOBS: MIGRATION OFFERS NEW OPPORTUNITIES AND OBLIGATIONS

Attitudes toward patriarchy in marriage tell only part of the story of how migration reorganizes gender roles and relationships within marriage. Hirsch and Hondagneu-Sotelo find that, following migration, couples divide household responsibilities differently. Men participate more in chores and caretaking, and women contribute financially to the household by entering the labor force. When men from Tlacuitapa migrate, they begin doing housework they did not do in Mexico. However, when wives or daughters join male migrants, the women resume responsibility for the bulk of the household labor. Female migrants from Tlacuitapa are thus entering the ranks of women the world over who are working the "double shift" of salaried labor and household chores.

Division of Household Responsibilities and Financial Decision Making

For many women, their formal occupation is only part of their daily work (Pedrero, Rendón, and Barrón 1997; Fernández-Kelly 1983; Hertz 1986; Garduño and Márquez 1995). Many female migrants discover that entering the labor force enables them to contribute to the family's finances, but it also increases their burdens as they retain their traditional, gendered role as homemaker and caregiver.

Women are primarily responsible for household chores and cooking in both Tlacuitapa and the United States, but the division of these tasks is slightly more egalitarian in the United States. For example, 92 percent of respondents indicated that in Tlacuitapa a woman is most often responsible for the cooking, and 90 percent reported that the woman does the household chores (see figure 7.3). In the United States, 57 percent of respondents indicate that the wife cooks most of the time, while 33 percent reported that the husband does most of the cooking. Likewise, 60 percent reported that women performed the household chores in the United States, while 1 percent reported that men are primarily responsible for these duties. While women still retain greater responsibility for the household, there is a post-migration increase in the frequency with which men do these tasks themselves or cooperate with their wives to accomplish them.

However, a comparison of migrant men whose wives are co-resident in the United States and those whose wives live in Mexico reveals a less egalitarian distribution of household responsibilities than initially indicated. In Tlacuitapa, males perform less than 5 percent of household responsibilities (figure 7.4). When males migrate to the United States, they begin performing the bulk of housework primarily because there are no women to perform these tasks. Once women join their husbands, couples revert to a less egalitarian distribution of household responsibilities that nearly mirrors the pattern prevailing in Tlacuitapa. This finding is consistent with Hondagneu-Sotelo's (1994) research on migrant bachelor communities.

Figure 7.3 Distribution of Household Responsibilities by Gender in Tlacuitapa and the United States

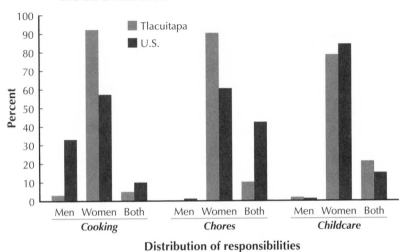

Distribution of responsibilities

Figure 7.4 Male Share of Household Responsibilities in Tlacuitapa and the United States

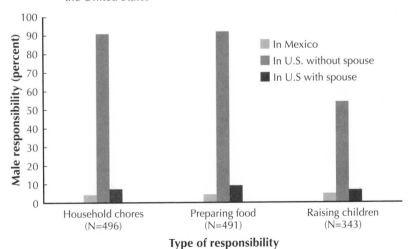

Type of responsibility

Households also divide other kinds of responsibilities. For example, women in Tlacuitapa have considerable power in financial decision making. Fifty-two percent of respondents indicated that in Tlacuitapa a woman is the primary financial decision maker in the family (figure 7.5). Seven percent of respondents reported that a man is primarily responsible for making financial decisions, and 41 percent indicated that financial decisions are taken by men and women jointly. These data suggest that women have a relatively greater degree of autonomy with regard to family financial management than do men, and that many couples are in fact operating within the model of companionate marriage described by Hirsch (2003).

Figure 7.5 Distribution of Household Financial Decisions by Gender in Tlacuitapa and the United States

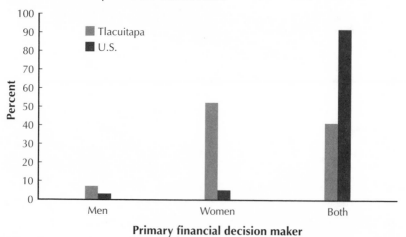

However, a significant change takes place in the context of migration. Respondents indicated that in the United States, financial decisions are made jointly 92 percent of the time, which represents an increase in shared responsibility but also a major decrease in the number of women taking primary responsibility for their families' finances. One explanation may be the high number of female-led households in Tlacuitapa, where women are deciding how to spend the remittances their husbands send from the United States.[17] Once families are reunited, earnings and decisions on how to use them become the responsibility of both husband and wife.

However, the fact that a woman receives remittances does not necessarily mean that she occupies a position of power within the family. A discussion with a woman whose husband has been in the United States for several years revealed her frustration at not knowing how much he earns. She has to ask him for money to feed and clothe their daughters and maintain their home, money that her husband is not always willing to send.

Modeling Divisions of Household Labor Post-Migration

In order to arrive at a more detailed understanding of how migration changes the balance of power within households, we conducted a series of multinomial logit regressions on the self-reported frequencies with which men and women perform various household activities. The "division of labor" questions used in the regression were only asked of married individuals, so the sample size is somewhat smaller than the patriarchy model (N = approximately 100 for each question). Also in contrast to the analysis of attitudes toward patriarchal marriage, the unit of analysis for this series of regressions is the household. That is, the models measure how well migration predicts the way a household organizes its labor, not how often a migrant, as compared to a nonmigrant, performs a particular task.

Because of this focus on the household, the independent variables are all household-level measures; for example, a family's level of wealth is included rather than an individual's income. Likewise, instead of a dichotomous variable reporting whether an individual has ever migrated, a continuous-scale variable for the number of months the husband and wife have spent in the United States is used. If neither the husband nor the wife has ever migrated, the value of each migration-related variable would be 0. The length of time a couple has been married is used as a proxy for the couple's age. The average age at marriage for survey respondents is 25 for men and 23 for women, and the standard deviation is

---

17. This would confirm research by Wiest, which describes female-headed households' handling of remittances in the absence of the husbands. However, larger household expenditures may require consultation with one's husband (Wiest 1973, 180–209).

5.6. Thus, if a couple has been married for 15 years, it is likely that both are around 40 years old. The U.S. model also includes whether a couple has U.S.-born children, to test Hirsch's (2003) argument that U.S.-born children are an important source of power for U.S.-based Mexican women. Finally, the U.S. model considers whether the husband and wife are co-resident in the United States, given the finding that, in the absence of a wife, a U.S.-based husband will do most of the housework, but when his wife arrives she performs most household labor. Conversely, the Mexico model considers the responses only for co-resident couples because if the husband is living in the United States, clearly he cannot be contributing to household chores in Mexico.

Table 7.3 Multinomial Logit Regression for Likelihood that Someone Other than Wife Takes Responsibility for Household Tasks in Mexico when Both Spouses Reside in Mexico

	Food Preparation	Household Chores	Childcare	Financial Decision Making
	β (Std. Error)	β (Std. Error)	β (Std. Error)	β (Std. Error)
Length of marriage	.039 (.037)	.032 (.030)	−.013 (.025)	**−.069*** (.021)**
Wealth	−.052 (.168)	−.072 (.110)	−.113 (.100)	.113 (.090)
Length of husband's migration	−.566 (.439)	.009 (.046)	.014 (.105)	−.031 (.028)
Length of wife's migration	.182 (.383)	.098 (.102)	.010 (.105)	**.960** (.021)**
Pseudo R²	.149	.050	.019	.186
N	107	101	90	111

Reference category: −1 (female responsibility).
* $p < .10$; ** $p < .05$ level; *** $p < .01$.

In both the Mexico-based and U.S.-based models, the dependent variable is "who performs the task the majority of the time," with possible answers being "wife," "husband," and "husband and wife together." The answers "husband alone" and "husband and wife together" were collapsed into a single category because of the assumption that the wife is the family member most commonly responsible for the chores under consideration. If anyone other than the wife alone is performing these tasks, it is possible to hypothesize a move toward a less patriarchal division of household labor. The omitted category for the models is "wife performs the task." The results therefore predict the likelihood that someone other than the wife will be performing a given task. Table 7.3 presents the Beta coefficients indicating the likelihood that a husband or a husband and wife living in Mexico are performing the household duties under consideration, and table 7.4 presents the Beta coefficients for the same likelihood in U.S.-based households.

Table 7.4 Multinomial Logit Regression for Likelihood that Someone Other than Wife Takes Responsibility for Household Tasks in United States

	Food Preparation	Household Chores	Childcare	Financial Decision Making
	β (Std. Error)	β (Std. Error)	β (Std. Error)	β (Std. Error)
Spouse in United States	−.967* (.508)	−1.86*** (.545)	−.539 (.573)	−.158 (.549)
Length of marriage	−.033* (.018)	−.031* (.017)	−.022 (.022)	−.010 (.025)
Wealth	.119 (.074)	.135** (.061)	.078 (.078)	.032 (.070)
Length of husband's migration	−.009 (.018)	.007 (.018)	.012 (.019)	−.016 (.020)
Length of wife's migration	.038* (.021)	.036* (.020)	.031 (.023)	−.014 (.028)
U.S.-born children	−.928** (.448)	−1.254*** (.454)	−.955* (.575)	.240 (.533)
Pseudo R²	.087	.146	.039	.019
N	145	142	106	144

Reference category: −1 (female responsibility).
* $p < .10$; ** $p < .05$ level; *** $p < .01$.

This analysis produced relatively few statistically significant findings, indicating that age, socioeconomic status, and migration experience are not strong predictors of the way households in Tlacuitapa organize their domestic responsibilities. Wealth has no significant predictive relationship to whether a wife is primarily responsible for household chores, nor does the husband's migration experience. Length of marriage, the proxy for age, is only significantly predictive when it comes to determining who makes financial decisions; the older a couple is, the more likely the woman is the family's primary decision maker. Interestingly, the longer a woman has spent in the United States, the less likely she is to be the financial decision maker for her family. This finding is consistent with others outlined below, which indicate that female migrants are more likely to be primarily responsible for certain household chores (see table 7.4).

The analysis for U.S.-based couples yielded stronger and more statistically significant results than that for Mexico-based couples. For instance, for the questions on food preparation and household chores, nearly every independent variable was predictive of how households organize their labor. Virtually none of the independent variables, on the other hand, is predictive of how couples organize their childcare and financial decision making.

Interestingly, the only independent variable that has absolutely no predictive relationship with the household responsibilities under consideration is the husband's migration experience. In other words, the length of time a man has spent in the United States has no bearing on how he and his wife divide their family's cooking, cleaning, childcare, or financial decision making. The more extensive a wife's migration experience, however, the more likely she and her husband together (or her husband alone) are responsible for the cooking and household chores. This bears out Hondagneu-Sotelo's and Hirsch's findings that couples who have been in the United States longer demonstrate a more equitable division of household responsibilities.

However, our analyses also found that a man whose wife is living with him in the United States is less likely to be doing the cooking and cleaning: co-resident spouses are more likely to report that the wife is primarily responsible for food preparation and household chores. Several explanations for this apparent contradiction are possible. Given that the proxy for age (length of marriage) is strongly predictive of the wife being the family member responsible for household chores, it could be that the age at which a woman migrates has an effect on how she and her husband divide their responsibilities. That is, women who migrate at a younger age and consequently have greater migration experience may be demonstrating more equitable divisions of household labor than women who migrate later.

Second, many co-resident couples are younger, mirroring the transition to family-based migration from Tlacuitapa to the United States, and are thus more likely to have young children. Indeed, these analyses indicate that couples with U.S.-born children are much more likely to report that the wife is primarily responsible for cooking, cleaning, and childcare. Consequently, the contradiction between co-resident spouses reporting greater female responsibility for chores and the length of a woman's migration experience increasing the likelihood that her husband is helping her may reflect a relatively young group of families with young children. As these families spend more time in the United States and these women enter the workforce in greater numbers,[18] it will be interesting to trace how their families begin to reorganize their domestic responsibilities and to see if and to what extent men begin to collaborate more regularly with their wives on the cooking and household chores.

Gendered Jobs: Employment and Migration for Men and Women

Historically, Mexican men have been their families' primary breadwinners. However, as a result of changing social conditions in Mexico and migration to the United States, more women are joining the paid workforce. Jobs held by Tlacuitapeños in both the United States and Mexico are highly gendered as "women's" or "men's" work. Additionally, changing labor opportunities and expectations have implications for gender roles, particularly as women renegotiate their domestic responsibilities.

The men we interviewed in Tlacuitapa work predominantly in construction (37 percent), agriculture (25 percent), and services (25 percent). Following migration to the United States, men's labor distribution changes; more than half of the U.S.-based men interviewed reported being employed in construction; 26 percent indicated they work in the service sector; and only 6 percent said they work in agriculture (see figure 7.6).

---

18. Tests were conducted to see if there is any connection between a wife's participation in the formal labor market and the way families organize their labor; neither whether a woman works nor her level of wages was significantly predictive of who is primarily responsible for the household chores.

Figure 7.6 Male Employment in Tlacuitapa and the United States, by Sector

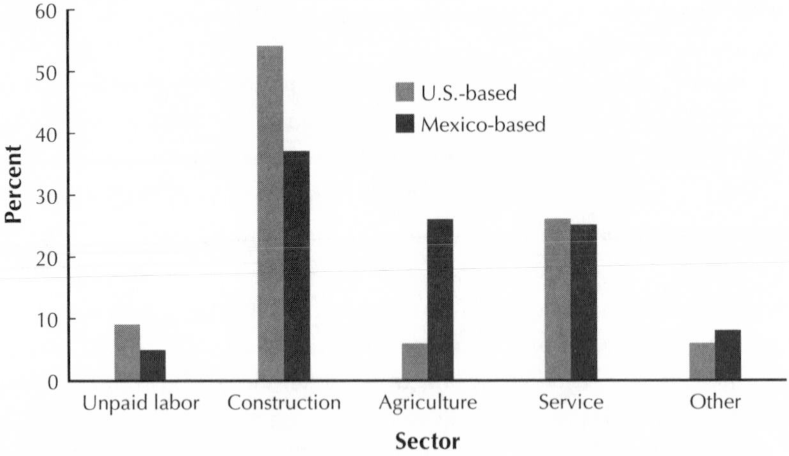

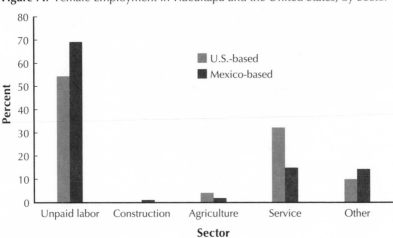

N = 372; U.S.-based N = 145.

The lack of jobs in Tlacuitapa has been documented as a major reason for men's migration since the era of the Bracero Program. Although migration frequently means better job opportunities for young men, it is not what parents hope for their children. As one informant stated: "I'm afraid that when my son grows up he'll go to the United States, too—that he'll look at our town and say, 'Well, this isn't working, so I'm leaving.'"

Figure 7.7 Female Employment in Tlacuitapa and the United States, by Sector

N = 440; U.S.-based N = 74.

Women in Tlacuitapa work mostly as housewives or in low-wage service-sector jobs.[19] The employment rates in services double for women migrants in the United States. Figure 7.7 shows the rates of employment by sector for women in Tlacuitapa and the United States.

The largest formal service-sector employer in Tlacuitapa is a shoe factory, with some eighty employees (seventy women, ten men). Seventy percent of the women employed there are between the ages of 15 and 20. In an interview with the factory manager, he reasoned that few men work in the factory because the wages are not sufficient to support a family. A few women also work in stores or local butcher shops, or as maids or store clerks; and a limited number of jobs were available in the factories that produce tortillas and *mole.*[20]

Women in Tlacuitapa also work in the informal sector, selling food items on the street corner or crocheting baby clothes at home. These jobs yield much lower incomes[21] and offer no possibilities for upward mobility. However, and not insignificantly, they do supplement family income.

The mere fact of having a salaried job does not immediately translate into greater power or equity for women in Tlacuitapa. Suzy earns US$40 a week at the shoe factory, but her pay is docked if she is caught talking while working. Other women told of wages being changed or withheld without notice or explanation. Thus, not only are women limited in the type of jobs available to them, but the treatment they receive on the job is sometimes unfavorable.

On the other hand, some working women gain independence. Because they earn an income, they no longer have to depend on their husbands for money. Some entrepreneurial women have established businesses in Tlacuitapa. One sells clothing purchased in the United States, and another has opened a tortilla business with her husband. In a society where women traditionally have had to ask permission to go anywhere

---

19. Even though many women earn money in the informal sector, the majority of women self-identified as housewives.

20. Many of these small businesses hire only family members and neighbors, effectively limiting women's free entry into the labor market in Tlacuitapa. In addition, migration greatly affects the viability and success of these businesses. A woman whose daughter owns a tortilla business stated that sales drop significantly when migrants are away.

21. Women's average earnings in Tlacuitapa are US$40 a week, compared to $271 for U.S.-based women.

other than to church, to market, or to visit relatives (Hirsch 2003), this role shift from homemaker to wage earner is radical.

In the United States, 46 percent of women migrants from Tlacuitapa perform paid labor (versus 31 percent in Tlacuitapa). Additionally, the share of women who self-identify as housewives after migration drops considerably, to 37 percent, compared to 60 percent in Mexico. However, once a woman obtains a salaried job, her marriage does not necessarily become more egalitarian in decision making and the division of household labor.

As discussed above, entry into the paid labor force has been used to explain increases in power and autonomy for Mexican migrant women. García and Oliveira argue, however, that it is not work per se that increases women's power and autonomy. Rather, it is women's control of economic resources and the importance of their economic contribution to family survival. When women's paid labor is viewed merely as secondary or supplementary, marital relations do not become more egalitarian (García and Oliveira 1994). The increase in Tlacuitapeño women's participation in the paid labor force post-migration confirms these researchers' findings: women's work outside the home is a move toward empowerment, but it does not automatically create egalitarian marriages.

As wage earners, migrant women earn considerably less than their migrant husbands. Although the average hourly wage for men and women migrants is nearly identical ($10 for women, $11 for men), women earn US$271 a week on average, while men average $513 a week. This difference is due primarily to the fact that women work fewer hours, reinforcing the view that women's wages are only supplemental to the husband's income.

Further, women are typically ten years older than men at the time of their first migration to the United States, meaning that men have had more time to acquire work experience and to develop social networks on which to draw when job searching. Male migrants also report better English skills.[22] Knowledge of English is an important measure of empowerment, because it gives men greater financial independence in case

---

22. Male migrants self-report comprehending English "well" 20 percent more frequently than female migrants. Of respondents who report speaking "a lot" of English, responses diverge further—20 percent of male respondents versus 8 percent of women.

of divorce or separation. And the disparity in English fluency suggests that migrant men have the potential for greater job mobility and professional careers, while women are likely to remain in dead-end jobs in the service sector.

Success does not come easily for men or women migrants. Our results suggest that the long work hours in the United States and migration itself affect family dynamics, creating new physical and emotional challenges. Ambivalence about working outside the home is common among migrant women. For example, María Guadalupe, a married migrant, told us that her life became very different when she relocated to the United States. She obtained a license to open a daycare center, and her paid employment eased her family's financial burden. Nevertheless, she described her life as very stressful, saying she felt pressured by her new work responsibilities: "Migration affected me physically; formerly I weighed 60 kilos and I dropped to 48 kilos. And as I weigh less with the stress of my job, I worry even more."

Many people we spoke with in Tlacuitapa reported that the long hours spent at work and commuting to and from work in the United States reduce the time fathers spend with their children. This may explain why men share more of the child-rearing duties in Tlacuitapa. Some women admitted that moving to the United States is not always as good as it is made to seem. "Those who have gone want others to think that the United States is a paradise, that you can achieve many things there that you can't here. . . . Those who have gone know the sacrifice, the effort to get their luxuries, the goods they bring from there, but they don't talk about this."

While migration creates new economic opportunities for male and female migrants, it can also create new burdens and obligations. Men and women in both the United States and Tlacuitapa must constantly negotiate a balance between work and family, with much of the burden for household responsibilities continuing to fall on women. The division of household labor within U.S.-based families does not differ significantly from that in Tlacuitapa-based families, but many U.S.-based women are working outside the home in addition to fulfilling their role as homemaker and caretaker. Thus, while incorporation into the workforce may increase women's autonomy and lead to more egalitarian marriage, the demands of the "double shift" continue to mitigate these increases and reduce women's empowerment in relation to men.

CONCLUSION

This chapter has shed light on how migration affects the balance of power between men and women in sending and receiving communities. From migration strategies to binational marriages to the organization of household responsibilities, migration shapes how men and women think about each other and what they expect from their partners and families.

Both qualitative and quantitative findings indicate that men tend to migrate either before marriage or without their partners, and they leave overwhelmingly in response to the economic incentive of work in the United States. Women, on the other hand, are still migrating to the United States primarily as tied movers, that is, as wives or family members of migrants. Because men are exempt from the de facto requirement of a "chaperone" for migration while women are not, patriarchal gender roles are maintained in the migration process.

Migration also shapes expectations surrounding courtship and marriage. When male migrants return to Tlacuitapa to find a spouse, they must act according to different gender norms than those prevailing in the United States. Expectations and ideas associated with masculinity and femininity, connected with understanding life in the United States, alter traditional ideals of what a partner should be. At times, this leads to conflict with older generations' views. Spouses in Tlacuitapa, particularly wives, must be willing to accept either a long-distance relationship or an international move. Consequently, binational families, with men in the United States and women and children in Mexico, are commonplace. Both men and women struggle with long-term separation from spouses and children, and both must renegotiate their gendered roles in marriage following migration. This separation takes a toll on all parties involved.

For women, migration to the United States offers a greater likelihood of employment outside the home. Yet this opportunity carries costs; many migrant women find themselves working more than they would in Tlacuitapa because they are also obligated to continue in the traditional role of primary caretaker. Once in the United States, being a mother, housewife, and now wage earner widens the scope of women's work. Whereas women in Tlacuitapa are not expected to help provide for the family financially, this becomes an extra responsibility in the United States due to the higher cost of living and the desire to send remittances to family members in Mexico.

Yet it is not only women who experience a shift in roles. Unaccompanied male migrants report that they do the majority of domestic chores in the United States, becoming their own caretakers while continuing to hold the traditional title of "provider." As a result of migration, couples experience a reorganization of balances of power and gender roles, even if only temporarily.

This reorganization of gender roles is reflected in the contradiction we found in our interviews in Tlacuitapa between the belief that migrant men are less "macho" and the data indicating that migrants are more likely to report patriarchal attitudes. This contradiction can be explained in several ways. First, migrants continue to act in ways they attribute to how things are done "back home," not realizing that social changes have occurred in their communities of origin. This "museumization effect" means that even as women are becoming more empowered in Mexico as a whole, migrants, unaware of changes at home, maintain more normative views of men's and women's marital responsibilities.

Second, migrant men who return to Mexico to find a spouse may be seeking more traditional women, who are willing to fill the role of homemaker, caretaker, and child bearer. Yet, in order to present themselves as attractive mates, they emphasize their modern, egalitarian views on marriage. This incongruity (looking for a "traditional" wife in one's community of origin while declaiming the virtues of an egalitarian marriage) explains in large part the seeming paradox outlined above.

Finally, both the family separation and family reunification that migration involves can provoke situations in which the woman is heavily dependent on her husband. In the case of separation, nonmigrant women must rely on their husbands for remittances. And for migrant women, their legal status and acculturation to life in the United States are highly dependent on their husbands, who tend to have better English skills, larger social networks, and more plentiful job opportunities.

In sum, while migration can empower women, women remain less empowered overall relative to male migrants.

References

Arias, Patricia, and Gail Mummert. 1987. "Familia, mercados de trabajo y migración en el centro-occidente de México," *Nueva Antropología* 9, no. 32.

Blau, Francine D., and Lawrence M. Kahn. 2006. "Gender and Assimilation among Mexican Americans." Presented at the NBER Mexican Immigration Conference, Cambridge, MA.

Cerrutti, Marcela, and Douglas S. Massey. 2001. "On the Auspices of Female Migration from Mexico to the United States," *Demography* 38, no. 2 (May): 187–200.

Chant, Sylvia. 1994. "Women, Work and Household Survival Strategies in Mexico, 1982–1992: Past Trends, Current Tendencies and Future Research," *Bulletin of Latin American Research* 13, no. 2 (May): 203–33.

Cornelius, Wayne A., David Fitzgerald, and Pedro Lewin Fischer, eds. 2007. *Mayan Journeys: The New Migration from Yucatán to the United States.* La Jolla, CA: Center for Comparative Immigration Studies, University of California, San Diego.

Cornelius, Wayne A., and Jessa M. Lewis, eds. 2007. *Impacts of Border Enforcement on Mexican Migration: The View from Sending Communities.* La Jolla, CA: Center for Comparative Immigration Studies, University of California, San Diego.

Curran, S. R., and E. Rivero-Fuentes. 2003. "Engendering Migrant Networks: The Case of Mexican Migration," *Demography* 40: 289–307.

Das Gupta, Monisha. 1997. "'What Is Indian about You?': A Gendered, Transnational Approach to Ethnicity," *Gender and Society* 11, no. 5: 572–96.

Dexter, Emily R., Sarah E. LeVine, and Patricia M. Velasco. 1998. "Maternal Schooling and Health-Related Language and Literacy Skills in Rural Mexico," *Comparative Education Review* 42, no. 2 (May): 139–62.

Donato, K. M., D. Gabaccia, J. Holdaway, M. Manalansan, and P. R. Pessar. 2006. "A Glass Half Full? Gender in Migration Studies," *International Migration Review* 40.

Fernández-Kelly, María Patricia. 1983. *For We Are Sold, I and My People.* Albany, NY: State University of New York Press.

García, Brígida, and Orlandina de Oliveira. 1994. *Trabajo femenino y vida familiar en México.* México, D.F.: El Colegio de México.

Garduño, M. A. A., and M. S. Márquez. 1995. "The Role of Stress in Exhaustion among Female Workers," *Cad. Saúde Pública.* [Rio de Janeiro] 11, no. 1 (January/March): 65–71.

González-López, Gloria. 2005. *Erotic Journeys: Mexican Immigrants and Their Sex Lives*. Berkeley, CA: University of California Press.

Hertz, Rosanna. 1986. *More Equal than Others: Women and Men in Dual-Career Marriages*. Berkeley, CA: University of California Press.

Hirsch, Jennifer S. 2003. *A Courtship after Marriage: Sexuality and Love in Mexican Transnational Families*. Berkeley, CA: University of California Press.

Hobcraft, John. 1993. "Women's Education, Child Welfare and Child Survival: A Review of the Evidence." London: Department of Population Studies and Centre for the Study of Global Governance, London School of Economics.

Hondagneu-Sotelo, Pierrette. 1994. *Gendered Transitions: Mexican Experiences of Immigration*. Berkeley, CA: University of California Press.

———. 2003. *Gender and US Migration: Contemporary Trends*. Berkeley, CA: University of California Press.

INEGI (Instituto Nacional de Estadística, Geografía e Informática). 2005. *Censo de Población*. http://www.inegi.gob.mx/est/contenidos/espanol/sistemas/conteo2005/localidad/iter/default.asp.

Kanaiaupuni, Shawn M. 2000. "Reframing the Migration Question: An Analysis of Men, Women, and Gender in Mexico," *Social Forces* 8, no. 4: 1131–47.

Levitt, Peggy. 2001. *Transnational Villagers*. Berkeley, CA: University of California Press.

Mehra, Rekha. 1997. "The Role of NGOs: Charity and Empowerment," *Annals of the American Academy of Political and Social Science* 554 (November): 136–49.

Mincer, Joseph. 2003. *Marriage and the Economy: Theory and Evidence from Advanced Industrial Societies*. Cambridge: Cambridge University Press.

Oishi, Nana. 2002. "Gender and Migration: An Integrative Approach." CCIS Working Paper No. 49. La Jolla, CA: Center for Comparative Immigration Studies, University of California, San Diego. http://www.ccis-ucsd.org/PUBLICATIONS/wrkg49.PDF.

Parker, Susan Wendy, and Carla Pederzini. 1999. "Gender Differences in Education in Mexico." Report for the World Bank. Washington, DC.

Pedraza, Silvia. 1991. "Women and Migration: The Social Consequences of Gender," *Annual Review of Sociology* 17: 302–25.

Pedrero, Mercedes, Teresa Rendón, and Antonieta Barrón. 1997. "Segregación ocupacional por género en México." Cuernavaca, Mexico: Centro Regional de Investigaciones Multidisciplinarias/Universidad Nacional Autónoma de México.

Reichert, Joshua. 1982. "A Town Divided: Economic Stratification and Social Relations in a Mexican Migrant Community," *Social Problems* 29: 411–23.

Rubio-Goldsmith, Raquel, M. Melissa McCormick, Daniel Martinez, and Inez Magdalena Duarte. 2006. "The 'Funnel Effect' & Recovered Bodies of Unauthorized Migrants Processed by the Pima County Office of the Medical Examiner, 1990–2005." Binational Migration Institute. http://immigration.server263.com/images/File/brief/Full%20BMI%20Report.pdf.

Smith, Robert C. 2006. *Mexican New York: Transnational Lives of New Immigrants.* Berkeley, CA: University of California Press.

Wiest, Raymond. 1973. "Wage-Labor Migration and the Household in a Mexican Town," *Journal of Anthropological Research* 29: 180–209.

Migrant recently returned from the United States is interviewed about his health history.

8   The Migrant Health Paradox Revisited

ELIZABETH ORISTIAN, PATRICIA SWEENEY, VERÓNICA PUENTES,
JORGE JIMÉNEZ, AND MAXIMINO MATUS RUIZ

The binational environment that migrants inhabit fosters unforeseen health implications for themselves and for their nonmigrating counterparts. Migration's impacts on disease, nutrition, work-related injuries, and use of health-care facilities are all important determinants of migrant and nonmigrant health, and there is heated debate among experts regarding whether being a migrant improves or imperils health. Our research yielded three findings that help resolve this issue. First, the migrants in our sample are healthier than their nonmigrant counterparts. Second, migrants with more exposure to the United States are not likely to report an increased number of infirmities, suggesting that longer stays in the United States do not necessarily lead to a decline in health. And third, in attempting to understand why migrants report being healthier than nonmigrants, we found that the obstacles to migration constitute a filtering effect, and only healthier Tlacuitapeños decide to make the journey north.

THE LATINO HEALTH PARADOX

At the core of the debate about the health of migrants in the United States is what is known as the Latino health paradox.[1] The Latino health paradox compares the overall health of Latinos living in the United States with that of other populations. Most Hispanic groups are classified as being of low socioeconomic status, yet they have relatively good health compared to other groups at similar economic levels. According to Patel et al. (2004, 707), "This mortality advantage is commonly considered a paradox both because socioeconomic standing is a well-established determinant of mortality and because Hispanics (primarily Mexican-Americans) have

---

1. We use Latino and Hispanic interchangeably in this chapter.

an elevated prevalence of several risk factors for mortality, including diabetes and obesity." In effect, despite health factors that should operate against them, Mexico-born Hispanics who reside in the United States actually enjoy better health than other ethnic groups living under similar economic constraints.

However, after controlling for age and other factors, the health of Hispanic immigrants reportedly deteriorates with time spent in the United States. "As immigrants adopt traditional American health behaviors over time, their health status begins to converge with that of the general U.S. population" (Kandula et al. 2004, 362). Following modernization theory, one would expect that the advanced health-care system and relatively healthy environment of the United States would make migrants healthier over time,[2] but the Latino health paradox asserts the contrary. As migrants continue living in the United States, they adapt to the U.S. lifestyle and begin to develop health profiles similar to those of native-born residents.

There are two competing explanations for this paradox, which are discussed throughout this chapter: the salmon bias and the healthy migrant effect. The salmon bias suggests that, because Mexican or other Latino migrants have a strong tendency to return to their home country after working temporarily in the United States or upon retiring or becoming ill, their illnesses and deaths are not captured in U.S. morbidity and mortality statistics, creating the *illusion* of a healthier migrant population.[3] The artificially depressed mortality rates for Hispanics may erroneously suggest that Mexican migrants are healthier than the native population (Palloni and Arias 2004). According to the second explanation, the healthy migrant effect, the difficulty of migrating prohibits all but healthy individuals from coming to the United States, and this selected-out cohort naturally displays better health levels overall compared to other groups.

Both the salmon bias and the healthy migrant effect emphasize the inherent difficulty involved in obtaining an accurate picture of overall migrant health. U.S.-Mexico migrants are a binational population by definition, and hence they are affected by factors on both sides of the border. Moreover, migrants' continuous movement across the border makes it difficult to draw a truly random sample of the population and hinders

---

2. For more information on modernization theory, see Inglehart and Welzel 2005.
3. This is a reference to the behavior of salmon, which return to their birthplace to spawn and die.

efforts to demonstrate a causal relationship between migration and health (Palloni and Ewbank 2004).[4]

Our study of health issues in Tlacuitapa necessarily suffers from some unavoidable limitations. First, a single community cannot be representative of all migrant-sending communities. Second, our data regarding migrants' health were self-reported, which may be less accurate than biometric survey data in representing an individual's actual health condition. Finally, the non-longitudinal nature of our study hinders our ability to prove a cause-and-effect relationship between migration and health outcomes. While we are mindful of these limitations, our results nevertheless engage the debate about the Latino health paradox and other contemporary questions on health and migration. Self-reported survey data, combined with qualitative interviews with migrants and public health professionals in the sending community, allow us to identify the variables associated with both migrant and nonmigrant outcomes.

In the following pages we present background information on health-care facilities in the sending community and examine the prevalence of self-reported infirmities among nonmigrants, active migrants, and returned migrants. We then analyze three logistic regressions that control for age and other factors in order to determine health differences between migrants, returned migrants, nonmigrants, and U.S.-based migrants. We also look at several factors that affect the health of migrants and nonmigrants, including nutrition, depression, labor accidents, access to health care, and the relationship between remittances and health-care expenditures.

HEALTH CARE FACILITIES IN TLACUITAPA

The most popular health facility in Tlacuitapa is the health clinic and adjoining pharmacy, which are overseen by Dr. Héctor Salvador López León. The clinic treats common illnesses and infections and also monitors the town's diabetic population. Cases that Dr. López León is not equipped to treat are referred to clinics in neighboring Lagos de Moreno, León, San Juan, or Guadalajara.

---

4. This problem is currently being addressed by the Centro de Investigación y Docencia Económicas (CIDE) and the Universidad Iberoamericana (UIA) in a joint longitudinal study, the Mexican Family Life Survey, which measures health indicators in the same population over time. For more on the Mexican Family Life Survey, go to http://www.radix.uia.mx/ennvih/main.php?lang=en.

Second in popularity among the people of Tlacuitapa is the public health center, the Centro de Salud, directed by Dr. Antonio Gallardo, a medical student doing his residency. He is assisted by a trained nurse, who is a permanent resident of Tlacuitapa. Town residents who are unable to pay for treatment go to the public health center for free medications such as basic antibiotics or cold medicines. These medicines, which are provided through government funding, typically run out before the next shipment arrives. A frustrated Dr. Gallardo talked about his center's shortcomings: "I cannot help a pregnant woman who is in an emergency situation. If the delivery is complicated, I cannot help her. This situation is very dangerous; I have no way to treat such patients." While the government's stated goal is to offer health services for everyone in need, this public facility clearly lacks many standard amenities.

One other health-care option in Tlacuitapa is to seek help from practitioners of traditional medicine, which run the gamut from a *huesero* (bonesetter) to an herbalist. Although traditional medicine is less popular since the population has become increasingly exposed to Western medicine, it remains available to returned migrants and nonmigrants alike. The huesero sets bones that have been dislocated or broken and treats sprains and general body aches, combining physical manipulation of bones (much like a chiropractor or physical therapist) with herbal remedies to manage pain. *Curanderos* use herbs in combination with a supernatural or spiritual element in order to treat their patients.

PRIMARY HEALTH ISSUES FOR TLACUITAPEÑOS

Tlacuitapa's general health profile is on par with those of communities of similar economic standing throughout Mexico (see Tapia Conyer 2006). Yet, according to the three individuals who provide health services in the town (Dr. López León, Dr. Gallardo, and the town's nurse), past and current migration patterns have altered the health landscape of this particular community.

The town's three health-care providers voiced similar concerns when asked about the general health of the community. Gastrointestinal infection was the most common complaint, but many Tlacuitapa residents suffer from more serious ailments, such as diabetes and high blood pressure. This is in line with health profiles across Mexico, where more than seventeen million people suffer from high blood pressure, and diabetes has become the third-most-common cause of death (Tapia Conyer 2006, 601, 559).

Diabetes and high blood pressure are major health concerns for migrants as well. The California Agricultural Worker Health Survey (CAWHS) reported in 1999 that just over half of the male subjects showed at least one of three clinical risk factors for diabetes (obesity, high blood pressure, or high serum cholesterol). Nearly one in five showed at least two of the three (Villarejo et al. 2000, 22).[5] While comparatively higher than numbers for the general U.S. population, these results appear to be in line with reported findings in Mexico, a fact that may indicate that health issues emerging in Mexico are also affecting Mexican migrants in the United States.

We found no consistent pattern among nonmigrants, active U.S.-based migrants, and returned migrants in terms of the prevalence of infirmities (see figure 8.1). Both U.S.-based and Mexico-based migrants are more likely than nonmigrants to report obesity and high cholesterol, pointing to the possible dangers of migration-related changes in dietary habits. Yet U.S.-based migrants are not consistently sicker than nonmigrants. For example, U.S.-based migrants report lower incidences of asthma, high blood pressure, and muscle problems. When assessing whether returned migrants are sicker than migrants still in the United States, the picture is clearer. Returned migrants report higher rates of asthma, high blood pressure, heart problems, and muscle problems than do migrants who stay in the United States, and they are only slightly less likely to report obesity or high cholesterol.

To determine the extent to which migration to the United States is associated with these infirmities, we must control for several factors via logistic regressions. The logistic regression models presented below assess whether migration experience is associated with health problems after controlling for sex, age, marital status, self-report of being overweight, times per week that respondent consumes fast food, and employment in construction or agriculture. In models 1 through 3 in table 8.1, "migrant" is a dummy variable that indicates whether the respondent has ever

---

5. Unlike our self-reported data, these results are based on a physical exam and full blood chemistry analysis.

migrated to the United States. In models 4 through 6 (table 8.2), "time in U.S." is a continuous independent variable that records the number of years the respondent has spent in the United States. The dependent variable in models 1 and 4 measures whether the respondent reported suffering from any of seven infirmities, including asthma, cancer, high cholesterol, diabetes, high blood pressure, muscle problems, and heart problems. In models 2 and 5, the dependent variable is a self-reported heart condition. In models 3 and 6, the dependent variable is a self-reported back or muscle problem.

Figure 8.1 Self-Reported Infirmities among Tlacuitapa Nonmigrants, U.S.-Based Migrants, and Returned Migrants, 2007

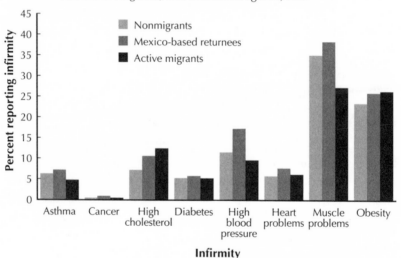

N = 849.

In the first three models, age is consistently significant in predicting negative health outcomes, which is to be expected; older people are more likely to be sick. A high consumption of fast food is positively correlated with all infirmities and with back problems, which is consistent with an expected health decline when consuming foods that are high in fat and sugar. Being a woman and working in agriculture predict back problems, which is consistent with physically demanding labor. Most important from a theoretical standpoint, migrants were significantly less likely to report one of the basket of infirmities or back problems, which concords with the argument that the explanation for the Latino health paradox is the fact that migrants are healthier than their compatriots who stay in Mexico.

Table 8.1 Factors Contributing to Health Problems (coefficients are reported as the odds ratio)

	Model 1 All Infirmities	Model 2 Heart Problems	Model 3 Back Problems
Migrant	**0.733*** **(.128)**	1.116 (.239)	**0.684** (.128)**
Time in U.S.			
Male	0.835 (.140)	0.787 (.170)	**0.591** (.138)**
Age	**1.047*** **(.007)**	**1.064*** **(.008)**	**1.027*** **(.006)**
Married	0.746 (.145)	0.881 (.216)	0.978 (.193)
Overweight	**1.991*** **(.342)**	**2.066*** **(.404)**	**1.563*** **(.271)**
Fast food	**1.101** (.047)**	1.081 (.065)	**1.082* (.047)**
Construction			1.423 (.410)
Agriculture			**1.751** (.490)**
Chi-square	81.03	91.99	37.83
Pseudo-R^2	.0761	.1353	.0396
N	797	789	798

* 90%, ** 95%, *** 99% confidence levels; robust standard errors in parentheses.
Note: In models not shown here, controls for levels of education and wealth did not have significant effects on heath.

Models 4 through 6 (table 8.2) test whether there is a correlation between length of migration and migrant health after controlling for the same factors as in the first three models. In this case, time in the United States correlated significantly with reporting one of the basket of infirmities and back problems, but the effect was negligible (odds ratio = 0.991, where 1.0 would be no correlation). In effect, contrary to the prevailing view of the Latino health paradox, more time spent in the United States did not change migrants' self-reported health. Age was once again a significant predictor that an illness would be reported. Being overweight also increased the likelihood that time in the United States would increase the probability of reporting an illness. Being overweight and consuming fast food are robustly associated with negative health outcomes.

Table 8.2 Time in the United States and Health Outcomes

	Model 4 All Infirmities	Model 5 Heart Problems	Model 6 Back Problems
Migrant			
Time in U.S.	0.991** (.009)	0.996 (.010)	0.996** (.010)
Male	0.811 (.173)	0.830 (.220)	0.782** (.244)
Age	1.051*** (.010)	1.062*** (.012)	1.036*** (.009)
Married	0.651* (.192)	1.053 (.394)	0.873 (.277)
Overweight	1.978*** (.457)	2.251*** (.002)	2.063*** (.496)
Fast food	1.073** (.050)	1.111 (.064)	1.050* (.064)
Construction			1.163 (.382)
Agriculture			1.232 (.470)
Chi-square	41.46	44.35	38.80
Pseudo-R^2	.0768	.1231	.0403
N	430	426	798

* 90%, ** 95%, *** 99% confidence levels; robust standard errors in parentheses.

The results of these first two sets of models show two general trends in our sample after applying various controls. The first set of models demonstrates that migrants are less likely than nonmigrants to report an infirmity. This suggests that people who have migrated are healthier than those who have never migrated. There are three possible explanations for this: migrants are positively selected for their health (the healthy migrant effect), sick migrants return to Mexico (the salmon bias), or—contrary to the Latino health paradox and in support of modernization theory—migrants become healthier with more exposure to more advanced medicine in the United States. The results from the second set of models show that, after applying proper controls, migrants are *not* more or less likely to report an infirmity as their time spent in the United States increases. This suggests that exposure to the United States is not associated per se with overall health outcomes.

Finally, in order to test if migrants are indeed positively selected by their health status or if the salmon bias is at work in our population, we constructed a third logistic regression using the same variables but adding a "returned migrant" independent variable (table 8.3).[6] The three dependent variables are the same as in the first two regressions.

Table 8.3 Factors Contributing to the Health of Returned Migrants

	Model 7 All Infirmities	Model 8 Heart Problems	Model 9 Back Problems
Returned migrant	**.650*** (.162)	**0.450**** (.157)	1.028 (.267)
Male	0.722 (.166)	0.675 (.189)	0.780 (.188)
Age	**1.045**** (.010)	**1.055**** (.011)	**1.036**** (.010)
Married	.756 (.253)	1.240 (.530)	0.746 (.263)
Overweight	**2.120**** (.525)	**2.607**** (.711)	**1.917**** (.476)
Fast food	1.061 (.052)	**1.131*** (.058)	1.041 (.066)
Chi-square	41.94	43.74	23.75
Pseudo-R^2	.0853	.1432	.0513
N	380	376	380

* 90%, ** 95%, *** 99% confidence levels; robust standard errors in parentheses.

Table 8.3 shows that returned migrants are *less* likely than U.S.-based migrants to report an infirmity, indicating that they are relatively healthy.

6. A returned migrant was defined as someone who had migrated to the United States but was living in Mexico in 2006.

This is strong evidence against the salmon bias as an explanation for the better health outcomes of the migrant population and tends, rather, to support the "healthy migrant effect" explanation. After controlling for age and sex, Tlacuitapeño migrants living in the United States are healthier, apparently because they were selected for their overall health by the rigors of migration.

This table shows further that self-reporting of being overweight is a consistently significant factor in the reporting of health conditions, along with increased consumption of fast food. These issues, coupled with the assertion that migration changes dietary habits, form a link between health and migration that is important for migrants and nonmigrants alike.

NUTRITIONAL CHANGES RESULTING FROM IMMIGRATION

Several studies have shown that migration to the United States produces changes in dietary habits, which can translate into a decline in migrant health. Two especially significant studies in this area focused, respectively, on dietary acculturation (Romero-Gwynn et al. 1993) and migrants' health indicators (Kandula et al. 2004). Though it is difficult to demonstrate a cause-and-effect relationship between nutrition and health within the migrant population due to selection biases and dynamic consumption patterns on both sides of the border, there are changes in nutritional patterns that occur upon migration that could potentially be linked with a decline in health. Medical anthropologist Seth Holmes argues that there is a significant decrease in the nutritional value of a migrant's diet within the first year of migration to the United States (Holmes 2006, 1778). Our study looks at the various ways in which nutrition has changed with migrants' time in the United States and compares those eating habits to those of nonmigrants.

A traditional Mexican meal consists mainly of "corn tortillas, beans, rice, potatoes, eggs, tomatoes, and chili peppers" (Kaiser et al. 2004, 1377). Most Tlacuitapeños consume this traditional diet; those with greater economic means commonly add a serving of meat. When asked about her food consumption, town resident María de Jesús stated, "We eat what we make at home—soup, beans. And when we have meat, we eat meat." When migrants come to the United States, they are exposed to new foods, new ways of preparing food, and an overall food "culture" that is dramatically different from their own.

One comparison that highlights the relationship between migrants' and nonmigrants' nutritional practices is their consumption of fast food. In our survey in Tlacuitapa, we asked, "How many times per week do you consume fast food?" In general, migrants reported consuming more fast food than nonmigrants; 53 percent of migrants consume fast food at least once a week, compared to 33 percent of nonmigrants. This suggests that migrants to the United States have become participants in America's fast-food culture, which could initiate a health decline among this population.

Several factors help explain the migrants' new eating habits. Fast food is quick and readily available. This is important to workers who simply do not have time to prepare balanced meals for consumption at the workplace. Héctor, a native of Tlacuitapa who now resides in Oklahoma City, told us it was simply easier to consume fast food because of his job. Héctor works in construction and patronizes whichever fast-food retailer is nearby. Another possible explanation for the popularity of fast food among this group is a lack of nutritional education. Perhaps if migrants were more aware of the negative effects of fast foods and snack foods, they would replace these products with more healthy options.

Consumption of fast food also varies by marital status: 77 percent of nonmarried migrants reported eating fast food at least once a week, compared to only 48 percent of married migrants (see figure 8.2). When they arrive in the United States, most male migrants must provide meals for themselves, something that in Mexico was done by their mothers, sisters, and wives. Absent the supporting structure of a traditional Mexican home, many migrant men avoid taking on new culinary responsibilities by opting for the convenience of fast food.

Finally, migrants' desire to assimilate can lead them to adopt poor eating habits. There were some 222,000 fast-food outlets in the United States in 2001, with combined sales of over $125 billion (Paeratakul et al. 2003, 1332). Mexican migrants quickly emulate the host society's preference for a quick and easy meal.[7] A study that analyzed the diets of Mexican Americans in different stages of the transition "from traditional Mexican diets to more mainstream American diets" found that "with increased acculturation and time in the United States, migrants consume fewer complex carbohydrates and more highly processed convenience foods that are high

---

7. Fast-food consumption has also been increasing in Mexico. The U.S. Department of Commerce reports that the fast-food industry in Mexico takes in about US$2 billion per year (http://www.buyusa.gov/mexico/en/250.pdf).

in sugar and fats" (Kandula et al. 2004, 361). These dietary changes can exacerbate deleterious aspects of the traditional Mexican diet that are not that healthy to begin with, such as the heavy use of oil and lard, dependence on starchy foods, and high consumption of sodas and other heavily sugared drinks.

Figure 8.2 Fast Food Consumption among Tlacuitapeños, by Marital Status

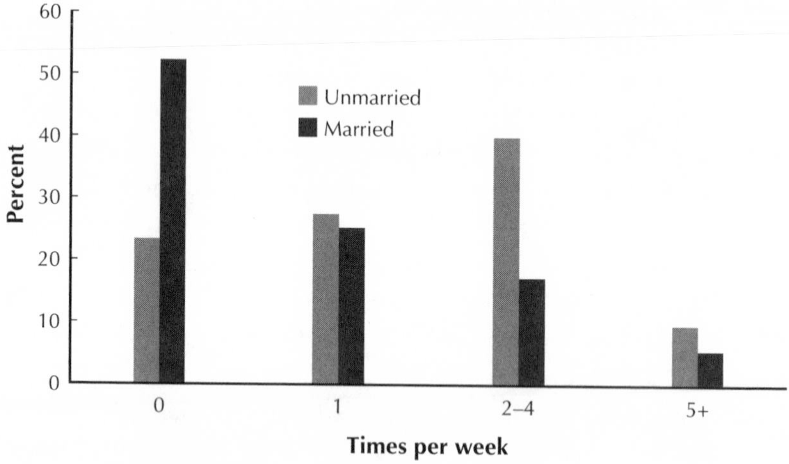

N = 391.

Consumption of fast food and other foods of low nutritional value can cause serious health problems. Rapid weight gain and obesity have been linked to heart problems and diabetes. In our survey, we asked, "After being in the United States, would you say you weigh more, weigh less, or weigh the same?" Fifty-nine percent of migrants reported weighing more after being in the United States. Only 8 percent reported weighing less; 33 percent reported weighing the same.

Obesity is prevalent among both migrants and nonmigrants from Tlacuitapa. In our survey, 25 percent of nonmigrants reported obesity problems, along with 26 percent of migrants.[8] Kaplan et al. (2004) found that "the prevalence of obesity among those with 0 to 4, 5 to 9, 10 to 14, and ≥ 15 years of residence in the United States was 9.4 percent, 14.5 percent,

---

8. In Tlacuitapa, 35 percent of females and 22 percent of males reported being overweight. According to the World Health Organization, nearly 45 percent of females and 30 percent of males over 30 years of age in Mexico suffer from obesity (WHO 2005).

21.0 percent, and 24.4 percent respectively" (p. 323). Obesity rates appear to rise with time spent in the United States, and this is directly linked to an increased risk of heart attack. We spoke with an informant who had suffered a heart attack because of a clogged artery. When asked the cause of his heart attack, he replied: "Food! A lot of Coca-Cola." He reported eating fast food almost daily because the work schedule at his construction job did not allow him time to eat elsewhere.

Immigration to the United States affects not only the habits of migrants but also those of town residents who remain in Tlacuitapa. A hot dog stand and pizza delivery truck now provide weekly service to local residents, and there has been an infiltration of new food products. American products line the shelves of the town's small grocery stores; one of the most prevalent items is Maruchan Cup o' Noodles.[9] According to Nazario, a grocery store owner, "The migrants ask for 'maruchan,' a soup from over there, so now I try to stock them." This product, high in sodium and fat, is one of the snacks most frequently requested by migrants and nonmigrants alike. It is important to note that remittances also support the popularity of such food products. Absent remittances, many nonmigrants in Tlacuitapa could not afford them. These processed food products have infiltrated the traditional Mexican diet, changing the nutrition of entire communities and making food habits among Tlacuitapeños relatively unhealthy on both sides of the border.

Of course, migrants' consumption of fast food is only one of several factors accounting for obesity among the Mexican population. Rivera et al. (2002) report that the Mexican population in general performs less physical activity as it has become more urban and has easier access to "inexpensive but high energy–dense foods" (p. 113). Further, nutritional changes are not the only threats posed by migration. Migration also affects the mental health of both migrants and nonmigrants, an issue that concerns health professionals on both sides of the border.

DEPRESSION

Although our questionnaire did not specifically address depression, we became aware of this issue when Tlacuitapa's health professionals spoke

---

9. Though Maruchan is a Japanese company, we classify its product as American because it has become part of U.S. snack-food culture and because migrants first encounter it in the United States.

of its pervasiveness. According to Dr. López León, anti-depressants are the most frequently prescribed medication for both migrants and non-migrants, and Dr. Gallardo said he observes signs of depression in some 40 percent of his patients, mostly among young wives of migrants. These patients complain of a variety of symptoms, which Dr. Gallardo identifies as signs of depression, such as tension headaches, anxiety, nervousness, and an overall desire for someone to listen. "They miss their loved ones who have migrated to the United States and are overwhelmed by loneliness, the lack of housework or something to keep them busy."

This was true for Leticia, a resident of Tlacuitapa whose husband left to work in the United States six years previously. After his departure she developed headaches and insomnia, for which she was prescribed sedatives. After seven months working in the sun as a construction worker, her husband developed a skin allergy and returned to Tlacuitapa, and in the years since her husband's return, Leticia's symptoms of depression have receded. Tlacuitapa is transformed during the annual fiestas, but the town is quiet and deserted during the rest of the year, and it is then that permanent residents like Leticia suffer from the absence of their loved ones.

We found that depression was prevalent among the migrant population as well. Many Tlacuitapeño migrants who had returned to their hometown for a short visit spoke of their distress when leaving their family behind and the strain of having to shoulder responsibility for supporting their many dependents. According to Dr. López León, migrants who arrive from the United States have elevated stress levels brought on by their responsibilities as family provider. Moreover, migration alters the traditional family structure, which also places a migrant at risk of becoming depressed. A study on the effects of transnational family relationships identified three areas that cause increased risk for depression upon migration: new definitions of family life, various forms of relational stress that begin in the preparatory stages of migration, and acculturative stress manifested in gender and generational relationships after migration (Falicov 2007, 5). A migrant who is separated from loved ones loses his or her access to emotional support.[10] Given the migrants' financial anxiety and

---

10. These finding are consistent with those from a 2005 study in Tunkás, Yucatán. Depression among migrants was provoked by the change in their social conditions and isolation from their traditional family unit. See Prelat and Maciel 2007.

uncertain future, depression rates continue to rise among Tlacuitapa migrants and nonmigrants.

LABOR ACCIDENTS AND THEIR ROLE IN THE IMMIGRATION EXPERIENCE

Moving away from the primary conditions that afflict our population, we also examined health complications that arise through work-related accidents and limitations on access to health care. As our earlier analysis shows, workers are affected by the physical demands of their occupations, a factor that further complicates migrants' health landscape and constitutes an additional obstacle for them to overcome after arriving in the United States.

Most male migrants from Tlacuitapa work in construction in the United States, a sector prone to work-related accidents. A serious accident may force a migrant to return home permanently or, at minimum, for a lengthy period of rehabilitation. We consider two categories of work-related injuries—nonfatal injuries and fatal injuries.

Nonfatal Injuries

The most common nonfatal occupational injuries are sprains and strains, accounting for nearly 44 percent of all work injuries in 2001 (U.S. Bureau of Labor Statistics 2004). Such injuries can have emotional as well as physical consequences. In our research, we met one person who had been injured at a car factory and another, Juan Pablo, who had suffered a back injury after falling thirty feet at a construction site. Juan Pablo was left with a broken nose, a laceration that extended from his eyebrow down his cheek, a broken arm, and several fractures in his hands. Juan Pablo said he did not receive appropriate medical attention; he was bandaged up and given medication at a local emergency room, but there was no follow-up care or evaluation. He later discovered that he would need extensive treatment. He required several operations, which kept him out of work for nearly a year. Many injured migrants are forced to return to Mexico in order to receive treatment or simply to wait while their injuries heal. Such timeouts imply huge costs that extend beyond the expenditures for health care because they also affect migrants' ability to provide financially for themselves and their families.

Fatal Injuries

Fatal injuries, though far less common, obviously result in much greater trauma for a migrant's family and community. In 2004, 5,703 workers died from fatal injuries in the United States (U.S. Bureau of Labor Statistics 2004). Latinos accounted for nearly 16 percent of the 2004 deaths, and from 1999 to 2002, Latino men accounted for an average of 94 percent of work-related fatalities among Latino workers in the United States. The risk factors associated with work in physically demanding economic sectors have a direct effect on migrants' health and family life. "They work in dangerous settings, and a variety of factors such as lack of training, inadequate safety equipment, and economic pressures further increase their risk for work injury" (Walter et al. 2002). Thrown into an unfamiliar work environment, migrants become even more vulnerable and prone to injury.

The death of Héctor Muñoz's father speaks to the possibility that a migrant will meet a tragic end. Héctor's father worked on a road-building crew and was repairing his machine when he was caught beneath it. As Héctor recalls, "I saw him, just saw pieces of him. She [Héctor's mother] doesn't know; that's why I'm talking in English. She thinks my dad's body was whole, but that wasn't true. It was just pieces; three or four bags of them." When we asked Héctor how the accident affected his family, he talked of the financial and emotional repercussions. The company gave the family minimal compensation, which only covered funeral expenses. Héctor's family filed a lawsuit, primarily to win some financial support for the mother. When speaking of the emotional strain, Héctor added, "You feel like the whole world is coming down on you."

ACCESS TO HEALTH CARE

The findings reported in table 8.2, along with our qualitative results, suggest that migrants are no more or less likely to report an infirmity with increased exposure to the United States. One possible explanation for this is that migrants are not accessing the U.S. health-care system.

Many migrants are unable or unwilling to take advantage of the U.S. health-care system, in part because of fear and in part because of a general lack of knowledge. Migrants in the United States have been blamed for "leeching" off of government aid programs (Smith and Edmonston 1998), and such accusations may decrease migrants' willingness to participate in social services and health care. Our research found that only four of the sixty-two migrants who became sick and received treatment in the United States over the past two years reported using Medi-Cal or another government program. The majority (38 percent) had their treatment covered by their employer, and 33 percent paid for treatment out of pocket (see figure 8.3).

Figure 8.3 How Do Tlacuitapeño Migrants Pay for Treatment in the United States?

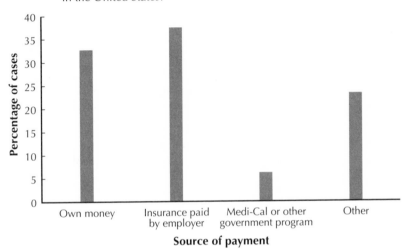

N = 64.

Both migrants and nonmigrants from Tlacuitapa view the U.S. health-care system as difficult to access. For nonmigrants, this constitutes one more obstacle that family members and friends must overcome if they decide to go to the United States. And migrants may be unsure whether their undocumented status means they have no right to access services in the United States, and they are often unaware of the steps to follow to obtain care. Marco San Román, the president of a labor union in the San Francisco Bay area, commented on the difficulty his fellow migrants experience when trying to maneuver their way through the health-care system: "A lot of them don't understand the system, how it works. I know, because I just went through it and it is crazy. . . . I don't know what to do, I don't know where to go. I don't know how to follow the law. Even people who have been there for a while don't know, not only the undocumented." This generalized lack of knowledge has caused many migrants to seek out providers of traditional health care or to stock up on medications when they visit Mexico.

Other factors that deter migrants from seeking health care are the comparative complexity of the U.S. system and the language barrier. María Luisa, a nonmigrant from Tlacuitapa, said she had heard that the U.S. medical system was simply too difficult to navigate: "They have to make appointments over there. Here, as soon as somebody comes in, they are seen. They don't have to make appointments. It's even harder if you don't speak English."

This sense of inaccessibility, which dissuades migrants from seeking health care in the United States, is not restricted to migrants from Tlacuitapa. According to the California Immigrant Policy Center and National Immigration Law Center (2006), "Undocumented immigrants have very little access to publicly funded health care programs and are reluctant to use services because of fear, and confusion over eligibility rules." The Mexican Health Ministry recently reported that "there are 2.1 million Mexican immigrants without medical insurance living in California, a third of all uninsured Mexican immigrants in the entire country" (Zúñiga et al. 2006, 29). Even *with* documentation, many Mexican migrants find the health-care system intimidating: "immigrants are much less likely to use primary and preventive medical services, hospital services, emergency medical services, and dental care than are citizens, even after controlling for the effects of race/ethnicity, income, insurance status, and health status" (Ku and Papademetriou 2007, 91). The lack of insurance and access to treatment makes the migrant community even more vulnerable.

One final factor that may deter migrants from using health-care facilities in the United States is their sense of being victims of ethnic discrimination. For example, when discussing health-care options available in Texas, Pablo said that being Mexican would prevent him from receiving treatment there: "Discrimination never ends for us." Eight of ten Tlacuitapeños surveyed said there was a lot of discrimination against Mexicans in the United States. There seems to be some basis for their belief: "Migrants not perceived to be a health threat to their host communities would be less exposed to discrimination and xenophobia, and more likely to be included as equal participants" (International Dialogue on Migration 2005, 24). The perception of discrimination has been a key point in studies of health care for minority groups. In examining the disparities that exist in the health care provided across different minority populations, the Institute of Medicine found that "ethnic disparities, whether real or perceived, are experiences that minority patients are likely to bring to the clinical encounter, and are thereby likely to shape their expectations, attitudes, and behaviors toward providers and health systems" (Smedley et al. 2003, 102). While our research does not provide conclusive support for this claim, the issue of discrimination and its effect on access to health care is one plausible explanation for migrants' low use of health-care facilities in the United States.

Many of our informants recognize the advantages that health insurance confers, and they lament the lack of health insurance in Mexico. María Luisa noted how vulnerable her family would be if her husband, a bricklayer, were injured at work: "If somebody suffers an accident here . . . there's nothing." For the people of Tlacuitapa, especially those who work at physically demanding jobs, knowing that their ability to make a living depends on not becoming ill or injured is cause for great concern. Feliciano Claudio, the local huesero, also expressed this vulnerability: "We don't have medical insurance here, no help from the government. . . . We just go along by the grace of God, with the little we earn here and there, or with help from our children."

Contrary to a widespread misperception, migrants do not come to the United States to exploit the U.S. health-care system. Our data suggest that many migrants are deterred from seeking health care in the United States for a variety of reasons, including unfamiliarity with the system, the language barrier, and fear of discrimination. And when they do seek health care, they are likely to pay for the services out of pocket or with help from their employer. Relying on their good health to endure, migrants do not allow their lack of health care to change their decision to remain in the United States to work. For many nonmigrants, having healthy relatives in the United States has become a crucial factor in their *own* health status; the remittances migrants send home have altered the way in which nonmigrants seek health care.

REMITTANCES AND HEALTH CARE

Though the medical facilities in Tlacuitapa are modest, migration has increased the likelihood that local residents will receive health care. In the years before remittances began flowing into the local economy, Tlacuitapeños were less likely to see a doctor or to use Western medicine, simply because they did not have the means to pay for such treatment. They relied instead on traditional medicine and natural remedies. Now, the inflow of remittances permits more extensive health coverage. In our survey, we asked recipients of remittances to identify the ends to which these funds were directed. Almost 30 percent listed medical expenses among the top three.

Across Mexico, the connection between remittances and health expenditures implies that major sending communities reap health advantages. According to a research team led by Elena Zúñiga, "there is evidence that remittances are encouraging greater expenditure on treating illnesses and meeting other health needs. Households that receive remittances spend an average of about 50 percent more of their financial resources on covering health expenses than households that do not receive any" (Zúñiga et al. 2006). Households in Tlacuitapa that receive remittances spend nearly 10 percent of their total household expenditures on health care, nearly twice as much as households that do not receive remittances (see figure 8.4).

Figure 8.4 Percent of Total Expenditures Used for Health Care among Households in Mexico, 2004

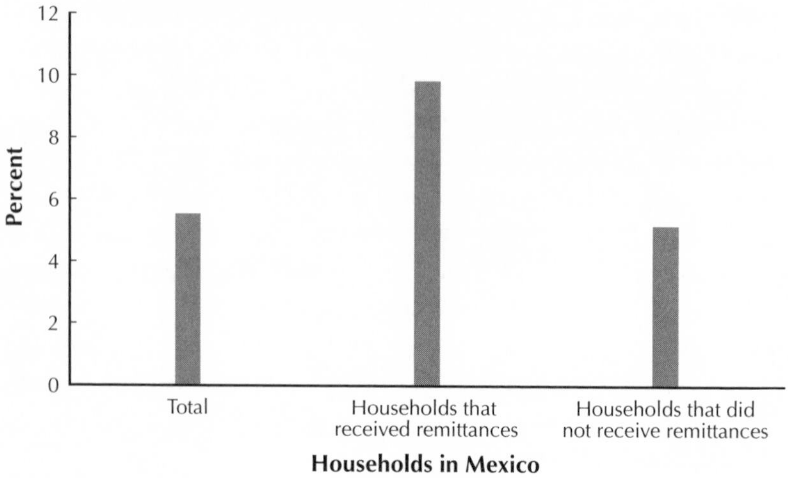

Households in Mexico

Source: INEGI 2004.

The ability to direct more money toward health care in the sending community may well improve efforts to control illnesses such as diabetes and high blood pressure. Thus, though migrants are reluctant to utilize health services while they are in the United States, the money they earn and send home has served to expand access to health services in Mexico.

CONCLUSION

Even though migrants in the United States face a number of health stressors—including changing food habits, depression, work-related accidents, and restricted access to the U.S. health-care system—our findings suggest that migrants are, nevertheless, a relatively healthy population. Yet they are at risk from some factors that affect health: Changing nutritional habits mean increased consumption of fast foods and a move away from the traditional Mexican diet for both migrants and nonmigrants. The mental health of both migrants and nonmigrants suffers from the effects of migration, with both populations showing a growing propensity toward depression. The dangerous working conditions in the labor-intensive jobs our population is likely to fill threaten the workers' ability to earn the wages that support them in the United States and their families in Mexico. Migrants in the United States show a reluctance to use health services, though this threat to their health is somewhat offset by the fact that their remittances serve to buy health care for family members in Mexico.

Returning to the challenge of explaining the Latino health paradox, our research argues for the healthy migrant effect, which operates to create a Latino population in the United States that is comparatively healthier than other groups due to their health-based selection from the general population in their community of origin. Migrants returning to Mexico show a strong health profile, demonstrating that the salmon bias is not at work in our sample; if the salmon bias were at work, we would expect to see a population of returned migrants that is substantially sicker than active migrants and nonmigrants. However, our findings also demonstrate that more time spent in the United States does not increase the likelihood that a migrant will report an infirmity, suggesting that healthy migrants make the journey to the United States, are able to maintain their health while there, and then return to Mexico. In the process, they experience a diversity of health environments on both sides of the border.

References

California Immigrant Policy Center and National Immigration Law Center. 2006. "Immigrants and the U.S. Health Care System." http://www.nilc .org/immspbs/health/Issue_Briefs/imms&ushealthcare_2007-01.pdf.

Falicov, Celia J. 2007. "Working with Transnational Immigrants: Expanding Meanings of Family, Community, and Culture," *Family Process* 46, no. 2: 157–71.

Holmes, Seth M. 2006. "An Ethnographic Study of the Social Context of Migrant Health in the United States," *Plos Medicine* 3, no. 10.

INEGI (Instituto Nacional de Estadística, Geografía e Informática). 2004. *Encuesta Nacional de Ingresos e Gastos de los Hogares.* Mexico: INEGI.

Inglehart, Ronald, and Christian Welzel. 2005. *Modernization, Cultural Change and Democracy: The Human Development Sequence.* New York: Cambridge University Press.

International Dialogue on Migration. 2005. *Health and Migration: Bridging the Gap.* Geneva: Migration Policy and Research Program.

Kaiser, Lucia L., et al. 2004. "Choice of Instrument Influences Relations between Food Insecurity and Obesity in Latino Women," *American Journal of Clinical Nutrition* 80.

Kandula, Namratha R., et al. 2004. "Assuring the Health of Immigrants: What the Leading Health Indicators Tell Us," *Annual Review of Public Health* 25: 357–76.

Kaplan, Mark S., et al. 2004. "The Association between Length of Residence and Obesity among Hispanic Immigrants," *American Journal of Preventive Medicine* 27, no. 4.

Ku, Leighton, and Demetrious G. Papademetriou. 2007. "Access to Health Care and Health Insurance: Immigrants and Immigration Reform." In *Securing the Future: US Immigrant Integration Policy: A Reader*, ed. Michael Fix. Washington, DC: Migration Policy Institute.

Paeratakul, S., et al. 2003. "Fast-food Consumption among US Adults and Children: Dietary and Nutrient Intake Profile," *Journal of the American Dental Association* 103, no. 10.

Palloni, Alberto, and Elizabeth Arias. 2004. "Paradox Lost: Explaining the Hispanic Adult Mortality Advantage," *Demography* 41, no. 3 (August): 385–415.

Palloni, Alberto, and Douglas Ewbank. 2004. "Selection Processes in the Study of Racial and Ethnic Differentials in Adult Health and Mortality." In *Critical Perspectives on Racial and Ethnic Differences in Health in Late Life*, ed. N. B. Anderson, R. A. Bulatao, and B. Cohen. Washington, DC: National Academy Press.

Patel, Kushang V., et al. 2004. "Evaluation of Mortality Data for Older Mexican Americans: Implications for the Hispanic Paradox," *American Journal of Epidemiology* 159, no. 7: 707–15.

Prelat, Sonia, and Alejandra Maciel. 2007. "Migration and Health." In *Mayan Journeys: The New Migration from Yucatán to the United States*, ed. Wayne A. Cornelius, David Fitzgerald, and Pedro Lewin Fischer. La Jolla, CA: Center for Comparative Immigration Studies, University of California, San Diego.

Rivera, Juan, et al. 2002. "Epidemiological and Nutritional Transition in Mexico: Rapid Increase of Non-Communicable Chronic Diseases and Obesity," *Public Health Nutrition* 5.

Romero-Gwynn, Eunice, et al. 1993. "Dietary Acculturation among Latinos of Mexican Descent," *Nutrition Today* 28, no. 4.

Smedley, Brian D., et al. 2003. *Unequal Treatment: Confronting Racial and Ethnic Disparities in Health Care.* Washington, DC: Institute of Medicine of the National Academies.

Smith, James P., and Barry Edmonston, eds. 1998. *The Immigration Debate: Studies on the Economic, Demographic, and Fiscal Effects of Immigration.* Washington, DC: National Academy Press.

Tapia Conyer, Roberto. 2006. *El Manual de Salud Pública.* 2d ed. México, DF: Intersistemas.

U.S. Bureau of Labor Statistics. 2004. *Work Health Chart Book 2004. Data from the Census of Fatal Occupational Injuries. Special Tabulation-Number and Rate for Fatal Occupational Injures by Selected Worker Characteristics, 1992–2002.* Niosh Publication Bo.2004-146. Washington, DC: U.S. Department of Labor, Safety and Health Statistics Program.

Villarejo, Don, et al. 2000. *Suffering in Silence: A Report on the Health of California's Agricultural Workers.* Davis, CA: California Institute for Rural Studies.

Walter, Nicholas, Philippe Bourgois, H. Margarita Loinaz, and Dean Schillinger. 2002. "Social Context of Work Injury among Undocumented Day Laborers in San Francisco," *Journal of General Internal Medicine* 17, no. 3 (March): 221–29.

WHO (World Health Organization). 2005. Global InfoBase. http://www.who.int/ncd_surveillance/infobase/web/InfoBasePolicyMaker/CountryProfiles/QuickCompare.aspx?DM=5&Countries=484&Year=2005&sf1=cd.0704&Sex=all&AgeGroup=15-100.

Zúñiga, Elena, Xóchitl Castañeda, Al Averbach, and Steven P. Wallace. 2006. "Mexican and Central American Immigrants in the United States: Health Care Access." http://www.healthpolicy.ucla.edu/pubs/publication.asp?pubID=196.

APPENDIX

Survey Questionnaire Administered to Persons with U.S. Migration Experience in Tlacuitapa and San Antonio de la Garza, Jalisco, January 2007

PERFIL DEMOGRÁFICO

¿En qué año nació Ud.?

¿En dónde nació?

¿Dónde vive Ud. actualmente?

¿Hasta qué año llegó Ud. en la escuela?

¿Alguna vez Ud. se casó o entró en una unión libre?

¿Su esposo/a ha vivido en los EE.UU.?

¿Por cuánto tiempo?

¿Cuántos hijos tiene Ud.?

¿En qué año nacieron?

¿Dónde nacieron?

¿En qué año emigraron?

¿A qué se dedica Ud.?

¿Cuántas horas trabaja por semana?

¿Ud. recibe un sueldo?

¿Cuánto gana?

¿Cuántos hermanos y hermanas tiene Ud.?

¿Qué posición ocupa Ud. en la familia? ¿El primer hijo, el segundo, el tercero etcétera?

¿Me puede decir cuántos parientes y de qué tipo (esposo/a, hermanos/as, padres etcétera) tiene Ud. que viven actualmente en los EE.UU.?

¿Cuántos hermanos y hermanas tiene que alguna vez han vivido en los EE.UU.?

HISTORIA MIGRATORIA

Antes de que Ud. se fuera a los EE.UU. por primera vez, ¿cuántos parientes tenía que ya vivían en los EE.UU.?

¿Estaba su esposo/a con Ud.?

Cuando Ud. se fue a los EE.UU. por primera vez, ¿tuvo que dejar a sus hijos en México?

¿Quién los cuidó?

Antes de salir de Tlacuitapa por primera vez, ¿a qué se dedicaba?

¿Ganó un sueldo?

En los últimos cinco años, ¿dónde ha pasado más tiempo? ¿En Tlacuitapa o en los EE.UU.?

¿Cuántas veces en los últimos cinco años regresó Ud. a Tlacuitapa?

[a personas entrevistadas en los EE.UU.]
Este mes (enero de 2007), ¿regresó a (Tlacuitapa/San Antonio) para las fiestas del pueblo?

[si "no"] ¿Por qué no?

Antes de irse la última vez, ¿cuánto tiempo pensaba Ud. quedarse en los EE.UU.?

En esta última temporada en los EE.UU., ¿se quedó más tiempo de lo que tenía planeado?

¿Por qué?

¿Conoce a alguien que se quedó en los EE.UU. en vez de regresar a Tlacuitapa?

¿Por qué se fue a los EE.UU. la última vez?

¿Se fue de Tlacuitapa porque no le iba bien en el pueblo, o porque en los EE.UU. había más oportunidades?

¿Cómo logró juntar o conseguir el dinero para financiar el viaje a los EE.UU.?

¿Cómo consiguió su último trabajo en los EE.UU.?

EXPERIENCIAS EN CRUZAR LA FRONTERA

¿Cruzó la frontera con papeles, o tuvo que entrar sin papeles (legales, prestados o falsos)?

¿Dónde consiguió sus papeles chuecos/prestados?

Si tuvo que comprar papeles, ¿cuánto pagó por ellos?

¿Cómo logró conseguir el coyote que usó?

¿Cuándo le pagó al coyote?

¿Hasta dónde lo llevó el coyote?

¿El coyote abandonó a alguien del grupo?

¿Recibió Ud. algún tipo de maltrato o abuso mientras cruzaba?

¿De parte de quién?

¿Qué tipo de maltrato o abuso?

¿Cuántas veces intentó cruzar la frontera, durante su último viaje a los EE.UU.?

¿Cuántas veces lo agarró la Migra en la frontera, en ese viaje?

Entonces, ¿pudo pasar o no?

¿Fue devuelto a una ciudad mexicana en la frontera, o lo llevaron a un lugar lejos de la frontera?

Si lo hubieran regresado a un lugar más lejano de la frontera, ¿esto disminuiría su intención de volver a cruzar, o no tendría ningún efecto?

¿Esto disminuyó su intención de volver a cruzar, o no tuvo ningún efecto?

¿Por cuál parte de la frontera pasó o intentó pasar?

¿Era una zona urbana o una zona rural?

¿Pasó Ud. por una garita?

¿De qué manera cruzó la frontera?

¿Cuánto tiempo pasó después de cruzar la línea hasta que llegó al lugar donde lo recogieron?

INTENCIÓN DE MIGRAR

¿Para este nuevo año, ha pensado en irse a los EE.UU.?

¿Por qué piensa así?

¿Qué tan probable es que Ud. consiga un trabajo en los EE.UU., la próxima vez que se vaya?

¿Qué tipo de trabajo piensa tener en los EE.UU., la próxima vez que se vaya?

¿Este trabajo será arreglado por algún pariente o amigo que ya vive en los EE.UU., o Ud. tendrá que buscarlo?

¿Cuánto piensa que va a ganar en ese trabajo?

¿Cuál es el sueldo mínimo que Ud. aceptaría por un trabajo en los EE.UU.?

PERCEPCIONES DEL CONTROL FRONTERIZO

¿Sabe algo o ha escuchado del proyecto de poner un muro en la frontera?

¿Ud. ha oído de la presencia de la Guardia Nacional americana en la frontera?

¿Cree que la Guardia Nacional trae o no trae armas?

¿Me puede poner en orden, empezando con la más difícil, las siguientes cosas que hacen difícil el cruce de la frontera sin papeles? Más Migra, el muro, la Guardia Nacional, Minutemen/vigilantes, clima extremo, rateros, policía mexicana.

Actualmente, ¿es fácil o difícil evadir la Migra, al cruzar la frontera?

¿Tiene algún familiar que se haya quedado en los EE.UU., por temor a la vigilancia fronteriza?

Actualmente, ¿es peligroso cruzar la frontera, si uno no tiene papeles?

¿Conoce Ud. a alguien que se fue a los EE.UU. y que murió al cruzar la frontera?

¿Sabe algo, o ha oído hablar, de la propuesta del Presidente Bush para trabajadores migrantes?

¿Qué es lo que propuso el Presidente Bush?

Si se aprueba un nuevo programa de contrataciones, ¿es más probable que vaya a los EE.UU. a trabajar, o no tendría ningún efecto sobre sus intenciones?

¿Alguna vez ha conseguido papeles chuecos en EE.UU.?

¿Piensa arreglar sus papeles para quedarse en los EE.UU.?

PROCESOS DE INMIGRACIÓN LEGAL Y DE CONSEGUIR CIUDADANÍA

¿Cuántas veces ha intentado arreglar papeles para algún familiar?

¿Cuánto tiempo duró el proceso?

¿Piensa arreglar papeles para algún (otro) familiar?

¿Cuánto cuesta arreglar papeles?

¿Alguna vez ha solicitado una visa para irse a los EE.UU.? (si la respuesta es "no", ¿Por qué no?)

¿Qué tipo de visa (la primera vez)?

¿Recibió la visa?

¿Cuál fue el primer año en que consiguió una visa?

¿Alguna vez se quedó Ud. más tiempo en los EE.UU. de lo que la visa permitió?

¿Alguna vez trabajó en los EE.UU. durante el tiempo que tenía su visa?

A veces, uno no sabe cuales son los verdaderos requisitos para obtener una visa de turista. Favor de decirme si es necesario pagar $100 dólares para obtener la cita, tener familiares en EE.UU., tener cuenta bancaria o ingresos, tener casa propia, tener un empleo en México.

¿Cómo aprendió acerca de los requisitos?

¿Ha solicitado una mica (*green card*)? (¿Por qué no?)

¿Bajo qué categoría solicitó la mica/*green card*?

¿En qué año la solicitó?

Si recuerda, ¿cuánto pagó por la ayuda de un abogado o un notario?

¿Recibió su mica/*green card*?

¿En qué año la recibió? (¿Por qué no la recibió?)

¿Ha pensado aplicar por una mica/*green card*?

¿Como se puede obtener una mica/*green card*?

¿Como aprendió sobre el proceso?

¿Cuánto tiempo necesita para obtener la mica?

¿Ha aplicado por la ciudadanía? (¿Por qué no?)

¿En qué año solicitó la ciudadanía?

¿En qué año recibió la ciudadanía? (¿Por qué no la recibió?)

¿Cuánto pago por la solicitud de ciudadanía?

Si recuerda, ¿cuánto pago por un abogado/notario?

¿Cuánto fue el costo de la solicitud?

¿Ha pensado en aplicar por la ciudadanía americana? (¿Por qué no?)

A veces, uno no sabe cuales son los verdaderos requisitos para obtener la ciudadanía. Favor de decirme si las siguientes cosas son ciertas o no. Es necesario tener una mica/green card, no tener ningún delito, no usar foodstamps ni welfare, saber inglés, salario mínimo de $1,500 al mes, tener conocimiento sobre el gobierno y la historia de los EE.UU., residencia de cierto tiempo.

¿Cómo aprendió sobre los requisitos para obtener la ciudadanía?

REMESAS E INVERSIONES

¿Alguna vez ha mandado dinero desde los EE.UU. para alguna obra pública en el pueblo?

Durante este viaje más reciente o actual a los EE.UU., ¿mandó dinero a sus parientes de aquí? (¿Por qué no mandó dinero?)

¿A quién se lo mandó?

¿Cuánto dinero mandó?

¿Con qué frecuencia?

¿Cómo mandaba el dinero?

¿Sabe Ud. en qué se gastó la mayoría del dinero?

Estando en Tlacuitapa, ¿ha recibido dinero de alguien en los EE.UU.?

¿De quién?

¿Para qué se usó la mayoría del dinero enviado de los EE.UU.?

¿Alguna vez ha invertido Ud. en un negocio?

¿Qué tipo de negocio?

¿En dónde?

¿Invirtió con dinero ganado en los EE.UU.?

Si quisiera empezar un negocio nuevo, ¿dónde lo pondría?

¿Cuál es la principal razón para no poner un negocio en Tlacuitapa?

¿Cuáles de las siguientes cosas tiene su casa en Tlacuitapa? Televisora, estereo, refrigerador, computadora, lavadora, vehículo.

¿Dónde realiza la mayoría de sus compras del mes cuando está en México?

¿Tiene Ud. cuenta bancaria, o es socio de una caja de ahorros en México?

¿Cuánto dinero trajo consigo, cuando regresó a Tlacuitapa la última vez?

¿Regaló alguna parte de ese dinero a sus familiares?

¿Cuánto, más o menos?

VIDA EN LOS ESTADOS UNIDOS

Durante su trabajo más reciente en los EE.UU., ¿el patrón le pidió algún documento de identificación?

¿Qué tipo de documento?

¿Tiene cuenta bancaria en los EE.UU.?

¿Es una cuenta en común con su esposo/a (*joint*), o es personal?

¿Tiene alguna propiedad en los EE.UU.?

Durante esta estancia más reciente en los EE.UU., ¿mandó a sus hijos a la escuela allá?

Cuando Ud. está en los EE.UU., ¿cuántas veces al mes se pone en contacto con su familia en Tlacuitapa?

Después de jubilarse, ¿dónde quiere vivir?

¿Le interesa más lo que pasa en la política de México, o en la política de los EE.UU.?

¿Tiene credencial de elector?

¿Votó en las elecciones mexicanas en el año 2006?

¿Regresó a México para votar, o votó por correo en los EE.UU.?

¿Ud. participó en las "marchas" de migrantes, en la primavera pasada?

CULTURA E IDENTIDAD

En el mes pasado, ¿cuántas veces asistió a misa?

¿Ud. asiste ahora a misa menos seguido o más seguido que antes de irse a los EE.UU.?

¿Ud. vería mal si alguien del pueblo se casa con una persona que no fuera de Tlacuitapa? ¿De México?

¿Cree Ud. que hay mucha o poca discriminación en contra de los mexicanos en los EE.UU.?

¿Ud. se identifica mucho o poco con los siguientes tipos de personas? Tlacuitapeños, jaliscienses, mexicanos, latinoamericanos, norteamericanos, estadounidenses, latinos, la gente del pueblo en EE.UU. donde vive Ud., la gente del estado en EE.UU. donde vive Ud.

¿Con cuál de las siguientes dos frases está Ud. más de acuerdo? Se debe permitir la inversión extranjera en la industria petrolera, para que crezca más. Permitir la inversión extranjera en la industria petrolera sería malo para el país.

Hay una ley que dice que un mexicano puede tener la doble nacionalidad. ¿Ud. está a favor o en contra de esta ley mexicana?

¿Ud. tiene la doble nacionalidad?

¿Su impresión de los mexicanos que se hacen ciudadanos norteamericanos es buena o mala?

Algunas personas dicen que tantas películas, música y libros extranjeros están dañando la cultura mexicana. Otros dicen que no es nada de malo. ¿Qué piensa Ud.?

¿Ud. diría que entiende bien o mal el inglés?

¿Ud. habla mucho, algo o nada de inglés?

ACTITUDES SOBRE EL PUEBLO

En su opinión, ¿la migración de gente de aquí a los EE.UU. ha beneficiado o ha perjudicado la economía del pueblo?

En su opinión, ¿la migración a los EE.UU. ha beneficiado o ha perjudicado las costumbres y las formas de vivir en Tlacuitapa/San Antonio?

Algunas personas dicen que un hombre, nacido en Tlacuitapa/San Antonio, puede progresar en la vida sin salir del pueblo. Otras dicen que para superarse, los hombres nacidos en Tlacuitapa/San Antonio tienen que salir. ¿Qué diría Ud.?

¿Y las mujeres? ¿Tienen que salir de Tlacuitapa/San Antonio para superarse, o pueden superarse sin salir?

¿Su familia ha participado en el programa Oportunidades?

¿Su familia participa en el programa Seguro Popular (seguro para la salud)?

¿Tiene Ud. o su familia terrenos agrícolas?

¿Para qué se utilizaron los terrenos en el último año?

¿Son terrenos ejidales?

¿Son propios?

¿Participa su familia en el programa Procampo?

LA VIDA FAMILIAR

¿Hasta qué nivel piensa Ud. que deben estudiar los varones?

¿Hasta qué nivel piensa Ud. que deben estudiar las mujeres?

En su opinión, ¿una buena esposa debe obedecer a su esposo en todo lo que él ordene?

En su opinión, ¿es obligación de la mujer tener relaciones sexuales con su esposo aunque ella no quiera?

En su opinión, ¿una persona cuya pareja no le obedece tiene el derecho de pegarle a su pareja?

En su hogar en Tlacuitapa, ¿quién prepara la comida, la mayor parte del tiempo?

¿Y en los EE.UU.?

En su hogar en Tlacuitapa, ¿quién hace las tareas domésticas (como lavar, planchar, limpiar), la mayor parte del tiempo?

¿Y en los EE.UU.?

En su hogar en Tlacuitapa, ¿quién cuida a los niños o les ayuda en sus tareas, la mayor parte del tiempo?

¿Y en los EE.UU.?

En su hogar en Tlacuitapa, ¿quién decide cómo se gasta el dinero?

¿Y en los EE.UU.?

¿Piensa tener (más) hijos?

¿Cuántos más?

Si ha sucedido algún conflicto con su esposo (pareja), ¿ha recurrido a la policía u otra autoridad?

LA SALUD

¿Ha tenido o tiene alguna de las siguientes enfermedades? Asma, cáncer, colesterol elevado, diabetes, hipertensión, problemas del corazón, infarto, problemas de espalda o músculos, sobrepeso.

¿Cuántas veces por semana Ud. se alimenta con *fast food* (comida rápida)? ¿Con comida de la calle/puestos ambulantes?

Algunas personas dicen que cuando los migrantes se van a los EE.UU., comienzan a usar drogas. ¿Ud. conoce a alguien a quien le haya pasado esto?

En los últimos dos años, ¿Ud. se ha enfermado o ha sufrido algún accidente en los EE.UU.?

¿Quién lo atendió? (¿Por qué se quedó sin tratamiento?)

¿Quién pagó la atención médica?

Al estar en los EE.UU., ¿diría Ud. que pesa más, pesa menos o pesa igual que antes de irse a los EE.UU.?

Si Ud. fuma cigarros de tabaco, ¿fuma más en Tlacuitapa o en EE.UU.?

Si Ud. toma alcohol, ¿toma más en Tlacuitapa o en EE.UU.?